HISTORY
of
MEDICINE

With commentaries

HISTORY *of* MEDICINE

With commentaries

ROBERT RICHARDSON, MA, BM, BCh, FRSM

HILARY S MORRIS, MA, DHMSA, FRSM

Quiller Publishing
Limited

First published in the UK 2005
by Quiller Press, an imprint of Quiller Publishing Ltd
The moral rights of the authors have been asserted

Copyright © 2005 Robert Richardson and Hilary S Morris

British Library Cataloguing-in-Publication Data
A catalogue record for this book
is available from the British Library

ISBN 1 904057 76 4

Designed by Jo Ekin
Set in AGaramond
Printed in England by Cromwell Press, Trowbridge, Wiltshire

Quiller Press
an imprint of Quiller Publishing Ltd
Wykey House, Wykey, Shrewsbury SY4 1JA, England
E-mail: info@quillerbooks.com
Website: www.swanhillbooks.com

Preface

We have written this book in the hope that it will prove to be a readily accessible window onto the history of medicine – both a pain-free grounding and a pleasurable route to revision.

The format we have adopted, which we believe to be unique among text books on the subject, enables Paul Baldassare (originally Bal-sarra-uzur) and his companion, Telesphorus, to discuss and pass judgment on events in a manner unavailable to writers of the more formal texts. These discussions are, nevertheless, all based on either historical evidence or authoritative opinions.

The names of the characters in the narrative, but not of those in the Commentaries or Sources, are listed at the end together with a mention of who they were or what they did. Within the narrative, Paul Baldassare's asides are in parentheses; modern additions, such as dates and explanatory notes, are in square brackets.

If we have succeeded in showing that learning can be an enjoyable experience and in implanting the urge to know more, then we shall have achieved our objective.

Robert Richardson
Hilary S Morris
2005

Foreword

This is a book that puts narrative medicine in its historical perspective. The history of medicine is set in its time and context and comes alive through the characters of Paul Baldassare and his companion. It is a truly novel approach.

We all have different styles of learning and I learnt best by listening to patients' stories. The authors' technique of creating dialogue and interaction between real, familiar characters in the history of medicine and Baldassare's subsequent debates with his muse will really appeal to interactive learners. Reading these chapters you feel you are having a learning experience in a small group. Enthusiasts of narrative-based medicine will delight in his story and the stories of the people he meets. This is reminiscent of the tradition of Plato's *Republic* where Socrates walks with Adeimantus and Glaucon down to the beach and creates a dialogue so that both sides can be explored before Socrates adds some words and then there is time for reflection.

History of Medicine suited my style of learning. The characters came alive and the timelines put their stories into context. The commentaries and sources give clues where to research further. This package is a stimulus to learn at different stages of development: it is inspirational to the young; it is a refreshing aide-mémoire for the more confident medical historian; and it provides a companion to ease the loneliness of the medical researcher. It opens doors and is a stimulus for those who want to let their minds run further – the dreamers.

Baldassare's journey is like my journey. We start off hoping to learn everything about medicine. All too quickly the search for total knowledge is elusive and finally we compensate by trying to find out more and more about less and less – the essence of specialism and super-specialism. Baldassare also represents the altruism of medicine in that in his search for knowledge he is teaching – the *OED* defines a doctor as a teacher, and in his search for history lies our history.

John C. Richardson
Emeritus Defence Professor of Primary Care and General Practice, University of Birmingham, UK
Hon. Senior Research Fellow in the Centre for the History of Medicine, University of Birmingham, UK

Contents

(continued overleaf)

(Contents continued)

[Timelines are shown at the start of each chapter, except for Chapters 11, 15, 19 and 22 where they are incorporated with those for Chapters 10, 14, 18 and 21, respectively.]

List of maps

Chapter 1

BC	3000 —	I Egyptian Dynasty
	—	Imhotep. Step Pyramid c.2700
	—	The Great Pyramid at Giza c.2600
	2500 —	
	} —	Old Kingdom III–VI Dynasties 2700–1900
	2000 —	
	—	Bronze Age in Britain c.1900
	—	Stonehenge c.1860–1560
	1500 —	
	—	18th Dynasty – Tutankhamun c.1350
	—	Exodus of the Israelites from Egypt 1230
	1000 —	
	—	Solomon built the temple in Jerusalem 961
	—	Foundation of Rome c.750
	500 —	Iron Age began in England
	—	Hippocrates 460–370
	—	Alexander the Great 356–323
AD	0 —	Birth of Christ
	—	Galen 129–c.200–216
	500 —	
	—	Birth of Muhammed 570
	—	Death of Alfred the Great 899
	1000 —	Battle of Hastings 1066
	—	Chinese circumnavigated and charted the world 1421–1423
	—	Black Death 1348
	—	Printing with moveable type 1444
	1500 —	Columbus 'discovered' America 1492
	—	Defeat of Spanish Armada 1588
	—	World War I 1914–1918
	2000 —	World War II 1939–1945

Medical beliefs in Mesopotamia
(*c.* 2700BC)

My father sat at the breakfast table playing with his porridge, occasionally raising the spoon to where he thought his mouth should be; porridge trickled down his chin. My mother had that familiar disgusted look on her face, but said nothing. She knew what answer she would get: "For a man's pleasure there is marriage; on thinking it over there is divorce" – and divorce usually meant being sold into slavery. But if *I* had behaved like that, she would have cuffed me round the head and snatched my bowl away: "If you can't eat properly, you won't eat at all." To which my father would almost certainly have added: "Pay heed to the word of your mother as though it were the word of god." He was a great one for spouting proverbs.

Sitting at the other side of the table, my mother was watching me closely. She knew why my father was so distracted – and, as it happened, so did I. He was busily hatching a scheme for my future and I didn't like what he had in mind one little bit. But she needn't have worried about me as I was already tucking into my bread and date syrup with my mind full of ideas of just how I could thwart my father's plans. My sister and two younger brothers, conveniently out of her way in the kitchen finishing their breakfasts, were no part of those plans. Soon they would be bundled off to the tablet house by our slaves – our school was called the tablet house simply because we scratched our lessons on tablets of baked clay.

My parents had named me Bal-sarra-uzur. At this time I was in my sixteenth year and my education at the tablet house had finished. My mother, for no reason other than to go against my father's wishes (or so I thought), had decided that I should stay at home and continue my studies with Ebih-Il, a friend of hers, and become a priest and wise man.

As all this happened a long time ago I had better do some explaining. First, though, you must forgive me if my memories of childhood are irretrievably blurred. As the centuries slipped away, these congealed into one amorphous day that began with the hour of my birth in the city of Kish in the land of Akkad, which you now know as part of Iraq. And it was, indeed, a very long time ago.

Kish was a prosperous city on the banks of the mighty Euphrates but, alas, it no longer exists. You see, the Euphrates is a flood river and has changed its course, not once but many times, reducing fields to desert and towns to ruin. But in my youth it brought trade and prosperity to Kish.

My home lay within the city walls, barely distinguishable from the many thousands of others and dominated by the monumental ziggurat [a pyramidal temple tower]. Outside the walls were gardens, rich with many plants you would recognize today: magnolia and rhododendron, cotoneaster and berberis, anemone and fritillaria ranged among sweet smelling herbs. Further away we grew our fruits and vegetables and, further away still, flocks of sheep and cattle grazed close to fields of barley, wheat and millet – all watered by the interlacing canals and ditches dug with such skill by our forefathers. Beneath the walls themselves and near the gates of the city lay the harbour full of craft busy with trade to the cities of the north and to the land of Sumer and the world beyond in the south.

Although you have probably never heard of Kish and probably never will again, in my time [about 2700BC] our ruler was king of both Akkad and Sumer, countries that fifteen hundred years later became known as Babylonia. Babylon (or Bab-ilim as it was then), lay some fifty miles to the west, and was still an insignificant desert village. Yet the shifting waters of the Euphrates were to bring her greatness and an immortality peculiar in the romance of history. (This is perhaps why I like to think of myself as a Babylonian – and who is there now who would challenge my assumption?)

My father was a merchant in the city. He was wealthy and as one indication of this he drank wine – he wouldn't be seen dead drinking the beer of what he referred to as the common man. But others were richer and that displeased him. Like so many rich men, wealth was his god and he just had to keep adding to it. "He who possesses much silver may be happy. But he who has nothing at all can sleep peacefully at night" was not among his repertoire of proverbs.

Not content with the well-earned comforts of home and the respect of the citizens, he had to listen to travellers' tales of unbelievable wealth waiting to be gathered in from distant places. If he had only listened and contented himself with dreaming… but no, he was taken with the urge to see and gather in for himself. That was bad enough; what made it a disaster was his determination to take me, his eldest son, with him. Neither my mother nor myself could make him see that if riches were there for the taking in Nubia's golden mountains, why in the name of the great god Abu did these tellers of tales come scratching at his door begging for food and shelter. No amount of pleading would shake him from his decision; he was determined, as he expressed it, to complete my education. I was developing other ideas of how to achieve that same end – and they didn't agree with my mother's plans either.

As the day of departure drew nearer, my father spent more and more time in one of the temples. Much incense was burned and many sheep slaughtered that their entrails might be staked out to reveal the fate of the expedition. The omens were consistently good – did not my father contribute handsomely to the welfare of the priests? But I knew better.

It was simple, really. You see my intelligence (in both senses of the word) was better. My mother, still a strikingly beautiful woman, had made all her decisions in recent years on the advice of this Ebih-Il who was an esteemed diviner and at whose house she was a frequent and welcomed visitor. Her scheme worked well enough until the breaking of my voice had opened my eyes to the ways of the world. I knew there was profit lurking somewhere in my new-found discovery, if I was content to bide my time. I was, and the time had come.

After breakfast my mother sent me off to Ebih-Il, but instead of discussing my education I put a proposition to him. It was that he should interpret truly the omens governing the expedition – and more particularly, my part in it – or I would immediately inform my father of my mother's infidelity. His response left me totally nonplussed.

"He already knows." He smiled like the slimey, fat toad he was. Why my mother saw anything in him was beyond me – but I was discovering that women are strange and unpredictable creatures. "Even so I will see what the future holds for you, if… " the smile broadened as he watched my discomfiture develop, "…if you will acquire for me the little statue of the god Abu that is your father's."

Of course I stole the wretched thing and brought it to him a few days later.

He made me stand before him like a child, seething inwardly at the man's insolence. "You were a fool, Bal-sarra-uzur, to believe me. But I shall keep to my side of our bargain, if only to teach you a lesson."

He gave me a very strange penetrating look before walking across to the window overlooking the river and began to intone. "I have offered incense and observed the oil and the water; I have summoned Ishtar, the Bringer of Dawn…." Suddenly he stopped and, with an overly dramatic gesture, clasped his hand to his chest. Sinking slowly to the ground, he began to make the most terrible gurgling, gasping noises before, so it seemed to my overwrought imagination, his body settled itself comfortably and lay motionless. Even diviners can come to an unexpectedly abrupt end if the gods choose to send death to visit them. There was only one sensible thing for me to do – and I did it. I picked up my father's little statue and hurried home. [I believe now that the man suffered a lethal heart attack.]

I make no secret of my terror. Beyond doubt I was doomed. For Ebih-Il to be called away by the gods when about to disclose the revelations of Ishtar opened the gateway to a perplexing array of omens. Inanna-Ishtar, child of the Moon god, the Morning and the Evening star, was also goddess of love and goddess of war. She was the comforter of man but, riding astride her sacred lion, she could bring him to destruction. I had little doubt which she had in mind for me.

My mother tore at her favourite green robe – the one she wore for her visits to Ebih-Il – took to her couch and refused to rise. My father lost patience with her, pointing out that other merchants had journeyed far afield to return safely and bring their wives great joy and comfort. He was not to know that the cause of my mother's distress lay elsewhere than with his departure. This restored my confidence as I now knew for certain that Ebih-Il had lied to me which meant that his divination would have been worthless make-believe. He had paid the price of his iniquity.

Soon my father's boats were fully loaded, some with barley, wheat, dates, fish oil, wool and skins for barter along the way; others, carefully disguised with objects of no worth, were filled with statuettes and heads of copper and bronze; figurines in polished black stone; necklaces and bracelets of gold inset with agate beads; silver bars; glass drinking vessels and much else besides of great beauty and value made from materials acquired on previous, less hazardous, journeys. He was staking his present wealth against a dream of untold riches – oh! gullible and foolish man.

But where there is trade, there also is corruption. It was no accident that our head boatman led us astray from the main channel and into the marshes of Sumer after we had passed the city of Ur. He said he was lost and would set out to find a guide. That night we were attacked. My father and many of his servants were killed – my mother would now have real cause to grieve – while those of us who survived were stripped and put in neck stocks; there was to be no escape.

At daylight, our captors examined us carefully. When they came to me, I stared at them in defiance. But instead of humiliating me as they had the others, I saw fear in their faces and they began arguing amongst themselves. At last they reached a decision and one of them took my head between his hands and gazed at me in wonder before falling to his knees to kiss my feet while another removed my stock. My garments and sandals were returned and I was given food to eat and beer to drink.

I have an aptitude for tongues and had acquired a few words of Sumerian from visitors to my father's house, sufficient to follow the substance of these peoples' talk. It seems they believed the colour of my eyes gave me the magical power to penetrate the secrets of the universe. For my eyes are blue, a blue as deep and intense as the sky at midday and enough to strike wonder into the minds of the superstitious and ignorant. Among my own people, this gift of Nature was rare, but not unique, and appeared, so I had been told, from time to time among those with ancestors whose seed, by one means or another, had found its way to Akkad from distant northern lands.

On that day they undoubtedly saved my life.

COMMENTARY

1) At the date when Bal-Sarra-Uzur began his journey (around 2700BC), society was becoming established and benefiting from a sense of knowledge and order; the development of writing allowed this knowledge to be recorded. Furthermore, the appearance of formalized education reinforced the social structure and led to the emergence of a professional class. With a king at its head, a hierarchy was established with a clear understanding of 'place' among the populace. The priesthood practised superstition rather than religion and the influence of the gods pervaded all aspects of human life. Since the concept of disease was so deeply embedded in the supernatural rather than the natural, there was little or no stimulus for change in the way medicine was practised.

2) The essential traits of folk-medicine and ancient medicine (see Source 2, below) are valid from before the start of this story and hold good until the lead-up to the time of Hippocrates (400BC). It can even be argued that the last remnants of this frame of mind exist to this very day, and are experiencing something of a revival in the face of growing concern and doubts over the effectiveness of orthodox medicine.

3) Clay tablets unearthed in Mesopotamia (the name means 'between rivers' – Euphrates and Tigris) in the 20th century record in some detail the lifestyle of the people of Akkad around 2700BC. Previously, in the mid-19th century over 30,000 clay tablets were discovered which also dated from this era; more than a thousand came from the library of Assurbinpal (668–626BC). Many of these are concerned with medicine, dealing with diagnosis, prognostication and pharmaceutical preparations.

4) By 3000BC cuneiform writing was in existence and five hundred years later, at the time of the First Egyptian Dynasty, hieratic

writing (a sort of truncated form of hieroglyphics) had been perfected and hieroglyphic writing itself was in use in Egypt. The importance of writing for communication of every description cannot be overstressed, besides which it leaves us with irrefutable proof of what was being said and done.

5) Disease was the result of upsetting a deity or jinn (the 'genie' of future fables) – wrongdoing of one sort or another. Treatment was directed towards appeasing his or her wrath. The herbal treatment offered by the priests was only a part of the business of placating the deity which included spells, incantations and the like. Healthy people avoided contact with a sick person in case they too incurred the wrath of the deity and were also struck down. This was possibly one of the first public health measures without the real implications being understood.

6) The interpretation of disease was omen-based. The most common form of divination was the inspection of livers of sacrificed animals (hepatoscopy) due to the belief that the liver was the seat of life. Clay models of livers have been found with markings which were probably used as a form of instruction (a primitive textbook). Soothsayers used animal entrails as a way of casting horoscopes.

7) Medical care was provided by members of the priesthood, some of whom may have had special training in the temples. However, as was the case for millennia to come, they directed their attention to the manifestations of disease and not its cause. The diseases and injuries suffered by the people of Akkad were similar to those we know (from mummies and frescos) were suffered by the contemporary ancient Egyptians – which, in turn, were little different from those suffered by the inhabitants of those parts of the world today. They include fractures, arthritis, tuberculosis, dental caries, hernias, poliomyelitis and parasitic diseases. Diseases were not identified as such, but their causes would have been the same as now, though they would have been a mystery to the people. The contagious nature of leprosy was understood with sufferers being segregated from the rest of society (as later outlined in Leviticus).

8) Over the centuries a demarcation in the treatment of the sick and injured emerged as different types of healers became responsible for specific medical tasks. Hence the seer (baru) specialized in divination, whilst the priest (ashipu) performed incantations and exorcisms. Later came the physicians (asu) who prescribed drugs and performed basic surgery and bandaging.

9) Communications with the north and the south were excellent, thanks to the river Euphrates, and encouraged trade as far afield as Egypt and North Africa. Trade was essential to the existence of civilization in Akkad. Grain, vegetables, dates, animal products such as meat, wool, leather and horn, fish and reed and plant-fibre products were available in abundance and were exported. However, wood, stone and metal were virtually absent and had to be imported. (The only wood they had came from the date-palm and was suitable only for rough work.) Metals, such as copper, gold and silver came from the mountains to both the north and the south. Bronze did not appear until 2000BC. The technology existed for the creation of beautiful and valuable jewellery, and of objects for use and display.

10) The agricultural area with its enormous yield of wheat lying between the Euphrates and the Tigris was to become the seat of endless wars. In fact, the whole of the eastern Mediterranean during the 18th century BC was in a state of upheaval on account of great population migrations. The military activities of Abraham, Isaac and Jacob recorded in Genesis – Chapter 13 onwards – took place at this time. Knowledge of wound dressings came primarily from the battlefields. One of the most common was dried wine dregs, salt, oil, beer and juniper blended with mud or fat.

SOURCES

1) "It is only by the successive testing of hypotheses and rejection of the false that truth is at last elicited. After all, what we call truth is only the hypothesis that is found to work best. Therefore in the opinions and practices of ruder ages and races we shall do well to

look with leniency upon their errors as inevitable slips made in the search for truth, and to give them the benefit of that indulgence which we ourselves may one day stand in need of."
Sir James George Frazer, *The Golden Bough*, 1963

2) "It is possible, as we shall see, that many myths, inventions, and bizarre cultural practices, such as mummification, circumcision, or the couvade, may have been transported by migrations from one place to another.... The civilized mind differs from the savage mind mainly in respect of a higher evolutionary development. In their reactions to folk-ways and settled custom, both exhibit the same inertia, fear of change, and aversion to the untried or unknowable.... It follows that, under different aspects of space and time, the essential traits of folk-medicine and ancient medicine have been alike in tendency, differing only in unimportant details.... Cuneiform, hieroglyphic, runic, birch-bark, and palm-leaf inscriptions all indicate that the folk-ways of early medicine, whether Accadian, Scandinavian, Slavic or Celtic, Roman or Polynesian, have been the same – in each case an affair of charms and spells, plant lore and psychotherapy, to stave off the effects of supernatural agencies. Wherever this frame of mind persists, there is no possibility of advancement for medicine."
Fielding H. Garrison, *An Introduction to the History of Medicine*, 1929
[Couvade is a practice among primitive peoples where the father feigns illness and takes to his bed at the birth of a child.]

Chapter 2

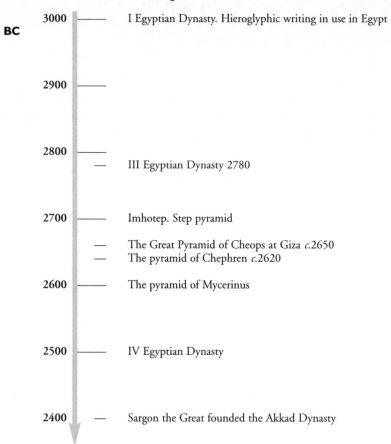

BC

3000 ——— I Egyptian Dynasty. Hieroglyphic writing in use in Egypt

2900 ———

2800 ———
— III Egyptian Dynasty 2780

2700 ——— Imhotep. Step pyramid

— The Great Pyramid of Cheops at Giza *c.*2650
— The pyramid of Chephren *c.*2620

2600 ——— The pyramid of Mycerinus

2500 ——— IV Egyptian Dynasty

2400 — Sargon the Great founded the Akkad Dynasty

Medical practice in Ancient Egypt
(*c.* 2700BC)

My recollection of the events of the next months – or it may have been years, I have no means of telling – is confused in all respects. Suffice it to say that I was passed from people to people and from country to country until eventually I found myself in Memphis in the hands of an ambitious nobleman who had acquired me with one intention only – the hope of advancement by presenting me to the king's vizier as a gift. Slaves from Kish were always in demand on account of our intellectual abilities, and the opportunity of finding one as young and as unusual as myself, arose but rarely. I was indeed a gift to be treasured.

My new owner's name was Imhotep. Being Pharoah Zoser's chief councillor he was second in importance only to those of royal blood. He was a kind man and made allowances for my early mistakes which soon became fewer as I mastered his language.

But he was more, much more, than just the pharoah's councillor. He was High Priest of Heliopolis and Recorder of Judgments – a sort of Archbishop of Canterbury and Lord Chancellor rolled into one. He was also an outstanding astronomer and mathematician. Yet all these seemed as nothing when compared to his greatest achievement: his invention of the pyramid that was to be his master's final resting place. Although this is now the majestic ruin you know as the step pyramid, when I arrived in Memphis it was fresh in its magnificent covering of dressed stone and surrounded by a beautiful white-panelled wall. Shining in the sun in all its glory, it stunned the eye from every angle.

With the passing of time we grew comfortable in each other's company and he began to treat me more as a son than a slave. He permitted me to eat at his table when we were alone and he undertook the completion of my education. Astronomy and mathematics gave me no trouble as I had been well taught at home – though our astronomy had been more liberally laced with astrology than his. But what he was insistent on teaching me were his beliefs about disease. In Akkad we believed that sickness and death were brought by the gods or by malignant jinn. That was why Ebih-Il had wanted my father's little statue of Abu; the image of the god was hard to come by, but the protection it could give was fearsome though not, as Ebih-Il discovered, when dishonestly obtained. My mind just would not accept that a human being would dare to interfere with the work of the gods or challenge the jinn. I argued from the analogy of a gift: when one person gives something to another, the gift is a thing apart from both. Yet, try as I might, I could not persuade Imhotep of the truth of our beliefs.

Imhotep studied me closely for a moment or two, no doubt deciding whether, after all, I was worthy of his continued effort.

"In your country," he said at last, "the priests study the entrails of animals to forecast the future?" It was a question. I nodded, sullenly. "When the livers are smooth and shiny, the omens are good?" I nodded again. "And when they are shrunken, discoloured, hard or knobbly, the omens are bad?" I bowed my head in assent. "These animals are afflicted," he continued, "not by a thing apart but by disease that has entered their bodies as an instrument of destruction. The priests can see this, even though they do not understand.

"The gods do, indeed, have powers to govern what we are; but much may happen in our lives over which they have no influence. You must learn that disease is not a divine affliction, but has causes that one day we shall understand. In my lifetime, I shall be able to do little more than look at a man who is sick and try to give what comfort I can." He sighed in despair at his helplessness. "When we know the causes and can observe their effects, then shall we be able to judge whether to treat or not."

It would, as Imhotep well knew, be many centuries before mankind again saw the healing art with his clarity of vision. But, as I stood beside him then, all I saw was an old man whose brain was becoming addled like an egg that has been kept too long.

I thought I might disconcert him by asking where he had gained his knowledge. "Through Thoth was I instructed in the mysteries of SA-HA-Hor, the protection round the falcon, where our Child of the Sun shall rest on his journey to paradise in the sky." As good an answer as any, I suppose, and one that showed he did believe in divine wisdom. And in all the years since, I have never heard a better explanation of the origin of knowledge. It will forever remain a closed book.

As his favourite slave – a position I was well able to defend – I was always at his side. Quite frequently we would come across an injured workman abandoned where he had fallen. When Imhotep thought he could help, he ordered me to have the man taken to his home. There, I would watch and listen while he went through what amounted almost to a ritual.

"First, I straighten the limb," he would say if the injury was a broken arm or leg, quite ignoring the man's screams. "Then I hold it firmly with slats of wood bound in place with linen. Lastly, I stiffen the linen with gums so that the man," who had by now often lost consciousness, "cannot undo my work."

When the injury was an open wound, he would save it from rotting by bathing it in willow water. "Now, as it is small, I shall pull the edges together with strips of gummed linen. But had it been a large gaping wound, I would have stitched them as my wife would a rent garment." On the first day of treatment he bound fresh meat over the wound; then on the following days he usually applied an ointment of grease and honey.

Yet, despite the evidence of my own eyes when I saw these injuries heal, I still did not believe him and made my disbelief plain. I refused to help him, saying that by doing so I would offend my gods. I could no more interfere with their work than I could command the rain to fall, the wind to blow or the rocks to stem the river's flow.

What really troubled me, though, were his writings about the sick and injured who were brought to him; I earnestly prayed these papyri would never fall into the hands of the pharaoh – such sacrilege would bring swift retribution, whoever the perpetrator. Some of his remarks were quite innocuous: when he felt powerless to help, he wrote that the man was to be left untreated or 'moored at his mooring stakes until the period of his injury passes by', a quaint phrase, but typical of the man in his whimsical moods. Other remarks were really outrageous, such as the statement that the pulse, which could be felt in different parts of the body, was related to the motions of the heart. And the observation that severe blows to the head or spine could cause paralysis, deafness, incontinence and other troubles.

I did not appreciate the wisdom of these writings until long years afterwards. But I did have a nasty suspicion that he was trying to indoctrinate me, so that his beliefs would not die with him.

When I had been with Imhotep for about two years and he still could not persuade me to his way of thinking – I refused stubbornly to be shaken from beliefs which had been instilled into me from childhood – he gave me, one day at our morning meal, a pleasant-tasting drink which, he said, would grant me insight into a matter of great importance.

"Bal-sarra-uzur, today we shall go to the temple where you must decide your fate. I shall ask you a question: 'Do you wish to stay on earth until mankind comes to understand the nature of disease?' " This seemed a strange question. After all, except for Imhotep, mankind already knew that disease came from the gods. My perplexity must have been evident. "You wonder why I should ask such a question? That is for you to discover. Your answer must depend on your beliefs."

Suddenly at that moment, I felt my life to be a dream. As the day progressed, its events floated in and out of that dream. How much was real and how much enchantment, I cannot say as the drink had undoubtedly made me hallucinate.

"Remember, Bal-sarra-uzur, if you wish to discover the answer, it will be a long time coming." Those were the last words I am certain I heard him speak.

* * *

At the entrance to the temple we were met by two priests. In my dream-like world I passed down long passages lit only by the light entering from small windows set high in the walls, through rooms where alabaster oil lamps suspended on the columns fluttered in the draught. The corridors were bare of furnishings but in the many halls stood golden altars and beautifully worked statues. The walls were covered with panels depicting day-to-day life. And wherever I looked, shaven-headed priests in their long linen robes were going about their duties.

"Wait," Imhotep instructed me in a voice that came from far away. "When the great door opens, pass through. I shall be ready to greet you." With that, he and the two priests left me.

The door at the end of the corridor where I was standing was massive and delicately worked in gold. On its far side lay the great hall of the temple. Already I could hear the chanting of the priests as they gathered there – or was the sound in my imagination? I believed I was about to be sacrificed and I welcomed the thought. Obeying the call of my gods seemed to be the only way to convince Imhotep that they were the masters of disease. I calmly decided I would answer: "Yes, I wish to stay."

Slowly the great doors parted. I remained motionless until they had swung back to their full extent. Opposite me, a long way away it seemed, Imhotep sat on a carved throne, inlaid with gold, silver and ivory, and raised on four steps. I scarcely trusted my legs to carry me as I walked towards the steps. I knelt and placed my brow on the lowermost. The chanting had stopped.

"Bal-sarra-uzur, you have been brought here for Imhotep to question you." A disembodied voice filled the hall. "Have you decided what your answer shall be?"

I rose and bowed deeply.

Imhotep, unfamiliar in the ibis-head mask he wore in his capacity of Recorder of Judgments, inclined his head.

"Bal-sarra-uzur, we have spoken together. Do you wish to continue on earth until mankind understands the nature of disease?"

I bowed deeply once again. As from afar I heard a voice: "Then I fear it will be for ever."

If you wish to dismiss this as nothing more than fantasy, the product of a disordered hallucinating mind, so be it. I can only assure you that it – or something closely resembling what I have described – did indeed happen. But, as I have said, it was all a very long time ago.

COMMENTARY

1) The first and most important comment is that no evidence exists to prove that Imhotep (his name signifies 'He who comes in peace') wrote the original of what has become known as the Edwin Smith papyrus. Neither is there any evidence that he did not. So, although to name him as the author may be wrong, it is a device to help in following the story of Egyptian medicine. Nevertheless, it took a man of exceptional intelligence and powers of observation to write this papyrus, and the chances of another such man as Imhotep existing without historical record are not great.

2) The introduction of papyrus, in sheets or scrolls, made writing a much easier task than scratching on clay tablets or inscribing on the walls of tombs and the like. Papyrus is prepared from the pith of the paper reed (*Cyperus papyrus*) which is cut into strips and pressed together. The Egyptian papyri have left us a lasting, if incomplete, picture of contemporary medicine and surgery.

3) Because disease and bodily suffering were considered to be the result of transgression of a sacred law, the influence of the priesthood effectively prevented any attempt at practical medicine. Moreover, the Egyptians would not allow the body to be desecrated as it had to be carefully preserved until the time of resurrection when body and spirit were reunited. Thus, although the Egyptians practised embalming and so acquired a working knowledge of anatomy, they did not put it to any serviceable use in medicine.

4) The building of the pyramids was responsible for a wide variety of injuries, much as can still occur on a building site today, despite health and safety regulations. For example: fractured limbs, head injuries, crushing injuries, soft tissue injuries and so on. Although Imhotep may not have originated the treatment of fractures and wounds, his descriptions are the oldest to have been recorded –

they could be regarded as the first texts on occupational health. Archaeological evidence shows that closed fractures usually healed well but that open fractures were mostly lethal. Imhotep's observations on the pulse and the possible effects of head injuries made no impact on medical practice.

5) There was no clear distinction between the priests who practised magical healing and the physicians who practised rational medicine/surgery – they were one and the same person. When it was obvious what had happened, for example a traumatic injury, the healer wearing his physician/surgeon hat, was intelligent enough to apply rational treatment. But when the cause was a mystery, as with disease, the healer as priest would, for instance, cast spells, use charms or amulets, or apply revolting concoctions to the patient's body in an attempt to drive out the demon within. Nevertheless, some of the treatments they used had therapeutic value; for example, willow water is significant because willow bark contains salicylic compounds which have a moderate antiseptic effect. (Aspirin is acetyl salicylic acid.)

6) These priest-physicians were unable to distinguish what was normal from what was abnormal. Furthermore, they did not appreciate that disease was an alteration of the structure or function of the body.

7) Throughout history there have been men who were so far ahead of their time that their contemporaries failed to grasp what they were doing or what they achieved. It is no wonder that Imhotep's observations did not take root in medical practice. Yet there must have been some appreciation of his work since his tomb became a centre of healing and, in the Greek period (probably around 700BC), he was deified and identified with the Greek god of medicine, Asklepios.

8) Imhotep's statements about the pulse and the effects of severe blows to the head show that he had truly remarkable powers of observation – something that was not seen again until the time of Hippocrates (430BC).

9) Little is known about the role of women in the medicine of ancient

Egypt. The one notable example was Peseshet who lived during the Old Kingdom (*c.*2575–*c.*2130BC) and was granted the title of Lady Overseer of Lady Physicians. From this we can assume that other women did practise medicine, but to what extent is unclear. Women healers do not appear to have been concerned solely with women's complaints since different papyri indicate that gynaecological disorders were an integral part of medicine (see Chapter 3, Commentary 8 and Source 3).

SOURCES

1) "Now if the priests of Sekhmet or any physician put his hands or his fingers upon the head, upon the back of the head, upon the two hands, upon the pulse, upon the feet, he measures the heart, because its vessels are in the back of the head and in the pulse… He says 'measure the heart in order to recognize the indications that have arisen therein… '"

The *Edwin Smith* papyrus

This shows that Imhotep appreciated that the pulse reflected the beating of the heart and, furthermore, that it could indicate something about the nature of the patient's disease. (See Chapter 11 and Galen's work on the pulse.)

2) "Thou shouldst say regarding him: 'One having a gaping wound in his head, penetrating to the bone, and perforating his skull. An ailment which I shall treat.'…Now after thou hast stitched it, thou shouldst lay fresh meat upon his wound the first day. Thou shouldst not bind it. Moor him at his mooring stakes until the period of his injury passes by. Thou shouldst treat it afterwards with grease, honey and lint every day until he recovers."

The *Edwin Smith* papyrus

Imhotep decides whether it is advisable to treat the patient or not. (Particularly in those times it could make matters worse by interfering.) Having decided that he could benefit the patient by treating him, Imhotep describes the treatment and then prescribes rest until the patient is over the worst.

3) "There is no force in the life of ancient man, the influence of which so pervades all his activities as does that of the religious faculty. Its fancies explain for him the world about him, its fears are his hourly master, its hopes his constant Mentor, its feasts are his calendar, and its outward usages are to a large extent the education and the motive toward the gradual evolution of art, literature and science. As among all other early peoples, it was in his surroundings that the Egyptian saw his gods."
James Henry Breasted, *A History of Egypt*, 1924

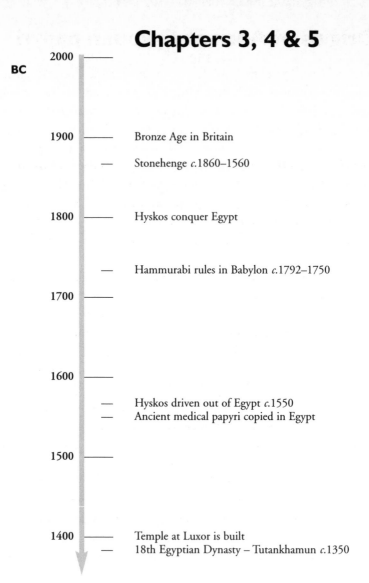

Chapters 3, 4 & 5

BC

2000 ——

1900 —— Bronze Age in Britain

— Stonehenge c.1860–1560

1800 —— Hyskos conquer Egypt

— Hammurabi rules in Babylon c.1792–1750

1700 ——

1600 ——

— Hyskos driven out of Egypt c.1550
— Ancient medical papyri copied in Egypt

1500 ——

1400 —— Temple at Luxor is built
— 18th Egyptian Dynasty – Tutankhamun c.1350

Origins of Ancient Egyptian papyri

(*c.* 1500BC)

In the early years, I was myself sceptical that anything had happened. I remained Imhotep's chosen slave and was by his side when he died, leaving me in the charge of a priest-physician to care for the sick – in which respect my beliefs were unchanged and now not even challenged. Imhotep's heretical ideas about disease were, like his writings, lost to sight.

With the passing years, my body showed none of the signs of aging; it retained its resilience and strength. Men looked at me strangely and began to avoid my company. When my new master also died, I slipped away from the temple and joined the river traders. I moved from boat to boat until eventually I became my own master. Nevertheless, I learned not to remain in one place for too long – I was stoned through the gates of more than one city. Time grew meaningless; perhaps the gods took pity on me as, alone in desert places, I would occasionally fall asleep in some natural shelter only to wake decades, maybe centuries, later refreshed and ready to journey on. Invariably, so it seemed in those days, the world and its people did not change.

In the reign of Amenophis I [*c.*1550BC], I was working in the temple of Ammon-Re in Karnak as an assistant scribe to Seneb, a priest-physician and keeper of the papyri, one of whose tasks was to record the remedies used in the House of Life. Regrettably, the healers in these Houses relied closely on what was contained in their cases of writings.

"See, Bal-sarra-uzur," Seneb called to me in his excitable manner, "here is an ancient papyrus from the ruins in Memphis."

I went over to him and started reading. The writing was, without doubt, in the hand of Imhotep. My heart beat faster and a lump came to my throat as I touched the ancient papyrus, my head full of memories. Seneb obviously did not appreciate the significance of what he was copying – if, indeed, he understood the hieroglyphs. (This is what you now know as the Edwin Smith papyrus after the man who acquired it at Luxor in 1862. The copy is believed to date from 1600BC.) With considerable self-restraint, I refrained from naming the author. My knowledge would only lead to the asking of unanswerable questions, the more particularly as Imhotep's fame now rested on his architectural achievements.

"By the bye," Seneb stopped writing and looked up at me. "I learnt a number of new incantations today. They expel the sickness of the year gone by, and grant protection for the one that is to come." So saying, he turned over the papyrus on which he was writing and began again on the back, speaking the words as he wrote: "O Flame-in-his-Face! Presider over the Horizon, speak thou to the Chief of the Hemesut House who makes Osiris, first of the land, to flourish." And so it went on. After a while he had me finish to his dictation. [The Edwin Smith papyrus, does, in fact, stop in mid-sentence.]

When we had done, he picked up another papyrus and read out a recipe for removing wrinkles from the skin. "It's made from the oil of the helbah seed. When you are old," he laughed, "it will keep you attractive to women!" Oh! Seneb you could not know what you were saying.

"But come," he went on, laying down the papyrus, "I have more important work for you." And he reached across the table to push a heap of papyri towards me. "These are for you to copy."

I took them to my table. They were a strange mixture; most were the usual recipes, yet others were quite old and Seneb could throw no light on their origins. But stranger still were their contents which seemed to bear no relationship to their age. As I worked my way through, I saw quite soon that they simply reflected the unchanging state of medical affairs. Herbal remedies in abundance; recipes including milk, honey, the fat of an amazing variety of animals and the salts of many minerals were all intelligently prescribed. Not so welcome were those that had their basis in magic and superstitious beliefs and were intended to repel evil spirits or attract benevolent deities; most revolved around the fluids and organs of the body and the excreta of man and animals, both real and fantastic. Unpleasant and irrational though these were, some of the more outlandishly sounding ingredients were merely secret names given to common herbs in order to preserve the priestly mystique.

One papyrus, however, aroused my curiosity. It was newly written, but whether derived from the writer's own observations or whether copied from another source, I could not discover. It told of the heart's movement and how this could be felt in many parts of the body: "the heart speaks out of the vessels of every limb" (You will find this in the Ebers Papyrus, obtained at Thebes in 1872 by Georg Ebers. It dates from 1550BC.) Imhotep's voice could still be heard even if only in the faintest of echoes.

As I copied on, curiosity gave way to unease. In my innermost heart I knew it was the gods who governed each man's destiny. Yet my continued existence on earth was beginning to persuade me that only in mankind's acceptance of Imhotep's teachings lay the route to my salvation. But alas! these faint echoes had always been swamped by folk medicine and superstition. For all practical purposes, the tangible evidence of his wisdom might have remained buried in the sands of Memphis. I was no nearer extricating myself from my predicament. So, after all these years, I decided the time had at last come for me to seek out new lands.

I left Seneb and without pausing to say goodbye, I travelled by boat down the Nile. Past Enet, Shem, Du-Kau, and Akhetaton. On past Menet Hufu until at length Imhotep's pyramid rose step-wise out of the mist. No longer resting alone in its magnificence, for now those of Khufu, Khafre and Menkaura and other long-dead kings thrust their threnetic peaks at the sky. (You would know them better by their Greek names of Cheops, Chephren and Mycerinus, respectively.)

On I went by Tyre and Sidon; and then I came to Byblus.

COMMENTARY

1) As the Euphrates and Tigris rivers brought civilization to the peoples of that part of the world, so too did the Nile to the ancient

Egyptians who also had an elaborate system of irrigation. The Nile *is* Egypt.

2) A theory of disease was even based on the Nile. In an attempt at a rational explanation of disease as opposed to a purely supernatural approach, Egyptian physicians viewed the body as a system of channels (vessels). This was based on the observation that, just as the Nile and its multitude of irrigation channels watered the land and made the fields fertile and productive, so a healthy body was one in which the 'channels' were clear and free from blockage. If the 'channels' did become clogged by bodily fluids, the remedy was to unblock them by means of purgatives, emetics or bleeding. Nevertheless, the treatment of disease remained under the dominant influences of religion and superstition.

3) Nine principal medical papyri have survived to modern times; the most important are the Edwin Smith and the Ebers. All date from around 1550BC and are almost certainly copies of much older writings – possibly even at third or fourth hand. What must have happened is that stray pages of ancient works were given to the scribes to copy onto papyrus scrolls; however, the scribes were without medical understanding and just copied what they were given without any sense of meaning or continuity. So what we have is a jumbled and uncritical selection of a variety of topics from long-forgotten medical texts.

4) The outburst of copying was not entirely by chance. The Hyksos (a nation formed from an amalgamation of different ethnic groups including the Semites, Horites and Indo-Iranians) had conquered Egypt soon after their formation in the 18th century BC. [It was the newly introduced war chariots, which the Hyksos deployed in large numbers, that gave them victory.] They were not assimilated and were driven out two hundred years later. This acted like a cultural renaissance for the Egyptians.

5) The Ebers is the longest of these papyri, consisting of 2289 lines on 108 pages and bearing the date of the ninth year of the reign of Amenophis I (1550BC). It consists of a few prayers and magical formulae but mainly of sections on a wide range of diseases

arranged according to the parts of the body affected. It is a compilation of earlier works in which superstition and sorcery were given full credence. Some of its original sources were apparently shared with the Edwin Smith papyrus; for instance, the observation on the pulse (see Chapter 2, Source 1) appears in both papyri.

6) The Edwin Smith papyrus is a roll more than 4·68 metres long written on both sides and consisting of nearly 500 lines. The writing on the front describes forty-eight surgical cases. It is remarkable for establishing relationships between lesion and symptoms and signs, and for grouping these into what we would now call syndromes (this advance is usually attributed to the Greeks). The author also is precise about his examination of the patient, the interpretation of the illness, whether to treat or not, details of treatment if he feels this will have a reasonable chance of success, and the establishing of the prognosis. Most significantly, the author realized that disease and injury had natural causes and were not due to supernatural influences. The writing on the back consists of incantations that are of a much later date.

7) It is of interest that J.H. Breasted, whose translation of the Edwin Smith papyrus was published in 1930, pointed out that in most of the case histories surgical manoeuvres were described under the heading 'Examination' whereas the giving of medicines appeared under 'Treatment'. This, he reasoned, indicated the difference in the esteem with which the work of surgeons and of physicians was held.

8) Apart from the Edwin Smith and Ebers, the main medical papyri are the Kahun which deals with women's diseases and veterinary matters; the Chester Beatty which is concerned with afflictions of the rectum and anus; and the Hearst which contains about two hundred and fifty prescriptions. It is probably not stretching things too far to suggest that the original works may have been divided into practical handbooks (surgery) and medical text books.

9) The Egyptians had at their disposal an array of herbal medicines, many of which had therapeutic value and are still found in

pharmaceutical products today. For example, they had acacia, anise, cassia, castor beans, castor oil, coriander, cucumber, cumin, garlic, poppy, saffron and wormwood. They also used mineral products such as alum, arsenic, copper, feldspar, nitre, sodium carbonate and bicarbonate, and sulphur.

10) On the evidence of the Edwin Smith papyrus, the Egypt of about 2700BC possessed a system of medicine that was a worthy predecessor of the Hippocratic. That it was not completely engulfed by the later magical vogue can only be assumed, since we know that Greek doctors derived some of their training and ideas from Egypt.

11) Evidence that the ancient Egyptians suffered from much the same range of diseases as occur today is provided by mummies and reliefs. The presence of tuberculosis, tumours of bone, parasitic infections (such as worms, and schistosomiasis – also called bilharziasis after Theodor Bilharz (1825–1862), the German who identified the parasite), hernias, smallpox and so on are all seen in mummies. And a temple relief shows a young man with the withered leg of poliomyelitis. There is also evidence of blindness almost certainly due to trachoma. Make-up was used both to enhance the appearance and, so they believed, to protect against such eye disorders.

12) The Egyptians paid much attention to cleanliness of body and home, probably for religious reasons. They washed morning and evening and before each meal using a type of alkali for soap. Since they ate with their fingers, water from a jug was poured over their hands at the end of a meal.

13) The Houses of Life were like colleges attached to the temples and were the meeting places of scholars and philosophers. Papyri were stored there and were copied, possibly for wealthy men who wanted a 'library' of their own. Papyrus was expensive and scrolls were hard to come by as the material was a royal monopoly. It was sheer good fortune that the original ancient papyri survived, to be found and copied many centuries later. Only the copies now survive.

14) Over-specialization has been held responsible for the later decline in Egyptian medicine. This notion of excessive specialization as recorded by Herodotus (*c.* 490–*c.*420BC) only becomes comprehensible when we realize that not only was the pharoah divine in his own right but that each part of his body was also divine and granted its own physician. The titles 'Guardian of the King's right eye', 'Shepherd of the anus' and so on, were at best merely ceremonial.

SOURCES

1) "If thou examinest a man having a dislocation in his mandible [jaw], shouldst thou find his mouth open and his mouth cannot close for him, thou shouldst put thy thumbs upon the ends of the two rami of the mandible in the inside of his mouth and thy two claws [the fingers of each hand] under his chin, and thou shouldst cause them to fall back so that they rest in their places."
The *Edwin Smith* papyrus

2) "I have formulae composed by the lord of the universe in order to expel afflictions caused by a god or goddess, by dead man or woman, etc., which are in this my head, in this my nape, in these my shoulders, in this my flesh, in these my limbs, and in order to punish the Accuser, the head of them who cause decay to enter into this my flesh, and feebleness into these my limbs."
The *Ebers* papyrus
This comes from the magic introduction and is possibly designed to reassure its user as to the papyrus's divine origin.

3) "Gynaecological examination must have been very detailed. It reached at least as far as the cervix, since remedies were described for uterine prolapse: 'remedy to cause a woman's womb to go to its place' (Eb. 789–793); for metritis: 'to cool the womb and expel burning out of it' (Eb. 820);.... Other prescriptions of the Ebers papyrus concern leucorrhea, metrorrhagia, vaginitis, means to

empty the uterus or to retain a threatening miscarriage."
Paul Ghalioungui, *Magic and Medical Science in Ancient Egypt*, 1963

4) "The practice of medicine they split up into separate parts, each doctor being responsible for the treatment of only one disease. There are, in consequence, innumerable doctors, some specializing in diseases of the eyes, others of the head, others of the teeth, others of the stomach, and so on; while others, again, deal with the sort of troubles which cannot be exactly localized."
Herodotus (*c.*490–*c.*420BC), *The Histories* II, 84

Mythology of the Eastern Mediterranean

(*c.* 1500BC)

In Byblus my heart sang.

Long ago, when I was a child, the people of Akkad had not been alone in viewing Nature's moods and seasons in terms of human experience; where else had we to look but at ourselves? We were born; we married; we gave birth and we died – and so, too, did the gods who governed our world. In their anger, they unleashed the wind, the rain, the thunder and the lightning. In their pleasure, they smiled and the sun shone on our fields. The plant spirits of our ancestors were transmuted into the gods of vegetation and were, like ourselves, life in conflict with death. Should they die and not be reborn, we also would suffer and die. So, to ensure their return, we played out the cycle of change in our worship. (You will no doubt see here the origins of homeopathic or imitative magic – like produces like.)

As I had discovered in my wanderings, there were numerous variations about this central theme, but the essence of them all was that the people's corn god had to be killed and descend into the underworld. There, his goddess would follow to strike a bargain with the resident deity that allowed her beloved to return to spend part of the year on earth – and woe betide him if he failed to report back to Hades for the remainder. With the passage of time, the rituals of death and rebirth were united in a single festival that varied only in degrees of licentiousness and cruelty from age to age and from culture to culture. And, also as time passed, people lost touch with the origins of their devotions and reached the ridiculous situation in which the god became his own enemy and was himself sacrificed to himself. The circumstances in which I reached Byblus accounted for my getting caught up as the lead player in one of these festivals.

* * *

The hands that pulled me from the sea were the rough calloused hands of fishermen. My ship had foundered in the last of the winter storms and the mounting agony of those days alone in the sea, when all my companions had perished, gave me further proof, if proof were needed, of the paradox of my mortal immortality.

It was my eyes that once again settled my immediate fate. When I managed to open the painfully swollen lids, I saw the face peering anxiously into mine draw back in wonderment; almost in reverence. The owner of the face lurched to his feet and started muttering to another member of the crew. When I next looked up, I had the distinct impression that my arrival was not unexpected.

"Tammuz." His voice was scarcely audible above the clamour of wind and sea. "Tammuz, you are welcome…" But I heard no more as I vomited horribly and lapsed once again into insensibility. The more unpleasant aspects of the mortality denied me were not to be evaded.

I dreamed that it was the dawn of the first day. A new life was born within me. I was warm and comfortable; my spirit was young again and the languor of sweet content pervaded my whole being. In the distance, women's voices sang to the accompaniment of a solitary flute. Perfume laden with the freshness of spring drifted over me on the faintest of breezes. But reality was not far away; the hands that washed my body with pure fresh water and bathed my sores in scented oil were the soft gentle hands of a mortal creature. I slept again.

When I awoke I was aware, through the mists that shrouded my mind, of another's presence. I felt her fingers touch my cheek, tentatively as if unsure of themselves. Then came certainty, and my face was caressed by those gentle hands; she kissed me. It was balm to my crusted and salt-laden lips.

I remained still, allowing my strength to return. When, at length, I roused myself sufficiently to view my surroundings, she had gone. I was lying on a vast couch and dressed in a robe of softest red linen. One side of the room was a single long opening, broken at intervals by decoratively carved pillars. From where I lay, I saw only the sea beyond, as if from a great height. I turned my head; what I thought to have been a room was but one part of a series of colonnaded cloisters surrounding a marble-tiled courtyard open to the sky. In its very centre, an elegant, cone-shaped obelisk drew down the warmth of the sun. The atmosphere had the innocence of youth. I continued to lie there absorbing the healing peace.

A movement, caught by the corner of my eye, made me raise my head. She was there after all, studying me from the shadow of one of the pillars. I watched as she walked across and kissed me, this time on the brow.

"Welcome Tammuz!"

"Why do you call me Tammuz? And the fishermen, too? It is not my name. I am called Bal-Sarra-Uzur."

After a moment's contemplation, as if bewildered by my failure to grasp what was so evident to her, she answered my question.

"In a dream the gods told me that Tammuz would not this year be chosen by the priests; he would be a stranger brought to Byblus by the sea. So, when the priests brought you here, I knew that you were to be my Tammuz."

She moved away while I lay back and gazed at her in wonderment.

"Who are you?" I was curious to learn what she believed.

She turned; my pulses quickened. "I am... " She stopped and, looking down, began twisting the ends of her sash between her fingers. The tears welled up. "I have no name. As a child I was taken captive and brought to Byblus. I was raised in the sanctuary of Astarte, the easier for her spirit to become my spirit. Tammuz, you are in my sanctuary now; I am Astarte!"

"Why do you still call me Tammuz, when you know my name is Bal-sarra-uzur?" I asked.

"Your body may be that of Bal-sarra-uzur, but your spirit is that of Tammuz. To the people of Byblus you are the god risen from the dead to be my lover. I am Astarte and *her* spirit is within *me*.

"Each year the chosen one of Astarte journeys into darkness to bring Tammuz back to his people. It is like this: Unless a stranger comes to the city in spring, the most handsome youth assumes the mantle of the god. It is a great and sought-after honour as the sacrifice ensures his immortality." I said nothing, as I did not see this as the ideal moment for questioning the delights of that condition. "If Tammuz is not reborn," she continued, "there will be no lover for Astarte and the harvest will fail. No children will be born and Byblus will fall into decay and ruin. You are my Tammuz!"

Astarte felt for my hand. "But who are you? You were pulled alive from the sea when any mortal man would have perished."

"My name truly is Bal-sarra-uzur and I come from Babylon in the east," I answered. "I am a physician who travels in search of understanding. But in moments of despair I believe my search to be in vain." She evidently didn't believe me as she continued to call me Tammuz.

In the days that followed, holy rites were celebrated in the courtyard, centred around the obelisk, the image of the goddess. We took no part. Our contribution began one morning when we were summoned early and ordered to leave the sanctuary. Descending a steep twisting stone staircase we took our places in the great procession already forming in the street below. For the whole of the day we journeyed inland climbing steadily, and all the while the flutes wailed and the people chanted a mournful lament, weeping and whipping themselves until their blood laid the dust at their feet.

"Astarte, why this misery?"

"Tammuz goes to his death and Astarte to her grief. It is of that they sing. We shall be alone and as surely as winter shall come so must Tammuz die." She looked at me and again there were tears in her eyes.

The next morning I awoke to find the people of Byblus gone; we were alone in a small stone temple prepared for our comfort and delight. I went outside into mountain air of inexpressible clarity and sweetness. If I were indeed to die there could be no lovelier place. The temple itself had been built in a cedar grove set in a natural amphitheatre high in the mountain. But high though we were, cliffs rose, precipice upon precipice into the eastern sky. Across the chasm, almost hidden in shadow, a river of crystal water sprang from a mighty fault in the rocks to disappear far below in the mists of the early morning.

I stood entranced, waiting for the sun to clear the cliffs. Goats were bleating as they browsed sure-footed among bushes on the precarious rock face. Wheeling in the sky high, high above, eagles maintained their relentless vigilance for unsuspecting prey; their majestic grace the only disturbing intimation of impending mortality in this earthly paradise.

The sun came to dissolve the mists and I watched the river plunging from pool to pool in a glorious tumble of falls until it again disappeared in a valley of deepening shades of green that carried it at last to the open sea. Butterflies rose in clouds to mate in the warming air, leaving beneath a profusion of sweet-scented flowers.

I was a god in the glory of his dominion.

Astarte held me from behind. "The waters of the river will soon be dyed with the blood of Tammuz and the anemones will be stained red."

"My love, Tammuz may die but Bal-sarra-uzur shall live. But how is Tammuz to die?" I asked.

"He hunts the wild boar, but one day Allatu, jealous of Astarte, breaks his spear on the rocks to leave him defenceless. He is killed by the boar. In due time, Allatu releases Astarte and she is saved by a priest from Byblus."

"Allatu?"

"She is the goddess who rules over the land of the dead."

"Then we are safe; no goddess can have power over me." And sitting by her side I told her my story.

When the river below turned blood-red – dyed with red earth swept along by its flood – we left the temple by the path to the east. Tammuz was dead, but this year his body would not be found and there would be no Astarte to grieve for him.

COMMENTARY

1) This particular myth is important because parallels can be found in Babylonia, other countries in the Middle East, Africa, Greece, Rome and even the New World. The ceremony was a blood ritual

which in early times was concerned with the annual growth and decay of vegetation and the vital importance of a successful harvest. Myths were created to explain the cycle of birth, death, and rebirth, and a variety of gods and goddesses were worshipped with the inevitable sacrifices. In these ceremonies the blood was shed to ensure the fertility of the earth. As a generalization, the more barbaric a people, the more bloodthirsty was their form of worship.

2) The inhabitants of Byblus really saw the reddish-brown swirl of mud, carried down by the River Nahr Ibrahim, spreading out to discolour the bright blue Mediterranean waters as the crimson life-blood of their god.

3) When Tammuz was slain by the boar, the drops of his blood fell to the ground and from them sprang the scarlet 'poppy' anemone.

4) In her haste to reach Tammuz's side, Astarte was caught by the thorns of a white rose bush. As she tore herself free, her blood touched the white flowers and dyed them red for ever. (It seems likely that she had been held up somewhere previously as the anemone blooms in the spring and the damask rose in summer – but that's mythology for you!)

5) To this day a mythological explanation of life, death, sickness and health may still be offered.

SOURCES

1) "Under the names of Osiris, Tammuz, Adonis, and Attis, the peoples of Egypt and Western Asia represented the yearly decay and revival of life, especially of vegetable life, which they personified as a god who annually died and rose again from the dead. In name and detail the rites varied from place to place: in substance they were the same."

Sir James George Frazer, *The Golden Bough*, 1963

2) "Hence it is said that the divine spirit is in the blood... as is taught by God himself."

Michael Servetus (1509–1553), *Christianismi Restitutio*, 1553
In this treatise Servetus described how the blood was turned to a bright colour in the lungs before being sent to the heart. This treatise was responsible for his death at the stake for heresy.

3) "Life consisteth in blood; blood is the seat of the soul; therefore the chiefest work of the microcosm is to be making blood continually."
François Rabelais, *Pantagruel,* 1533
Rabelais (*c.* 1495–1553) was a physician and a priest.

Medical practice in Babylon
(*c*. 1500BC)

The road to Babylon was long. Yet I was irresistibly drawn to the city, perhaps to escape a mythological death but more, I believe, to witness the great changes taking place in the country of my birth.

Hammurabi [1792–1750BC], king of Babylon, had been dead for two hundred or more years when I came to Babylon, but his influence was still felt. He was an excellent and humane man who had achieved political stability among the petty states of Akkad before conquering Sumer and establishing himself as supreme ruler of Babylonia. He took an innocent pleasure in referring to himself as King of the Four Quarters of the World. Although the kings of Akkad before him had been the human agents of the gods – unlike the pharaohs who were divine in their own persons – Hammurabi did not assume divinity in any form. Nevertheless, to ensure a favourable reception when the time came, he dedicated his achievements to the gods and had them inscribed on a mighty block of basalt. Some said that these were laws handed down to him by the gods but, as this thoroughly pragmatic monarch remarked, if the people chose to believe this and it made them happy, who was he to disillusion them.

Shortly after leaving Byblus, Astarte became convinced that Allatu was following us. The Queen of Darkness had been cheated of Tammuz and now, said my companion, in her vengeance demanded the soul of Astarte. No amount of reasoning on my part could shake this conviction; the Astarte at my side was a mortal child of circumstances, not an immortal goddess.

The first proof of what to her was Allatu's wrath came when we reached Kadesh. I had returned from bribing a camel-master to find Astarte frightened and weeping. With shaking hands she showed me a piece of cloth stained with blood that had risen into her mouth.

"Allatu has come to destroy me. We cannot deny the gods what is rightfully theirs and hope to escape their anger." Her voice was muffled and faint. She coughed and her blood flowed again.

I knelt and took her hands. They were cold. "It will pass," I said with a confidence I was far from feeling. The wings of the little bird of hope fluttered only feebly within my heart: I had seen many die from a simple beginning like this.

Yet pass it did and we set out into the desert. The journey was harsh and even the strongest amongst us suffered. At Derez Zor we boarded a boat to take us down the Euphrates to Babylon. Astarte was a very sick woman. Her flesh had begun to fall away; she craved for spiced dishes but would not eat, and by nightfall her tiredness was extreme even though she had rested through the day. When I took her in my arms at night, her skin was drenched with sweat and she would start the morning by coughing away the decay that was rotting her body.

Despite her pathetic physical deterioration, all her senses were heightened and she was happy, confident that once we reached Babylon, we would be under the protection of the goddess, Ishtar, and all would be well again. There was an unnatural quality about this confidence which disturbed me.

Arrived at Babylon, Astarte was carried ashore on her couch, while I acquired a house and servants (money talks in all eras!) and went to seek a physician. In the market place my enquiry was met with the choice between a practitioner of medicine or of magic. My puzzlement was evident.

"You are a stranger here?" I answered that I was newly arrived from Phoenicia and that my wife was wasting away.

The man thought for a while. "You should, I think, discover the divine intentions of this sickness." And he gave me directions to a practitioner of the magic art.

I found the man in a temple where he took my money before bidding me breathe into the nostrils of a sheep. Astarte should have done this, but when I explained that she was too sick to be moved, he agreed that I, as her husband, would serve as well. He then sacrificed the beast and removed its liver. This, he examined with great care, consulting various charts before giving me a magic formula. It was, need I say, useless for any purpose. Not much had changed since the days of my youth.

Walking away, I heard a voice within my head – perhaps the echo of Imhotep's – insisting: "Find a physician. Find a physician." I obeyed. The man who accompanied me home was clean-shaven and, besides a bag of herbs, carried a libation jar and a censer, the insignia of his calling. As he studied Astarte, I saw a look of hopelessness momentarily cross his face. Nevertheless, he prescribed a number of herbal concoctions which, he said, would ease the pain of her breathing and help her to rest more peacefully.

When I mentioned that I also was a physician but from a distant land, he was eager to tell me of the reforms introduced by Hammurabi, as he believed these to be unique to Babylonia.

"We have many herbal remedies that banish sickness. (He was correct in this, as some of the herbs had medicinal properties that you would recognize today, though others were quite useless. The physician's skill – or luck – lay in prescribing the correct one.) We physicians are rewarded according to the nature of the sickness and the worth of the sufferer. *Our* worth is judged by what we decide to treat and what we decide to leave to those who rely on magical potions! If we fail to banish the sickness or the sufferer dies, we have a penalty to pay, which likewise depends on the worth of the sick man. Yet we fare better than the surgeons; if they are inept, they are liable to lose their hands. Fortunately, most of their work is setting broken bones and removing the impediment that clouds the sight [cataract] – and they are skilled at both."

When the physician had left, I returned to Astarte. Her cheeks were flushed with a hectic fever but from their sunken sockets her eyes blazed with her desperation to live. She struggled for breath while I could only watch her agony.

Then, at the end of a day when the wind had whipped the desert sand into a fury and hidden the sun from view, I sensed her life was finally slipping away. I hurried to her room. Her eyes were shut, but her cracked dry lips were moving. I bent down to listen.

"Allatu has come for me at last. Goodbye, Tammuz."

And there was no stopping her life's blood as it poured from her mouth.

Despite my reluctant acceptance of Imhotep's belief in the natural cause of disease, death still remained a mystery to me, and with the passing of the centuries I felt I had every justification for continuing to believe that it could be nothing other than a divine intervention.

COMMENTARY

1) To the Babylonians, disease and suffering were the consequence either of wrongdoing or of being possessed by devils. The sick were, therefore, far more likely to try to placate the deity they had upset than to consult a physician.

2) The Code of Hammurabi is a block, or stele, and had some two hundred and eighty laws inscribed on it, ten of which were applicable to doctors. It deals with case laws covering economic provisions, family law, civil law and criminal law. It is one of the first, if not the first, indication of professionalism in medicine and the care of patients. Medical men were held accountable for their actions and instances of misconduct were covered by a legal framework. Punishment ranged from fines to amputation of a hand and even execution. The Code also established the fees that doctors could demand for their services. (The stele is now in the Louvre in Paris.)

3) Although the Code is associated with the name of Hammurabi, civilized communities had probably lived by it for many centuries. The fact that the laws resemble the Mosaic laws indicates a common heritage. The Code records that the physician was a representative of the healing god, Ea, and so could be regarded as a sort of priestly person. The physician is, however, clearly distinguished from the surgeon. Likewise, the distinction between magical procedures, religious procedures and medical procedures – such as herbal treatments – was also clearly defined. The specific references to abscesses of the eye would suggest that eye infections

were common. The Code might seem to indicate that Babylonian medicine was fairly advanced (compared to that in other countries), but that this was not the case can be deduced from Comment 1, above. Thus the reasons for the absence of any progress in medical practice were similar to those in previous eras.

4) The apparent severity of a craftsman's punishment when things went wrong should be measured against those meted out to other professionals which could involve execution. It is possible that these punishments were not always enforced – otherwise recruits to the healing profession might have been few and far between.

5) During the reign (c.1792–1750BC) of Hammurabi the small city state of Babylon was transformed into the large territorial state of Babylonia. Although he achieved control of the waters of the Euphrates – essential for a nation dependant on irrigation agriculture – the last years of his reign were beset by almost constant warfare over the distribution of water. Unfortunately, the Babylonian method of irrigation eventually led to the silting up of the channels with resultant salination of the soil and loss of fertility.

6) The Babylonians believed that sheep (and some other animals) could foresee the future in a way that human beings could not, and that this ability was somehow revealed in the shape of their livers, the peculiarities of which had much to do with the determination of good or bad omens.

7) The goddess Astarte was identified with Ishtar, Aphrodite, Venus and other goddesses in different countries. She was the goddess of love and war (see Chapter 1).

8) The Babylonians originated the decimal system; divided the year into twelve months, the week into seven days, the hour into sixty minutes and the minute into sixty seconds; and they divided the circle into 360 degrees.

SOURCES

1) "If a doctor has treated a freeman with a metal knife for a severe wound, and has cured the freeman or has opened a freeman's

abscess with a metal knife, and cured a freeman's eye, then shall he receive ten shekels of silver.

"If the son of a plebian, he shall receive five shekels of silver.

"If a man's slave, the owner of the slave shall give two shekels of silver to the doctor.

"If a doctor has treated a man with a metal knife for a severe wound, and has caused the man to die, or has opened a man's abscess with a metal knife and destroyed the man's eye, his hands shall be cut off.

"If a doctor has treated the slave of a plebian with a metal knife and caused him to die, he shall render slave for slave.

"If he has opened his abscess with a metal knife and destroyed his eye, he shall pay half his price in silver."

The Code of Hammurabi

[A craftsman would earn about one-fiftieth of a shekel a day.]

Chapter 6

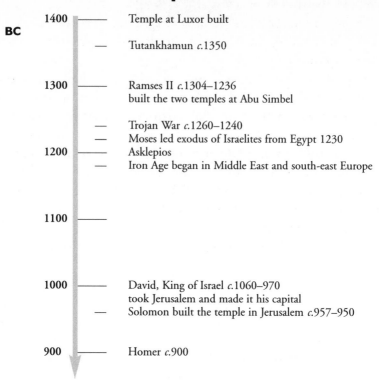

BC

1400 — Temple at Luxor built

— Tutankhamun *c.*1350

1300 — Ramses II *c.*1304–1236
built the two temples at Abu Simbel

— Trojan War *c.*1260–1240
— Moses led exodus of Israelites from Egypt 1230
1200 — Asklepios
— Iron Age began in Middle East and south-east Europe

1100 —

1000 — David, King of Israel *c.*1060–970
took Jerusalem and made it his capital
— Solomon built the temple in Jerusalem *c.*957–950

900 — Homer *c.*900

Greek medical mythology

(*c.* 1200BC)

Far away in the northern sky the storm clouds gathered over Mount Olympus. The purpled edge of darkness hung from the vault of heaven to be rent asunder by brilliant flashes of anger as Zeus hurled his thunderbolts one by one into the earth beneath. Behind the little town of Tricca the hillside lay enveloped in a swirling, eddying curtain of mist. All Thessaly trembled and waited for the god to speak.

The pebbles on the track glistened in opalescent light, as down the centre the mist condensed into human form, attenuated wisps falling away on either side only to roll in again at once as if to mask his progress. The man walked slowly, his head bowed deep in thought. His sandled feet trod with confidence, the weighty staff in his hand more an encumbrance than a help. The robe, gathered over his left shoulder, bared his chest; its hem was wet. At the man's side trotted a short, bare-footed creature shrouded in a hooded cloak. As he drew closer, the man sensed my presence and raised his head. In his clear, wise eyes was recognition.

Puzzled at this, I studied him closely. Yes, there was something familiar about him. Little of his face was visible, hidden as it was by a luxuriant beard shimmering with minute droplets of mist. In my mind's eye I began to picture the face as if shaven. Recognition continued to elude me until he spoke.

"Surely, Bal-sarra-uzur, you have not forgotten me?"

The emotion that filled my breast was overwhelming. When I had last heard that voice, it had spoken a different tongue but so powerfully did it bring memory flooding back that I lost my hold on the present. I believed I was with Imhotep again being led into the swirling mist to stand before him in the temple. I heard him speak.

"Imhotep is dead, but his spirit lives on within me. It is Asklepios who speaks with his voice."

Unashamedly, I embraced him, holding tightly until a measure of control had returned. Then, my voice still unsure of itself, I asked, "Master, why are you here? What are you doing? Is Thessaly your new home?" While questions poured from me, the storm drew closer; then in a moment of inspiration, I saw the purpose of our meeting.

"Master, you have come from Zeus with my release. I cannot live for ever!" Desperation overcame me. "If you love me as a son, you will obey the gods and end my agony!" I fell to my knees before him and kissed his hands.

He waited before giving his answer.

"Bal-sarra-uzur, truly I love you, but I no longer have power to change your destiny. My purpose now is to bring the knowledge of Egypt to this land. You should be glad for it will add to man's understanding of disease. The seeds of a new civilization lie here in Greece and when they awaken their glory shall be unsurpassed. But your life, Bal-sarra-uzur, must continue; it is for others yet to come to achieve your salvation. There can be no other road to release!" I am certain I glimpsed a tear in his eye; the depths of my misery were no secret to him.

Together we walked on down the path, the unnatural light casting deep shadows among the rocks. The track was steep and the stones underfoot loose and treacherous. As we crossed the bed of the stream, Asklepios spoke again. "If I cannot bring you rest from this life, I can," he looked at the little figure perched on a rock, "I can give you a companion. Telesphorus is my son; he shall go with you to share your burden and bring strength when your soul is in torment."

Telesphorus looked up at me; as he did so the hood fell back. Never had I seen such an impish face. It was the face of a child, a youth, a young man, an old man – it was the face of a being for whom age had no meaning. The expression was full of devilment but quite without malice. His chin was small and pointed; his nose upturned; his eyes were the blue of gentian and tilted imperceptibly upwards at their outer corners; his ears set high and coming to the faintest of points were made to catch the slightest sound; his blond hair lay close to his skull in tight little curls. Immediately, I sensed a bond between us.

"Telesphorus," I said, lingering over the syllables, "will you do as your father says?"

"Yes, Bal-sarra-uzur, I shall do so willingly. You see," he twisted his head to glance at his father, who gave an imperceptible nod, and then turned back to me, "my father has the blood of gods flowing in his veins. So I am immortal and the prospect of accompanying you, even to eternity, holds no terror – in fact, I shall make it a pleasure for both of us." He jumped off the rock, grinned and winked at me.

Great drops of rain now started to fall, marking their arrival with little pits in the dust. Glancing back, I saw Zeus descend from Mount Olympus out of the darkened sky; as his thunderbolts came closer, roars of fury shook the earth.

"Imhotep was mortal," Asklepios said, "but I am truly immortal – Apollo was my father although he entrusted my upbringing to Chiron, the centaur." I must admit that, at first, I doubted the truth of his claim as the gods were liberal with the distribution of their seed and no self-respecting family in ancient Greece (and, later, in Rome) was without a god among its ancestors. But I soon realized that, as he said, he was a true immortal. "So well did Chiron instruct me in the art of healing that Zeus is in a rage." He paused for a moment in contemplation. "It appears that the population of the Underworld is declining and Hades holds me to blame!" His voice smiled at the thought.

"I want you to meet two of my daughters," Asklepios said as we reached the welcome shelter of his home. "They may help you understand man's attitudes to disease." In answer to his call, two exquisitely beautiful girls, dressed simply in white with golden fillets binding their fair hair, appeared from an inner room. There was humanity and compassion in their gaze. But there was something else besides – an impression that their love would never be won by mortal man. They were symbols of what mankind sought on earth, but would, it seemed, attain only in heaven.

Asklepios introduced them to me. Then, reading my thoughts, he went on, "Hygeia and Panacea will always be sought by man – and, as you will discover, he will do so with increasing intensity the more his knowledge expands. Hygeia, he will seek to grant him health throughout his life; Panacea, to cure him of all his ills. In his ignorance, he will confuse the one with the other. And when I am gone, they will take their places on Mount Olympus, for ever inaccessible to earthbound mortals."

At these words, the blackened sky became a moment of purest silver accompanied by a roar that shook the house, reverberating back and forth among the hillsides until its echo faded and died.

"My children," Asklepios rose to his feet, "Zeus demands my life and I must go to meet him. Bal-sarra-uzur, you have my son Telesphorus for company on the road ahead. Though he may not appear so, he is wise and through him you will discover much about the nature of man. Learn and profit."

He bowed his head and remained silent for a while before kissing each of his children in turn. Then, placing Telesphorus's small hand in mine he walked to the door and into the night.

Still grasping Telesphorus by the hand, I followed. The rain had ceased. There was Asklepios, a serpent wound halfway up his staff. Suddenly the heavens split asunder, a tearing blinding flash drowned the darkness and a mighty sound filled the night. Asklepios stood still, gazing upwards, the central point of an ethereal brilliance that dimmed the fury of the thunderbolt.

* * *

"Do not lose heart." Telesphorus was already sympathetic to my predicament. "Greece is about to change the world with a glory that shall echo down the centuries. Now, though, I want you to fix your eyes on the greatness of Athens and remember: What is time but an illusion. When, tomorrow, we arrive in Pindar's bright and violet-crowned city, it shall be eight hundred years from today."

COMMENTARY

1) The influence of Egyptian medicine undoubtedly spread to other countries, primarily along the trade routes which carried both

knowledge and medical preparations. Nevertheless, the Egyptian influence on Greece has to be treated with circumspection: the Mycenaeans were certainly receptive to foreign ideas and practices but the Greek mainland appears to have been more resistant.

2) The ancient Greek character tended to be independent and argumentative, neither of which sat comfortably with a powerful priesthood. Consequently, physicians and religiously-inclined healers practised in reasonably friendly competition. The followers of Asklepios became known as Asclepiads – of which there were many families. The temples of the cult, known as Asclepieia, resembled the spas of today: after prayers, a bath in the mineral spring and massage with sweet-smelling ointments, the patient was introduced to the rite of temple sleep. In the night the priest visited him or her in the guise of the god. If the patient was awake the priest offered medical advice; if asleep, the advice came in a dream which the priest interpreted in the morning; he then prescribed an appropriate treatment, for instance, blood-letting, a purgative or perhaps an emetic. If the treatment was successful the patient left a thank-offering to Asklepios, usually in the form of a model of the diseased part in clay, wax or even silver or gold. In some temples the cure was achieved by a sacred dog or snake licking the diseased part in the night.

3) The Greeks clung outwardly to many old traditions and still practised religious and magical rites, but there is no evidence that they stood in awe of them. For instance, they worshipped Zeus but joked about his private life – which would have made headlines in the tabloid press!

4) In Greek mythology Telesphorus was indeed a son of Asklepios; Hygeia and Panacea were two of his daughters – their names are now part of our language. The image of Telesphorus, with or without that of his father, later appeared on coins and medallions and, until the 18th century, he featured with his father in the frontispieces of books.

5) Although Asklepios is shown on the Timeline as having lived around 2000BC –that is, later than the Siege of Troy – the fact that

Homer placed him at the earlier date may be regarded either as poetic licence on Homer's part or as evidence of the general unreliability of dating events in the distant past.

6) By the 6th century BC the cult of Asklepios had become a major influence in the treatment of the sick. Beside the supposed healing powers of Asklepios himself, there were the centres of healing based around temples of health. The finest remains of such a temple are still to be seen at Epidaurus. At an Asklepion, health was restored with a combination of treatment, rest and instruction on how to lead a healthy life.

SOURCES

1) "The 10th General Assembly of the World Medical Association adopted a medical emblem to be used in providing complete protection to civilian doctors, their assistants and medical civil defence units which are not and cannot be protected by the Red Cross under the Fourth Geneva Convention. The emblem is a straight vertical stick and a serpent represented by a sinuous line over the stick with two undulations on the left side and one undulation on the right side, displayed on a white field."

Resolution adopted by the 10th General Assembly of the World Medical Association, Havana, 1956

An excellent resolution, but not one to be relied on to give protection in the world as it is today.

The emblem represents Asklepios's rod and serpent – not to be confused with the caduceus (the herald's wand) of Hermes (Mercury in Roman mythology) in which two serpents are entwined up the staff. Notwithstanding, the caduceus has, since the Renaissance, been used as a medical symbol. In 1902, for example, the caduceus was adopted as the official insignia of the United States Army Medical Department!

2) "For, Aesculapius is a healing force which emanates from the

substance of the sun and comes to the aid of the souls and bodies of mortals…. That is why images of serpents are added to those of these gods [Aesculapius and Salus, as Hygeia was called in Latin], because they enable the bodies of men as it were to throw off the skin of disease and to quicken again to their former strength, just as snakes revive every year by sloughing their old skin."
Macrobius (c.400AD), *Saturnalia*, I,20

3) "Leaning on his staff, with its entwining serpent, Asklepios revealed himself to every mortal who came to him in distress. The sick who, with unquestioning faith, had laid themselves down to rest in his sanctuaries were healed by him in their dreams. He held out a helping hand to any who invoked his aid. He became a saviour, mightier than any other divinity of Antiquity. He was gentle and kind to all who sought healing at his hands. He was powerful and universally loved at the time when Christianity came into the world, and became one of its strongest opponents."
J. Schouten, *The Rod and Serpent of Asklepios*, 1967

4) "Agestratos was unable to sleep on account of headaches; as soon as he came to the abaton [temple of healing] he fell asleep and had a dream. He thought that the god cured him of his headache and, making him stand up, taught him wrestling. The next day he departed cured, and after a short time he competed at the Nemean Games and was victor in the wrestling."
From a votive stone found at Epidaurus

5) In the *Iliad* Asklepios is described as a chieftain of Thessaly from whom Achilles learnt about medicine. In his turn, Achilles passed on this knowledge to his friend Patroclus who put it to practical use. Eurypylus, wounded with an arrow in the thigh, was carried to a tent where Patroclus "laying him at length, cut out with a knife the bitter, sharp arrow from his thigh, and washed the black blood from it with warm water. Then he applied a bitter, pain-assuaging root, rubbing it between his hands, which checked all his

pains; the wound indeed dried up and the bleeding ceased."
Homer (8th century BC), *Iliad*

6) "O bright and violet-crowned and famed in song, bulwark of Greece, famous Athens, divine city!"
Pindar (*c.*518–*c.*438BC), *Fragment 76*

Chapter 7

	500	Iron Age began in Britain
BC	490	Battle of Marathon
		The doctrine of the four humours developed during this century
	460	Birth of Hippocrates
	450	
	447	Building of Parthenon began in Athens
	431	Start of Peloponnesian War (Athens v Sparta)
	430	Outbreak of the plague of Athens
	404	
		Athens surrendered to Sparta
	400	
	356	Birth of Alexander the Great
	350	
	347	Death of Plato
	323	Death of Alexander the Great
	321	Death of Aristotle

Plague of Athens and teachings
of Hippocrates
(430–c. 425BC)

In the harsh realities of a city under siege, I would have believed myself free of the world of mythology had it not been for the continued presence of Telesphorus in my life and the perception that ancient myths remain as tributaries of the stream of human consciousness. The evolution of mythology to explain the inexplicable did, after all, reveal an astute insight into the nature of man and an imagination uninhibited by a deeper understanding of the physical world.

(I make no apologies for my emphasis on mythology. I can vouch for the fact that the creatures of that world were as alive to the Greeks of some two or three thousand years ago as were the inhabitants of other countries of whom they had only heard tell. The true interpretation of the past is lost with the passing of time, but vestiges of an ancient spirituality lie not far below the surface of any culture – call it part of the race memory if you will. And since much of it has no counterpart today, you find its manifestations inexplicable and perplexing – perhaps even threatening. You must yourself have noticed how the attitudes of some of your patients – and not only the less educated – towards their illnesses, real or imagined, are heavily influenced by considerations of this nature of which they are probably totally unaware.)

Our arrival coincided with the invasion of Attica by the confederacy of Peloponnesian states [431BC] and to my chagrin we were swept along with the mass of people driven to take refuge in the city. As it was scarcely an auspicious introduction to a glorious new world, I feared Telesphorus had made a serious miscalculation.

"No, Master," he assured me. "This is but a temporary blemish on the face of beauty." I would not myself have described the conditions we met in quite such a romantic manner. Indeed, before long the blemish began to suppurate when the plague, which had come up from Aethiopia through Egypt and Libya, broke out in Piraeus [430BC]. Rumour had it that the Peloponnesians had poisoned the wells, but when the pestilence spread to the high city it became yet more deadly – and rumour gave way to the fear of uncertainty since the water here was from springs and safe from poisoning. Many who attended the sick were themselves quick to die, a point not lost on those self-styled physicians whose interests lay more in the rewards than in the love of their work. They fled the city in unseemly haste at the first opportunity and to no one's great loss: their remedies were as unremarkable in their effectiveness as were all the supplications to the gods or the enquiries of the oracles.

Among the few trained physicians who remained was the Coan, Hippocrates. He came from a family of Asclepiads whose origins could be traced back to Asklepios. (I told you, did I not, that a god among one's ancestors was a prerequisite for a good Greek family!) They regarded themselves as highly trained healers and were extremely jealous of their reputation. They lived an itinerant existence visiting villages and towns that were too small to make it worth the while of any physician to settle in the neighbourhood. Hippocrates's fame was widespread, from his birthplace on the island of Cos in the east, through Attica and Thessaly to Thrace in the north. His mere presence at the bedside was reputed to revive the dying. But the charisma of the man was never more evident than in the midst of the moral and physical squalor reigning in Athens. No matter where his patients lay, he was always dressed in clean linen, his hair and beard neatly combed, his nails trimmed and his gentle hands well cared for.

Hippocrates had a vision of medicine which he carried before him all his life. At his home in Cos and on his travels he was constantly teaching, to the extent that at times his everyday conversation seemed to be a series of aphorisms. (Much as the writings of your Mr Shakespeare are full of quotations!) I first met him soon after the outbreak of the plague. He had been up since dawn writing.

"This is the time of the day when I find it most convenient to record my yesterday's observations," he explained after we had exchanged greetings. "I set down every detail, even when events have not gone as I might have hoped. Only in this way will we learn what is normal in nature. I am trying to understand disease by classifying what I observe."

Speculation about disease in general, and its causes in particular, had, he told me, been rife for some while; most importantly, the notion that it was something abnormal had at last been appreciated. But lacking anything other than the simplest idea of the structure of the body and being in almost total ignorance of how it functioned, the only features of disease that were in the smallest degree comprehensible were those recognizable by one of the five senses. With different diseases having symptoms in common, this led to awesome confusion. Yet it was a start and gave Hippocrates the inspiration to bring order of a sort out of chaos.

The reason for my visit had been to seek his advice on the treatment of the plague. "State the past, know the present, foretell the future," was his enigmatic reply. "So far as any disease is concerned, strive to help, or at least to do no harm. The art of medicine is threefold: the disease, the patient, the physician. The physician is a labourer for the art."

After a moment's pause, he continued: "Those who make supplication to the gods and enquire of the oracles waste their time. It may well be that the gods rule in heaven and earth, but their influence on our destiny is remote. In medicine natural causes prevail. Diseases are natural events.

"But you asked about the plague. Alas! no physic is of use in these cases. Give barley gruel unless the patient suffers excessively from thirst when water and honey will be best. As to its prognosis, all I can say is that our natures are the physicians of our diseases."

Evidently, he had no better idea than I had. Nevertheless, he was devoting his questioning Greek mind to the problem. Besides grouping illnesses according to their dominant symptoms, he told me he was dividing them into acute and chronic, and into epidemic, endemic and sporadic. As he saw it, until a disease was identifiable as a disease, its cause would remain a mystery and until its cause was known, it could not be adequately treated.

The more Hippocrates talked, the more encouraged I became. His understanding of disease was sufficient to show the way ahead. How I hoped this would satisfy the gods and ensure my release!

I next asked him what he considered to be the cause of the plague. The immediate cause, he said, was the mass of people crowded into the city as this laid them open to attack by an ubiquitous noxious element. What this noxious element was, or where it came from, he was unable to say. And this, regrettably, showed me that any rejoicing on my part would be premature. Hippocrates's difficulty was that he did not know that disease could spread by contagion [transmission of disease by direct contact with an infected person or object] though towards the end of his life there were those such as Isocrates [436–338BC] – and later Aristotle [384–322BC] – who were convinced that phthisis [tuberculosis – usually referring to tuberculosis of the lungs] spread by a corrupt exhalation of the breath. But until the nature of this corruption was known, the concept remained another of the speculations that abounded in medicine.

"Disease may also come," he continued, "when our digestions are disordered, or from outside sources such as the climate or the geography of the region. If the cause of the disease can be removed, the natural forces within our bodies will overcome the damage it has produced. As physicians, we can help these forces by seeing to the patient's diet and hygiene and the exercise he takes." (How, he would have rejoiced when the immune system was discovered.)

When the plague had ceased to ravage Athens, I left the city and journeyed with Hippocrates to his home on Cos. At many places on the way he revealed that, when the occasion demanded, he could be an excellent surgeon as well as the incomparable physician I knew him to be. Among the operations he performed was cutting for stone in the bladder – though this was an undertaking he would only allow trained fellow Asclepiads to perform; no one else should even attempt the operation. The only occasions on which Hippocrates refused to carry out a necessary operation were when he considered the patient might lose too much blood.

For a while I remained on Cos as his guest. My greatest pleasure during these months was to listen while he taught, gathering his pupils under a plane tree. On one of these occasions I learnt about the doctrine of the humours which was to develop over the ensuing centuries and underpin – or haunt, depending on your viewpoint! – medical practice for the next thousand and more years. You will even catch echoes of it in your own time. (For the sake of readier comprehension I have taken liberties with his style of speech.)

"From the scientific standpoint," he began, "the doctrine of the humours had its origins about a hundred years ago with Pythagoras [*c*.582–*c*.507BC] – though the medical connection was not immediately made apparent. Pythagoras had spent several years in the temples of Egypt working on a system of numbers that extended back into the astrological recesses of Babylonia and Chaldea. His elucidation of the ancient meaning gave physicians the key to the prognosis of fevers since he believed that certain numbers were endowed with mystic values. On certain days after the onset of a fever, its behaviour determines the prognosis; on certain other days, we know the patient will take a definite turn for the better or the worse.

"But besides working with numbers, Pythagoras challenged the age-old belief that the heart was the seat of life, the soul, the emotions and the intellect; he proposed instead that the mind and the intellect resided in the brain. We have no means of proving his proposition, but his reasoning was persuasive. He also maintained that animals as well as man have a soul and that when the body dies, the soul becomes incarnate again in another body.

"On his return to Crotona, he introduced the doctrine of the four elements – earth, fire, air and water – which, in turn, possessed the qualities of cold, heat, dryness and moisture. These qualities he termed contraries – heat and cold were active contraries; dryness and moisture were passive contraries. Everything in the world consisted, he said, of different mixtures of the four elements.

"This philosophical theory was the inspiration for the idea that the body contained four humours, all of which were to be found in the blood."

At this point he called to one of his assistants and, holding his arm by the wrist, he made a swift cut into a vein at the bend of the arm. Another assistant caught the flow of blood in a transparent beaker. At a sign from Hippocrates, he placed the half-filled beaker on a table and bound a towel round the arm.

A far-away look came into Hippocrates's eyes. "Long, long ago in the confused and misty beginnings of their existence on earth our ancestors saw that life ebbed away when blood flowed from a terrible wound. Blood and life were one and the same to them and now, to our philosophers, blood is become the essential fabric of their theories.

"When you watch the blood in this beaker," he came down to earth again, "you will see the humours appear, though if you had a fever the definition of the changes would be clearer."

As we watched, a layer like a bright red jelly began to form on the surface.

"That," he said, "is blood, the humour."

Next, a transparent yellow fluid seemed to be extruded.

"That is yellow bile."

Left behind was a dark-red jelly from which a pale greeny-white layer finally separated. I was to learn later that the dark-red jelly was regarded as black bile – thus completing the four humours. Hippocrates did not admit of its existence – most confusing!

"And that final layer," said Hippocrates, "is the humour that is called phlegm. When the blood has come from someone who is ill with a fever, the phlegm may appear more quickly on the surface. Each humour, according to the philosophers, is formed and stored in a different part of the body: blood in the heart; yellow bile in the liver; and phlegm in the brain – a most convenient site!"

"This doctrine of the humours is distorted by some physicians," he spoke with feeling, "who maintain that man is nothing but blood [in the humoral sense]; others that he is only bile; and yet others that he is only phlegm. Each pretends, indeed, that there is a unique substance – chosen at random – which changes its appearance and properties under the influence of heat or cold, becoming thus pleasant, bitter, black, white, and anything else. This is not so! It is utter stupidity!" His indignation was wonderful to behold!

The following summer Hippocrates announced that he would be returning to Greece and asked whether I would accompany him. When I declined, saying that I had long planned to visit the school at Cnidos on the neighbouring peninsula, he stopped what he was doing and led me by the arm into the shade of the plane tree.

"Have you ever met a physician who was trained at Cnidos, Balthasar?" he asked. (I had learnt the wisdom of adapting my name to suit the locality.)

"No," I replied.

"Then I must warn you against their teachings. The Cnidians think more of the disease than of the patient. They see in every symptom a disease which must be treated. This is wrong; you must look to the good of the whole patient. The nature of the body can be understood only as a whole."

A note, almost of anger, had entered his voice. Many times I had heard him rail against those who, with only limited instruction, practised medicine. But this was the first occasion I had heard him speak so vigorously against a school of physicians.

"Why do you feel so strongly about the Cnidians? Surely theirs is only a different approach to the complexity of disease?"

"That may be so." His tone spoke his true feelings more than the words. "But only by observation and appraisal do we learn how the significance of a symptom can vary according to circumstance. In every patient there is a natural balance which must be sought out and restored by gentle and varied treatment.

"Medicine is an art, and the artist is a man who refuses to put the pleasures of the senses or the comfort of the body before the satisfaction of his artistic sense." I now realized that my questioning had turned his thoughts to ethics, one of his favourite topics. "There are some who call themselves physicians who use their position of trust to debauch the women in the patient's household, who cannot keep the secrets learned at the bedside and who dress and behave in an unbecoming and ostentatious manner. These men do not uphold the dignity of our profession; you should have nothing to do with them."

Dear Hippocrates could be rather pompous when the mood took him! "When you first see a patient, do not discuss your fee," he went on. "If you do, you may lead him to suspect that unless he agrees to your terms you will leave him to his fate. This may be harmful, particularly if the disease is acute. Hold fast to your reputation rather than to profit. It is better to reproach patients you have saved than to upset those who are at death's door."

I left Cos the next day. Hippocrates's parting words to me were: "Love of the art and love of mankind go together." I never saw him again, though his teaching has remained with me and will, I suspect, still be in my heart when I am finally granted peace.

COMMENTARY

1) Hippocrates did actually exist (though some scholars dispute this). He was an itinerant practitioner of medicine, based on the island of Cos in the eastern Mediterranean and, according to Plato (428–347BC), was from a family of Asclepiads. With Hippocrates, we see the influence of the individual on the development of medicine.

2) Hippocrates was the probable author of a number of treatises, but what we now know as the Hippocratic collection consists in the writings of many authors around that period. [The aphorisms put into Hippocrates's mouth in the text are taken from treatises in the collection.] The collection is free of religious and supernatural influences and represents a major step forward in medical thinking. The doctrine of the four humours provides a model whereby the cause of illness can be explained without resort to these influences. Over the centuries there had been a gradual build-up of the rational approach to medicine and the Hippocratic school was its culmination. (There is more about Hippocrates in the opening paragraphs of Chapter 8.)

3) The plague of Athens is significant in the history of public health in that it contrasts the destruction wrought by disease with the benefits of community life. The nature of the plague, despite

Thucydides's excellent description, remains a matter of speculation: it might have been bubonic plague, despite the omission of any mention of the typical buboes (swelling of the lymph nodes); it might have been smallpox, typhoid fever, typhus fever or a now extinct form of a disease that would be recognizable as such today. Alternatively, since it lasted for some five years, it might have been a combination of all the 'plagues' that might be expected, given the circumstances. The true interpretation of many past diseases becomes lost, not only with the passage of time, but also because reliable descriptions were non-existent.

4) Pythagoras did not originate the doctrine of the four elements, he simply brought it back to Greece from Egypt. Nevertheless, at some time during the century and more after his death, the doctrine of the four humours developed from a bringing together of the four qualities (hot, cold, moist, dry) with the doctrine of the four elements.

5) The four humours were not figments of the imagination; they have modern equivalents. First, blood when shed is red (blood, the humour), then, as coagulation proceeds, serum (the yellow bile of the ancients) is extruded. The dark-red jelly (black bile – which they believed was formed and stored in the spleen) consists of red blood corpuscles enmeshed in fibrin; phlegm is what we now call the buffy coat and consists mainly of white blood cells and platelets. Admittedly, the eye of faith must have been required as the buffy coat really only appears as such after centrifugation. But if you think about it, the ancients were nearer the truth – as we understand it – than they could possibly have imagined. Apart from the more esoteric changes that take place during disease, one extremely common alteration (in trauma, haemorrhage, infections and many other conditions) is leucocytosis, the increase in circulating white cells that shows itself in the increased depth of the buffy coat – and it was excess of phlegm that was blamed for so many diseases.

6) War was a prominent feature in Greek history. Frequent references to battle wounds, some of which were successfully treated, may be

found dating from the Homeric era. By the time of the Peloponnesian war (431–404BC) a number of surgical techniques were recognized as appropriate for battlefield casualties.

7) The Peloponnesian war was started by the Peloponnesian states, led by Sparta, in order to restore independence to the Greek maritime states which were the subject allies of Athens, the dominant state, both on land and at sea. During the first few years of the war, fortune favoured first one side and then the other, before eventually the last Athenian fleet was beaten by Lysander in 405BC; the city was besieged and Athens finally surrendered the next year leaving Sparta the supreme state.

SOURCES

1) "For the disease (which took first the head) began above and came down, and passed through the whole body; and he that overcame the worst of it was yet marked with the loss of his extreme parts; for breaking out both at their privy members, and at their fingers and toes, many with the loss of these escaped. There were also some that lost their eyes, and many that presently upon their recovery, were taken with such an oblivion of all things whatsoever, as they neither knew themselves, nor their acquaintance."

Thucydides (460–399BC), *History of the Pelopennesian War*

2) "I swear by Apollo Physician and Asclepios and Hygeia and Panacea and all the gods and goddesses, making them my witnesses, that I will carry out according to my ability and judgment, this oath and this covenant:

"To hold him who has taught me this art as equal to my parents and to live my life in partnership with him, and if he is need of money to give him a share of mine...

"I will apply dietetic measures for the benefit of the sick according to my ability and judgment; I will keep them from harm and injustice.

"I will neither give a deadly drug to anybody if asked for it, nor will I make a suggestion to this effect. Similarly I will not give to a woman an abortive remedy. In purity and holiness I will guard my life and my art.

"I will not use the knife, not even on sufferers from stone [in the bladder], but will withdraw in favour of such men as are engaged in this work.

"Whatever houses I may visit, I will come for the benefit of the sick, remaining free of all intentional injustice, of all mischief, and in particular of sexual relationships with both female and male persons, be they free or slaves.

"What I may see or hear in the course of the treatment or even outside of the treatment in regard to the life of men, which on no account one must spread abroad, I will keep to myself, holding such things shameful to be spoken about.

"If I fulfil this oath and do not violate it, may it be granted to me to enjoy life and art, being honoured with fame among all men for all time to come; if I transgress it and swear falsely, may the opposite of all this be my lot."

The Hippocratic Oath

The oath has been translated and variously modified down the ages. For instance, substitution of God, Christ and the saints for Asclepios and his family would have made it acceptable to the early Christian church. There are some apparent contradictions between the oath and what we know was practised by Hippocratic doctors; thus the prohibition of surgery is at odds with the surgical treatises that deal in detail with the subject.

3) Among the Hippocratic aphorisms are the following:
    On prognosis: "In order to prognosticate correctly who will recover and who will die, in whom the days will be long, in whom short, one must know all the symptoms, and must weigh their relative value."

    Taking a history: "Leave nothing to chance, overlook nothing: combine contradictory observations and allow yourself enough time."

Study the patient and his circumstances: "Observe the nature of each country; diet; customs; the age of the patient; speech; manners; fashion; even his silence; his thoughts; if he sleeps or is suffering from lack of sleep; the content and origin of his dreams… one has to study all these signs and to analyse what they portend."

Chapter 8

Aristotle and Alexander of Macedon
(370–321BC)

Hippocrates was correct in his opinion of the Cnidians. Their narrow-minded concept of disease did not, in reality, differ greatly from that of my Akkadian ancestors: both behaved as if disease existed as a thing apart from the body. Since there was nothing for me to learn, I hurriedly took my departure from Cnidos.

When I had been with Hippocrates I had been able to share the clarity of his vision. But on my return to Greece I found that the essence of his understanding of disease was in danger of being drowned in a torrent of medical philosophy. The first signs of this had appeared while Telesphorus and I had been making our journey through time to Athens and, indeed, Hippocrates had approved some of its aspects. But so many physicians and philosophers were now expounding such a variety of theories on the nature of disease that my immediate difficulty was to discern the main stream of thought. My confusion was not eased by the fact that many of these theories were subsequently ascribed to Hippocrates – as were a number of aphorisms that I know were not his. In consequence, my recollection of those times is hazy and I now find it difficult to be precise about the chronology or who said what.

Before moving on I needed, for my own peace of mind, to know whether Hippocrates had really advanced the understanding of disease or whether his work had been without a sure foundation.

"Balthasar," Telesphorus had the voice of one who knew the past but had also visited the future, "Hippocrates stood at the gateway, but the gods denied him admission as he lacked the keys to the doors beyond. Before a physician can understand what is truly abnormal, he must have a complete understanding of what is normal. This was not granted to Hippocrates, although in many instances he did appreciate that what he saw was, in fact, not normal." [This may seem self-evident, but once again we must forget what we know if we wish to reach into the minds of people who lived before our knowledge was acquired.]

"Hippocrates understood that diseases had their patterns," continued Telesphorus. "His attempts to classify them were to enable the same disease to be recognized as such by all physicians. He knew that, if it could be identified, every disease had its cause; but with observation his sole instrument, he could do no more than identify certain responsible conditions. He understood also that treatment could influence and, sometimes, cure a disease – but, more importantly, he knew that the body had the power to recover by itself, unless overcome by the severity of the disease.

"Although his work is treated with disdain by some of the present schools of philosophy, it contains elements of true understanding which will always survive. Even so, for this to happen knowledge of his teachings must be spread throughout the world.

"I know you rarely accept my advice," there was a wicked twinkle in his eye as he said this, "but I think we should journey to Mysia to meet Aristotle [384BC–322BC], not so much because he is a great and influential philosopher, but for where his friendship will lead."

I asked no questions as Telesphorus would never allow me to base my decisions on a knowledge of future events. We simply made our way across the Aegean Sea to Mysia.

* * *

I first met Alexander of Macedon [356–323BC], the last of the gods to walk this earth, when I came to Pella with Aristotle. The philosopher had been summoned by King Philip [382–336BC] as tutor to his thirteen-year-old son.

Aristotle had spent much of his youth in Pella when his father was physician to Amyntas II, Philip's father. I like to imagine it was this hereditary influence that added the scientific drive to his philosophical inclination. At any event, after studying under Plato [427–347BC] in

Athens, he left for the court of Hermeias in Mysia, already believing himself the superior of his dead master. There he stayed for five years during which he described, mostly from his own dissections, nearly five hundred animal inhabitants of the island of Lesbos and the countries around the Aegean Sea.

He was one of the most restless characters I ever encountered; always searching for facts, facts and more facts. Every scrap of information he obtained he fitted into his plan of the animal kingdom – even if some of the facts became a trifle bent in the process. When he had no first-hand knowledge he borrowed a description which, more often than not, had been gleaned from some traveller's fanciful imagination – he was just as gullible as my poor father.

On our arrival in Pella, Aristotle persuaded King Philip to establish a school in an ancient grove of the nymphs. Paths were cut where he might walk while teaching and in the very centre a belvedere was constructed, ostensibly for his rest.

Alexander's fellow pupils were selected personally by Philip from the noblest families in the land. Amongst them were Ptolemy [c.367–283BC] and Hephaestion [d.324BC] the tall, dark, curly-headed boy upon whom Alexander came to rely as the only intimate friend in his life. All were to form the Companions of the Grove of the Nymphs, the elite of Alexander's invincible army.

In the belvedere, Aristotle continued his own work.

"There are similarities and differences between the various forms of animal life," he said to me on an afternoon when Alexander and his friends were exercising their horses. "According to these all life is arranged on a ladder of ascending perfection with man standing on the topmost rung. See here!" he commanded and led me to a table where he had displayed a row of hens' eggs with part of their shells removed. "There you have one animal developing from an embryo to its state of perfection. The truth in microcosm illustrates the truth in the macrocosm."

In his excitement, his lisp became more obtrusive; but more distracting was the way he looked at me, not in the eye, but over the top of my forehead. I think he believed the gods came to learn from him and it was to them he was really speaking.

"This egg," he pointed to one on the left, "is three days old. You can just see the first signs of life in that small red pulsating spot. That is the heart."

He went along the row showing me how, as the eggs became older, more of the developing embryo became visible – the body, the head and the enormous eyes.

"Organs appear in order of their importance; the first is the heart – when its motion ceases, death is inevitable. It is the source of the body's innate heat and the seat of sensation and thought. It is home to the soul."

I looked at him quizzically. He responded to my challenge. "Are you not aware of its action when you experience pleasure or pain?" That, I could not deny.

"But," I asked, "how do you reconcile this with the views of Pythagoras and Hippocrates who maintained that the brain was the seat of the intellect?"

"Who was Pythagoras? Who was Hippocrates?" Sometimes the arrogance of the man was beyond endurance.

"Did they study the animal body as I have done?" he went on, irritated with me for having doubted his word. "No, of course they did not, otherwise they would have found the brain to be without sensation. They were like Plato who concerned himself not with facts but with theory. Balthasar, I have told you before and I tell you again, knowledge must be built on the evidence of a man's senses. They may at times lead him into error, but only by the accumulation of facts can he hope to arrive at the truth.

"No one can doubt the dominance of the heart. Do not my observations tell me that pneuma is responsible for the transmission of both sensation and movement? Does it not convey information from our senses to the heart and is it not the medium through which the expanding and the contracting of the heart bring about movement? Plato refused to trust the evidence of his five senses; he was overwhelmed by his belief that mankind would arrive at the absolute truth through inspiration. But I tell you he was seeking an escape from reality!

"The true duty of the brain, Balthasar, is to cool the innate heat of the body."

Aristotle, by this time, was pacing up and down the belvedere, twisting and untwisting the girdle that held his robe in place, and lisping furiously.

"You see, this is in agreement with my observations that there exist four fundamental qualities, the hot, the cold; the wet, the dry. Each one of these pairs is the opposite of the other. All matter is made up of one from each pair in combination. Thus air is hot and wet; earth is cold and dry. Fire is hot and dry; water is cold and wet. These last two are pertinent to our argument for the fire in the heart must be prevented from overheating the body. This the brain does by secreting a special water we call pituita or phlegm. The lungs help also, by cooling the blood."

I was about to remonstrate with him by pointing out that variations on this theme had been in circulation for many years; that Hippocrates had held rather similar views – which doubtless would have impressed him not at all – when he suddenly stopped his perambulation, looked straight at my forehead and said:

"I have wasted enough time. I am eating with Philip tonight and must change my clothes. Goodbye, Balthasar. You are wiser now than you were two hours ago." And with that his frail, undersized body disappeared through the trees.

Some months later Aristotle introduced into his teaching his beliefs on the soul and on the nature of procreation. Alexander listened with great attention for he was deeply concerned about the mystery of his conception. Philip himself had cast doubts on the legitimacy of his son's birth. His wife, Olympias, the sacred prostitute of Samothrace, had been visited by Zeus in a dream on the night before the wedding ceremony. The lightning of the god had struck fire deep within her womb and the astrologers unhesitatingly interpreted the dream to mean that Zeus and none other had impregnated the beautiful Olympias. By her behaviour and continual worshipping at the altar of Zeus-Ammon, Olympias did nothing to dispel the rumour. Zeus was the father of her son. (This should come as no surprise if you recall what I said about the gods becoming entangled in Greek family trees – and only the greatest of them would suffice for the greatest of earthbound monarchs. Ammon, the ram-headed god of the ancient Egyptians was identified by the Greeks with Zeus.)

Aristotle, quite unintentionally, explained for Alexander how this could be.

"Concerning reproduction," he said, "you must understand that the function of the female is to provide the material for the new birth. It is the function of the male to provide the soul, the principle of life. You may view the female part, the material, as the unformed clay to which the hands of the potter give form. The potter contributes nothing material. Thus, since the semen of the male is an accidental and not an essential, it is possible for the principle of life to enter the womb without physical contact." [To oversimplify matters, this is a statement of the possibility of virgin birth (the offspring being the incarnation of divine powers), belief in which is as old as religion itself. For Alexander, it was confirmation that he was indeed the son of Zeus-Ammon.] A strange look of exultation came into Alexander's face. He continued walking by Aristotle's side, but his thoughts were far away.

Aristotle, seemingly unaware that his pupil was no longer listening, continued: "You may distinguish that which has life from that which has not by the presence of this soul, or psyche, which gives form and leads to the development of perfection. The soul in man has three parts: the vegetative which is concerned with nourishment and reproduction; the animal, which is sensitive; and the rational which is intellectual. The lowest of these is the vegetative; the highest, the rational. Plato would have had us believe that the intellectual or emotional soul was immortal. In his ignorance he failed to relate theory to observed fact and held firmly to what he wished to believe." The contempt for his old master's opinion was awesome.

"From what I have said, you can see why love appears in different guises. The love determined by the vegetative soul drives a man to reproduce himself; it is crude and vulgar. The love which a man can experience through the rational soul transcends the needs of the body; it can be felt by a man for a man; it opens the way to a state of greater understanding." Alexander exchanged glances with Hephaestion; they put their arms around each other's waists. "Thus the female with her defective soul," continued Aristotle, aware of the effect of his words, "is imprisoned within her material body; only a man is capable of transcending all intellectual and spiritual limitations."

Alexander was twenty-one when he left Pella at the head of thirty thousand infantry and seven thousand cavalry to conquer the world.

* * *

The lands of Ammon were under the heel of the foreign invader; in Egypt the Ram-headed god of the Hidden Sun had been defiled by the Persian conqueror. Alexander, the chosen one of Ammon, would restore for the last time the true religion. This was written in his stars.

He was received with rejoicing in the city of Jerusalem where his coming had been foretold by the prophet Daniel. And in Egypt he was crowned Pharaoh in Memphis with all the mystic circumstance known to that ancient people.

Shortly after the ceremony, Alexander marched with a small body of troops down the western side of the Nile delta until, at Rakoti on the shores of the Internal Sea, he founded the first and greatest of the cities that would bear his name.

The plans were drawn up under his guidance and the sites of all the buildings marked out on the ground: Where the temples would rise to the glory of Ammon, sacrifices were offered and a papyrus was unrolled in symbolic gesture where the library would preserve the written knowledge of the world.

* * *

In Babylon, Alexander was feted. He had fulfilled the prophesies and released the lands of Ammon from bondage. The armies of Darius III, King of Persia, had been outmanoeuvred and then defeated.

Whether Alexander was militarily correct to pursue the person of Darius is not for me to judge. Perhaps he was, as the continued presence of the defeated monarch was a threat to the security of his new empire. But this I do know: from the moment that Alexander set out from Babylon in pursuit and left behind the lands of Ammon, he ceased to be a god and became a cruel, brutal conqueror. At times his actions were tinged with madness. The gods were done with him and he was treading with increasing swiftness the path to his inevitable destruction.

* * *

Darius was murdered by Bessus, his own cousin. Bessus was betrayed by Spitamenes, his own general, and delivered into Alexander's hands. Spitamenes was slaughtered by his own wife, who came to Alexander carrying her husband's head. But still Alexander strode like an avenging Achilles through the Persian empire. His troops suffered in full measure from the harshness of the climate and the countryside, and only the force of his personality supported by not a few murders of friends both good and bad, enabled him to stave off mutiny.

* * *

One prince of Bactria remained unsubdued. From his impregnable mountain fortress, Oxyartes refused to acknowledge Alexander. He considered himself safe since the walls of his stronghold rose in continuation of the precipice at whose foot we were encamped. When Alexander demanded his surrender, Oxyartes replied that only if Alexander's men grew the wings of eagles could they take the fortress.

But grow wings they did and took the fortress.

Oxyartes had a daughter, Roxana, whom Alexander took as bride in 327BC. After Alexander's death in Babylon four years later, Roxana and her child fled to Greece where both were assassinated. The power-hungry generals were not running the risk of any challenge to their authority by supporters of the dead Alexander.

COMMENTARY

1) Aristotle's insistence on empirical investigation (resting on trial or experiment) when studying the natural world was to result in a methodology that remained the framework of scientific research for much of the following 2000 years. Dante (1265–1321) described Aristotle as 'Master of men who know'.

2) The foundation of Alexandria at the mouth of the Nile ultimately led to a seat of learning that many would argue has still to be surpassed. Ptolemy, one of Alexander's generals, became ruler of Egypt in 323BC and its king in 304BC. He was intent on creating a lasting monument to the great Alexander: the museum and library testified to this desire. Greek scholars came in their numbers to this new centre where it appeared that all restrictions on learning would disappear once and for all.

3) The perplexities of the ancients over the location of the Intellect, the Soul and the Heart should not be taken at anatomical face value, since all was not as it might seem to be to modern eyes. Concepts have changed and words have lost their ancient meanings – sometimes beyond recall; in particular, the intellect of today is not the Intellect as it was understood in the distant past. Although it may appear that the ancients (from Pythagoras onwards) were delving into the mysteries of anatomy and physiology, their arguments were, in fact, on a far more esoteric, spiritual plane. For them, the Intellect (by means of which man discerns what lies beyond the earthly plane) resided in the Heart – not the anatomical heart, but the Heart that is the centre of the soul.

4) Pneuma is difficult to translate. Literally it means breath, but in the ancient context it refers to the spirit or soul.

5) The brain was believed to cool the innate heat of the body by secreting pituita (from the Greek meaning 'spit') or phlegm (another name for the same thing). At the start of its career phlegm was something that cooled heat, but over the centuries the Latin and Greek words changed their meaning to the precise opposite: inflammation, or something regarded as produced by heat. [The

occurrence of words with contradictory meanings is not uncommon. 'Cleave', for instance, can mean to stick together or to split apart; 'sanction' can mean to prohibit or to permit; and just think of 'wicked' today.] The reason the disease of the eye known as cataract got its name was because the phlegm pouring down from the brain like the cataracts on the Nile was supposed to cloud the lens.

6) The cult of Ammon, symbolized by a ram-headed idol, suddenly appeared about two thousand years ago. It coincided with the astrological age of Aries (the ram). Alexander was the chosen one of Ammon and his task was to free the lands of Ammon from the Persians who were suppressing the cult of Ammon. He is usually depicted with ram's horns on either side of his head.

7) Hephaestion was a true friend to Alexander and there was a strong homosexual element to their relationship – nothing out of the ordinary in those pre-Christian times. Nevertheless, men can have a strong bond with each other without the need to attribute a homosexual element.

8) A similar happening to the taking of Oxyartes's stronghold brought an end to the siege of Sardis when Cyrus the Persian took the city of Croesus the Lydian, c.546BC. (Herodotus, *The Histories*, I, 84)

SOURCES

1) Alexander's coming to Jerusalem was prophesied in Daniel, 11, v.2-5: "And now will I show thee the truth. Behold, there shall stand up yet three kings in Persia; and the fourth shall be far richer than they all; and by his strength through his riches he shall stir up all against the realm of Grecia.

"And a mighty king shall stand up, that shall rule with great dominion, and do according to his will.

"And when he shall stand up, his kingdom shall be broken and shall be divided toward the four winds of heaven; and not to his posterity, nor according to his dominion which he ruled: for his

kingdom shall be plucked up, even for others beside those."
Most modern scholars hold that the Book of Daniel was written some two hundred years after Alexander's time. Thus the prophesy was probably based on written tradition – unless you prefer to believe that it sprang fully formed from the writer's imagination.

2) "No physician, insofar as he is a physician, considers his own good in what he prescribes, but the good of his patient; for the true physician is also a ruler having the human body as a subject, and is not a mere moneymaker."

Plato (*c.*427–347BC), *Republic*, Book I, p.342
Plato was a contemporary of Hippocrates and this quotation indicates that the ethical side of medical practice was as much a consideration in those early days as the purely medical side.

3) "Nature does nothing in vain."

Aristotle (384–322BC), *Politics*, Book I, Ch. 2.
This conclusion was echoed by Galen and consequently governed medical thinking until relatively modern times.

Chapter 9

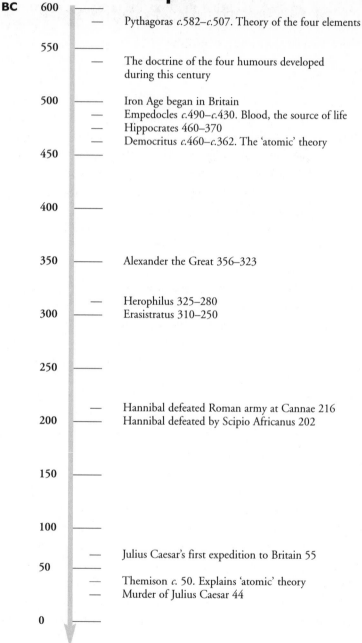

BC 600

Pythagoras *c.*582–*c.*507. Theory of the four elements

550

The doctrine of the four humours developed
during this century

500

Iron Age began in Britain
Empedocles *c.*490–*c.*430. Blood, the source of life
Hippocrates 460–370
Democritus *c.*460–*c.*362. The 'atomic' theory

450

400

350

Alexander the Great 356–323

Herophilus 325–280
300
Erasistratus 310–250

250

Hannibal defeated Roman army at Cannae 216
200
Hannibal defeated by Scipio Africanus 202

150

100

Julius Caesar's first expedition to Britain 55
50
Themison *c.* 50. Explains 'atomic' theory
Murder of Julius Caesar 44

0

Anatomy, physiology and the confusion of Greek medical philosophy

(321–30BC)

In the wake of Alexander's army, and at his express command, came scientists, philosophers, physicians, artists, sculptors, writers, astronomers, all bearing with them the seeds of learning that they might disseminate them throughout the world to testify to the greatness of Greece and of Alexander. The heart of this intellectual empire was Alexandria in Egypt. Its influence would remain undimmed for close on a thousand years.

When I resumed the burden of my life after Alexander's death, it seemed appropriate that I should visit Alexandria. There, in Ptolemy's museum, I rubbed shoulders with philosophers and scientists from the far corners of the earth. The confusion inspired by the diversity of their opinions led of necessity to compromise – except among the physicians. They argued, and the more they argued, the further did their views diverge.

This, it is not to be wondered at, had the effect of making medicine one of the most popular subjects, for the Greek mentality rejoiced in endless argument. Because of their profound respect for the human body, the Greeks, anatomically speaking, were disinclined to lift even a solitary finger to uncover what they could not see. The Alexandrians – and those who were not Greeks behaved like Greeks – gave their imaginations free rein to explain these unseen mysteries. For these philosophers, disputation was more important than experience; the human mind alone was noble enough to seek out the truth.

Nevertheless, two men gave me cause to hope. Both Herophilus [335–280BC] and Erasistratus [310–250BC] were intent on expanding knowledge through observation and experimentation; for them, there was more to anatomy than the display of naked bodies at athletic contests.

I had no difficulty in finding Herophilus. He was dissecting the body of a man who had been executed for the murder of his wife – confined within walls, the stench was already worse by far than that of any day-old battlefield. Herophilus's demonstrations were necessarily few, but always popular despite the assault on the senses, as dissections of the human body were a novelty and, once the initial distaste had been overcome, excited immense curiosity. Among the onlookers was Erasistratus.

While Herophilus displayed the convolutions of the brain and distinguished the two major parts of the organ, Erasistratus held his peace. But when the anatomist moved down the table and opened the belly, Erasistratus began to breathe more deeply and run his fingers through his beard. This was the moment he had been waiting for. The structure of the body was unchallengable and there for all to see, but the functions of its various parts were speculative and Erasistratus believed himself to be on safe ground as he had experimented on live criminals condemned to death. (This has always been open to doubt as, had either man left a written account of his work, nothing has survived. I was never witness to a live dissection, but I have no reason to question its veracity.) Herophilus removed the liver and put it on one side. He then turned his attention to the stomach and duodenum.

"When food has been eaten," he declaimed, "it enters into the stomach where it undergoes coction. This means that the food is triturated, dissolved, heated and fermented. It then is in a semi-fluid state and passes out of the stomach to be taken up by the body."

"Herophilus," boomed Erasistratus. All eyes turned to him. "How do you know this?"

"Hippocrates stated it was so, and… "

"Ha! Hippocrates said so! And you seriously expect us to believe that just because a flatulent old man said it was so, it is so? Why, it is nothing more than a cookery lesson!"

Erasistratus was getting into his stride. Most of the onlookers were becoming bored with Herophilus's pedantic and long-winded commentary and were ready for an argument. It was part of the expected entertainment.

"I was born on Chios and was taught by Chrysippus [*c.*340BC] on Cnidos. And where did he," pointing an accusing finger at Herophilus, "learn his medicine?" The sneer with which the word medicine emerged had been well rehearsed. "I will tell you. On the island of Cos. Herophilus is the imitative ape of Hippocrates. At Cnidos I learnt the true medicine."

The conflict between the two men seemed incapable of resolution. Whatever Herophilus stated, Erasistratus went to great lengths to challenge. Nevertheless I believe their animosity was the driving force behind their achievements.

"I do not form my opinions from what others have done, but on what I myself have done." Erasistratus thumped the table and glared around the room, daring anyone to contradict him. No one did. "In my experiments," he went on, "I have shown that the stomach, by its movements, breaks up the food into a multitude of small particles. These constitute the chyle. The chyle is of two parts. The first contains the elements of bile and is carried to the gall bladder. The second contains the elements of blood and is carried to the vena cava. Dispute that if you can, Herophilus!"

Herophilus knew he was no match in public debate for the bombastic younger man; but however much Erasistratus annoyed him, he was prepared to make allowances since he appreciated that, in their different ways, both were working towards the same ends. Ignoring the tirade, he proceeded with his dissection. Suddenly he looked up.

"Erasistratus," he said with a sparkle in his eye. "You do sometimes agree with me and even make use of my studies when it suits you? No! do not deny it. You know my work on the pulse, of its variations in rate and rhythm in certain circumstances. And you agree with it?"

"Yes." Erasistratus was grudging with his acknowledgment.

"And as there is another point on which we agree," Herophilus continued, "would you explain the function of respiration while I expose the lungs?"

In a less belligerent tone than before, but with evident ill-nature, Erasistratus began.

"We owe the fact of life to pneuma, that most subtle vapour which pervades our whole being. The air we breathe enters our lungs and from there is taken to the heart which contracts and dilates in response to a force inherent within it. In the heart the air is changed into pneuma, our vital spirit, which is then carried to all parts of the body by the arteries. That part of the pneuma which reaches the cavities of the brain undergoes a further alteration into animal spirit for dispersal to the different structures of the body through the nerves, which are hollow. When we make a movement we do so because our muscles shorten by becoming distended with animal spirit.

"Further, the blood in our body is contained within the veins, at the ends of which are innumerable invisible communications with the arteries. When an artery is cut, the pneuma first escapes; then the blood from the veins and heart is able to flow through these communications and also escape.

"But when we come to consider disease, I utterly reject the belief that it is due to disorder of some hypothetical humour, as propounded by Hippocrates and his ignorant followers." Not for long could Erasistratus refrain from disparaging the Hippocratic method. "Fundamentally, disease is due to plethora. There is too much blood and starvation is the treatment."

Herophilus had reached the limit of his patience. "If that is your belief, you are a greater fool than I took you for. If the diseased body contains an excess of blood, the treatment is to bleed the patient. But you refuse to do so because that is Hippocratic practice!" With that he slammed his knife on the table and stormed into his inner room.

* * *

The emergence of the new civilization in Greece that Asklepios had foretold had been more in the nature of an eruption than an evolution. Where it had originated remained a mystery and I often thought that Imhotep's answer to my question of where he had gained his knowledge was as applicable to the Greeks as it had been to him. Thanks to Telesphorus I had seen the eruption in medicine at its magnificent best, but I was also witness to its inevitable petrifaction in the stream of philosophical lava that flowed from the initial explosion. Herophilus and Erasistratus had been the last to escape.

In the final analysis philosophers are in the enviable position of being able to talk arrant nonsense and yet be listened to with respect by others who believe they are expounding a profound truth. [Cicero (106–43BC) was of much the same mind when he wrote: "Nihil tam absurde dici potest quod non dicatur ab aliquo philosophorum"! – "There is nothing so ridiculous but some philosopher has said it."] Eventually, when I had suffered from nearly two hundred years of absurdities, I decided that enough was enough.

"Telesphorus." Who else could I consult? "Telesphorus, explain what is happening. I have listened and tried to understand, but these interminable arguments about animal spirits and vital spirits, about pneuma and humours make no sense. Far from leading to a greater understanding, they are destroying Hippocrates's teachings. If physicians cannot build on sure foundations already in place, what hope is there for me?" Despondency had become a continuous burden. I could see no end to my earthly existence.

"Bal-sarra-uzur." Whenever I was seriously troubled, Telesphorus would revert to calling me by my original name. "I regret that most of what you hear makes sense only to the speaker. Our philosopher-physicians are shut away in their Alexandrian towers – which is just as well for the rest of humanity."

I could not argue with that. The generality of mankind was as well, or as ill, served as it ever had been by any herbalist or itinerant physician or surgeon.

"Once again, we should undertake a journey with deliberate intent – this time to seek enlightenment. I believe Themison [c.50BC] to be the one man capable of pulling together the tangled threads of Greek medical speculation."

And so it was that we made our way to Laodicea where the road to the west divides, one fork taking the traveller towards Ephesus and the other, the more northerly, to Smyrna.

Themison proved to be a kindly man of middle years who made us welcome. When he began to talk, however, I feared I was about to be subjected to yet another one-sided theoretical diatribe.

"The body is composed of an infinity of minute particles. I claim no credit for this discovery; it was first proposed nearly four hundred years ago by Democritus [c.460–362BC] and then Erasistratus gave it his approval. Nevertheless, contrary to the belief of those who maintain that there are four elements, these particles are all of a similar nature – but I see you knew this." Although he gave me a curious look, far from being offended, he seemed pleased to have an audience prepared to listen intelligently.

"My contribution has been to explain how these solid, atomic particles may be responsible for disease. They may become too tightly packed, too loosely packed, or too tightly in one part of the body and too loosely in another. The simplicity of this indicates how we should choose our treatment. In the first case, we produce relaxation by blood-letting, purgation and fomentations. In the second, we administer astringents – cold baths, alum, vinegar. In the third – ah! the third is the challenge to the physician as he must do whatever he thinks to be necessary."

He was not at all put out by this lame ending; indeed he regarded it as the quality that gave the essential twist of complexity to ensure that when other less worthy theories had been long forgotten, his would endure.

At this point, Themison rose and crossed the room to remove the top of a lamp. This was in the form of a flat decorated plate with a hole in its centre.

"You must have realized, Balthasar, that my philosophy as a Methodist is Epicurean and can never be acceptable to the Stoics. Consequently they have devised a theory that is as different from mine as it is possible to get." He held up the lamp top. "It is as if our medicine is the solid plate, while the Stoics build their medical philosophy on the centre hole!" His face began to crease until, unable to contain himself any longer, he gave way to sobs of laughter.

It was a merry sound and I must admit that the thought of the Stoic physicians contemplating nothingness appealed to my sense of the absurd and I, too, began to laugh. Nevertheless, Themison was showing me, quite unintentionally, how great was the gulf that divided the different schools of medical philosophy. Insofar as the hole in the top of the lamp served to control the flame, so was that nothingness – the pneuma – held to have perfectly reasonable functions to perform. By formalizing themselves into distinct schools, physicians were successfully restricting their freedom of thought. When Themison had dried his eyes on the sleeve of his robe, he continued with his exposition.

"The Pneumatists, as we call them, have quite lost their way. They call upon their recollections of Pythagoras and Aristotle and now maintain that too much heat causes the pneuma to expand and to move more rapidly in the body so that the person becomes excited. Too much cold causes it to contract and move more slowly: the person becomes sluggish. Excess of heat and dryness produces acute diseases and excess of cold and moisture leads to chronic diseases."

When Themison saw that I was about to question him, he held up his hand and continued.

"I have still to mention two other schools of medical philosophy, if only on account of the numbers of their adherents. There are the Empiricists who say: 'The patient is ill. Use your own experience or what you have learnt from the experience of others to treat his complaints and do not concern yourself with the whys and wherefors.' They reject the need for dissection as they say you only see what is dead and learn nothing about the living! And there are the Dogmatists who take the Hippocratic stand that disease is caused by a lack of balance in the bodily humours but have carried it to such extremes that it now defies recognition."

I must admit to becoming more than a little confused by all these different philosophies as they seemed so at odds with each other. However, when he mentioned the doctrine of the four humours I began to pay attention.

"The originating force behind all these theories," he said, "is the doctrine of the four humours – though, I admit, many philosophers have, over the years, not been struck squarely by its impact and have been sent spinning away at a tangent. One of their greatest difficulties has been to account for the warmth of the body.

"Pythagoras's theory of the four elements tells us that heat is associated with perfection and strength, and cold with things underdeveloped," he explained. "This is why, a short while after Pythagoras's death, Empedocles [*c.*490–*c.*430BC] restated the theory of the four elements and, in one of his moments of poetic inspiration, concluded that the source of heat – of life itself – was the blood.

"Next the philosophers reasoned that innate heat must require cooling and this, they maintained, was achieved by the pneuma inhaled during respiration. After all, Balthasar, they had to find a purpose for respiration, particularly as Aristotle had said that Nature did nothing in vain. However, they extended the function of the pneuma by saying that it was carried to the brain where it was responsible for producing thought and the movements of the body. When pneuma is prevented from reaching the brain, we lose consciousness." (Change pneuma to oxygen and think of the implications.)

"Eventually, the philosophers brought together all the theories and observations at their disposal, and saw how they could help Nature. They believed that phlegm was responsible for most diseases and, being stored in the brain, was ideally situated to pour down and drown the organs beneath – over the eyes to cause cataract; onto the lungs to cause consumption; into the abdomen to cause dropsy; into the bowels to cause dysentery; and into the rectum to produce haemorrhoids. Nature attempts to deal with this, they said, either by losing the phlegm through the nostrils or by drying up the excess with fever. If the excess is not drained and reaches other parts of the body it produces inflammation or leads to abscesses.

"At this point the philosopher-physicians excelled themselves. Phlegm was a humour contained in the blood and was increased in disease. Why not give Nature a helping hand by removing blood from the patient? That, Balthasar, is why blood-letting is now an integral part of the doctrine of the four humours and is regarded as the best means of removing diseased material from the body.

"As time went on, the physicians discovered that an imbalance between the humours could also be rectified by purging, enemas, hot and cold baths, creating issues to promote the flow of phlegm [pus] and much else, usually unpleasant, besides."

Suddenly, Themison stopped. "I sense you are not what you seem." He looked searchingly into my eyes as if seeking an answer to his uncertainty; not finding it he shook his head in disappointment and, since he showed no inclination to continue talking, Telesphorus and I made our departure.

(If you think this account of the Greek period unnecessarily confusing and at odds with itself, then, believe you me, you should have lived through it! And, what is more, it got worse before it got better. Nevertheless, the persistence of the doctrine of the four humours until displaced by your modern scientific approach was no mean achievement.)

COMMENTARY

1) The Alexandrian school witnessed the differentiation of subjects, in the sense that the structure of the body (anatomy) was studied separately from the function of the body (physiology). Anatomy was favoured by the fact that dissection of the human body was permitted – a freedom not found in mainland Greece.

2) Balthasar's and Telesphorus's observations on the chaos that descended on medical thinking in Alexandria are valid. No general agreement could be reached about the basic principles on which the theory and practice of medicine should be organized. The academic climate in such a centre of learning made it almost inevitable that religion would increasingly become a lesser element in the arguments of the philosophers.

3) Also valid is Themison's account of the various medical philosophies. It serves as the commentary on the doctrine of the four humours and how it developed and became confusing.

4) Neither Herophilus nor Erasistratus left any written record. As so often happens with our knowledge of ancient history, we have to rely on accounts written many years – perhaps centuries – after the

event. However, we may be fairly confident that Herophilus made extensive anatomical studies and that Erasistratus, the physiologist, applied working models to different parts of the human body.

5) "That part of the pneuma which reaches the cavities of the brain undergoes a further alteration into animal spirit for dispersal to the different structures of the body through the nerves, which are hollow. When we make a movement we do so because our muscles shorten by becoming distended with animal spirit." This concept is not so ridiculous or far-fetched as it might seem considering that the 'muscles' of some robots of the present electronic age are powered by compressed air conveyed to them along tubes.

6) "Further, the blood in our body is contained within the veins, at the ends of which are innumerable invisible communications with the arteries. When an artery is cut, the pneuma first escapes; then the blood from the veins and heart is able to flow through these communications and also escape." This shows how perceptive the ancients could be in their gropings towards the truth. Erasistratus realized that the capillaries must exist some two thousand years before they were seen under the microscope. His error in believing that the arteries contained pneuma which had to escape before the blood could flow from an artery is attributable to his intellectual honesty, as he had never seen a corpse whose arteries had bled when cut.

SOURCES

1) "They [the Ptolemies] hold that Herophilus and Erasistratus did this in the best way by far, when they laid open men whilst alive – criminals received out of prison from the kings – and whilst these were still breathing, observed parts which beforehand nature had concealed."

Celsus (25BC–50AD), *De Medicina*

Some believe that the Ptolemies were so eager to help their scientists that they released condemned criminals into the hands of the anatomists. Whatever the truth of this, Alexandria was an attractive place for scholars, since conditions in most other countries did not favour serious study.

2) "When the thorax or chest expands, the lungs also undergo dilatation and fill themselves with air. This air, entering first by way of the trachea, ultimately reaches the anastomosing terminals of the bronchial tubes, from which locality the heart by the act of dilatation, draws into itself, and then, immediately afterwards contracting, sends it by way of the artery (the Aorta), to every part of the body."

Galen (129–c.200-216) writing about Erasistratus's views on pneuma. Erasistratus was evidently aware that the heart contracted and dilated under its own steam and he must have guessed that the heart valves existed, otherwise the contraction of the heart could not have sent the pneuma to every part of the body. What is missing is the equation of pneuma with blood.

Chapters 10 & 11

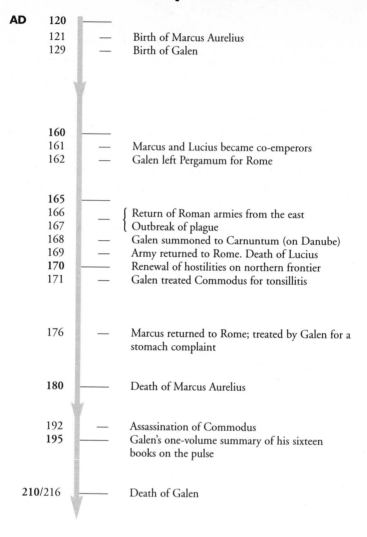

AD		
	120	
	121	— Birth of Marcus Aurelius
	129	— Birth of Galen
	160	
	161	— Marcus and Lucius became co-emperors
	162	— Galen left Pergamum for Rome
	165	
	166	— { Return of Roman armies from the east
	167	{ Outbreak of plague
	168	— Galen summoned to Carnuntum (on Danube)
	169	— Army returned to Rome. Death of Lucius
	170	—— Renewal of hostilities on northern frontier
	171	— Galen treated Commodus for tonsillitis
	176	— Marcus returned to Rome; treated by Galen for a stomach complaint
	180	—— Death of Marcus Aurelius
	192	— Assassination of Commodus
	195	—— Galen's one-volume summary of his sixteen books on the pulse
210/216		—— Death of Galen

Rome: Marcus Aurelius and Galen – I
(AD166–169)

Telesphorus had many talents, yet the one I prized most highly was his ability to dissolve time. As I lived through the days of my life, I experienced the moments as other men did, but when they had passed they contracted into what they really were: insignificant fragments lost in the universe. The more I saw of medicine, the more I felt the gods must be playing tricks on me, using me for their amusement. I was fast returning to my conviction that the beliefs of my childhood were true – or at least as true as we would ever know in this life – and that some divinity did indeed govern our fate. An appeal to the gods was still as effective – or as futile – as any bleedings, purgings, or enemas devised by man.

One day, Telesphorus took it into his head that the time had come when I should visit Rome. The reason he gave was that 'Romans' now inhabited the far corners of the known world and Rome itself was master of a vast empire – though, as he said, not without a certain difficulty in places.

For some two or three hundred years Rome had been the flame around which the moths of Greek medicine had fluttered. They had no opposition in establishing themselves, despite the bad name they earned, as the Romans considered the practice of medicine beneath their dignity. Their good fortune was further enhanced when Julius Caesar [*c.*101–44BC] conferred the full rights of Roman citizenship on all foreign physicians – not that this did anything to improve the quality of their work. Although occasionally a foreigner would rise to a fashionable eminence, most Roman citizens, wisely perhaps, were content to rely on their household gods; when they fell sick they merely consulted the appropriate god and treated themselves with a herbal remedy.

* * *

I waited at Tivoli while Telesphorus went on to the city to prepare for my arrival. Rome was no place for a newcomer – particularly a physician – lacking an outward display of wealth. But I knew I could rely on Telesphorus to ensure I made a sufficiently dramatic entry.

He returned to announce the acquisition of an imposing residence on the Palatine hill and the seeding of a formidable reputation.

"Galen is most anxious to make your acquaintance." This surprised me as the man was well known to hold his fellow physicians in low regard. "It is more than ten years since he left Alexandria and he wishes to discuss the teaching of his work in the university." That more than explained his interest.

Telesphorus paused; he evidently had not finished his report but I gave him no encouragement to continue; his uncertainty amused me.

"I replied," he hesitated again. "I replied that the greatest physician in Egypt, Paulus Alexandrinus, would be pleased to meet the greatest physician in Rome." The words came in a rush; I had never seen Telesphorus so embarrassed.

"Telesphorus, what else did you say? I know the reputation of this man. His standing as the most – indeed the only – fashionable healer in Rome is such that he believes no other can even aspire to be his equal. And he has wealth, both from his own labours and by inheritance."

"Ah, Master, you see he holds Hippocrates in high esteem and his ambition is to build upon the work of his predecessor, which he says was left unfinished… "

"Yes, yes! I know," I interrupted. "But what did you say that will annoy me?" I was finding Telesphorus's reluctance to come to the point somewhat exasperating.

"… so that he himself will be recognized as the greatest physician the world has known." Telesphorus was not to be hurried. "But he also intends that when he has completed the work begun by Hippocrates, nothing will remain to be discovered and the name of Galen will reign supreme and for ever unchallengable!"

"And what did you say?"

"I told him my master had studied all the books on medicine in the Alexandrian library and had compiled a summary of all medical knowledge to which he had added his own commentary." Telesphorus's eyes remained firmly fixed on the floor as he related the conversation. "I said this outshone the *De Re Medicina* since you were a physician and Celsus [25BC–AD50] was not. I also told him you had discovered an unknown text by Hippocrates which you had included in your book and had been able to prove its value in the treatment of your patients."

"Telesphorus! You know I did no such thing!" I was astounded and could only hope that he had some equally facile explanation to extract me from what could be a most difficult situation. "And what text am I supposed to have found?"

"It was only a short one, Master, and concerned with the humours." Telesphorus was almost contrite. "I said you had found a hitherto overlooked passage in *On Airs, Waters and Places* which clarified Hippocrates's views on how changes in the weather affected the balance of the humours in the body and in that way led to disease. It also made it plain that the movements of the heavenly bodies did not, of themselves, cause disease. This, Master, will gratify Galen as it confirms him in his contempt for astrological predictions and magical remedies."

The reputation of Paulus Alexandrinus (I rather liked the authoritative ring of my new name) was secure. If Galen should challenge me, I knew I could match him in any argument about Hippocrates. I also knew that Telesphorus was aware of this and I strongly suspected that it was he who had been amusing himself at my expense.

* * *

Rome was a city with two natures: each in its own way the creation of the other. Despite the congested clamour of its streets, its physical manifestation cast a spell on me from the moment I rode through the Nomentanum gate. Ovid's epithet could not be bettered. The eternal quality he had sensed entered my spirit. But, alas! their own creation was in the process of destroying the creators. It was no longer the Romans who ruled, but the city itself.

As I soon discovered, the population had become exhausted by the perpetual demands of its home; the emperors governed in the name of Rome and through the fear of Rome. The inhabitants of the slums often found escape from the misery of existence in the collapse of their tenements. The wealthy submitted to the will of Rome, all initiative and inventive vigour drained from them by the requirements of office of one sort or another.

Besides his ability to dissolve time, Telesphorus seemed to have another, less desirable, talent. He had, once again, introduced me to a city ravaged by plague. When I drew Telesphorus's attention to his unfortunate habit, he merely shrugged his shoulders as if to imply that wherever he took me epidemic disease would not be far away.

"Paulus Alexandrinus," I think he, too, liked the resonance of the name he had given me, "it is time to visit the Illustrious Galen – as some describe him – for he intends to leave the city and I believe you might profit from his commendation."

Galen received me with a degree of circumspection; not every day did he meet a fellow physician with a reputation as impressive as the one Telesphorus had laid on me. At first, as we talked of matters of no consequence, I felt no warmth towards him and could well appreciate how his prodigious intellect would ruffle the feathers of lesser mortals. But when I explained that even though my own knowledge of medicine was unequalled in Alexandria, I had come to Rome to learn the manner in which he had extended the teachings of Hippocrates, his reserve began to fall away.

I sat back and studied him. As we talked on, my first impressions required adjustment as now the true Galen was beginning to appear. He was a driven being; a man fearful in the knowledge that time was not on his side if he was to achieve the divine purpose. For the task he believed the gods had set him was to display the entire fabric of medicine and, through his writings, to lead the world to an understanding of disease. Did he, I wondered, have an over-inflated idea of his own abilities? Or had he been blessed (or, more likely, cursed) with a sufficient intensity of purpose to reach his goal? It did, though, seem to me that if ever a man possessed the necessary mental equipment, it was Galen. Yet beneath his intellectual and practical skills lay an indefinable quality that served to explain his popularity among those fortunate to experience this aspect of his character. I saw now why Telesphorus had been so anxious that I should meet him – and on terms as near equal as Galen would allow.

Then I noticed that he, in turn, had been studying me. His face held much the same expression as had been in Themison's quizzical gaze. And, like Themison, Galen, too, was unable to find what he was seeking, though he saw enough to take me into his confidence.

"I have always been suspicious," he said, "of those who maintain that disease is sent by the gods through the movements of the planets. My own belief," and his voice made it plain that it was more than belief, "is that disease is caused by an imbalance of the humours brought about by changes in the diet or in the weather or by differences in the climate from one region to another. But, Paulus, your... your... " Telesphorus's status had evidently bewildered him.

"Telesphorus is my student and assistant," I helped him out.

"Yes. Your assistant tells me you have discovered an unknown work of Hippocrates." He smiled for the first time. It came slowly, as if rarely permitted. Indeed, I suspected that it was only permitted when there was something to be gained. At this point I was in half a mind to keep my 'discovery' to myself, but the other half decided to accept Telesphorus's judgment that Galen was a man worth cultivating. I withdrew from my sleeve a document I had written in the Hippocratic style the previous evening.

"I made a copy of a passage not known to scholars – certainly I can find no mention of it in the works of Celsus." So saying I handed him the sheet of vellum I had used for my deception. He read it. He read it again.

"Paulus!" He gripped my hand – he was not given to shows of emotion. "This gives the lie to those who argue against me. We are truly, every one of us, individuals who must be treated as such when ill.

Now I can go further. But first, you can assure me that this is a true copy of what you read and that the writer was indeed Hippocrates?"

I think I could have said that the writer was the great god Pluto and he would still have accepted it, such was his desire to be proved correct. Nevertheless, I gave a true answer: "It was beyond any doubt written by one of the Hippocratic school of physicians."

"Then I am indebted to you. I have been labouring to show that the balance of a man's humours is reflected in his temperament. And this passage indicates clearly that Hippocrates was of like mind, although he does not commit himself to a plain statement."

With difficulty I hid my perplexity. I had not the least idea of his meaning. I need not have worried.

"A man's temperament," he continued without pause, "is soon discovered by the watchful physician. The treatment of sickness is to restore the equilibrium of the humours."

He then launched headlong into an account of his correlation of the humours with human characteristics.

The truth of what I say walks the streets of Rome as, indeed, they do of any city," he began. "Those who are of a fiery, swift and passionate nature and are given to silent rages have the sanguine temperament; their constitution is hot and humid and they are ruled by the blood of their humours. Many native inhabitants of this country are of a sanguine temperament. When they fall sick they are to be treated with medicines possessed of a similar temperament. Dill and fenugreek are of the first order since their heat is imperceptible to the senses. Caustics are of the fourth and last order."

Scarcely pausing for breath, he pounded his way through the other three temperaments, the choleric, the melancholic and the phlegmatic. "Those of a choleric disposition are given to anger and pride; they have a hot and dry constitution and their ruling humour is yellow bile. You yourself will have noticed that many Egyptians are of this temperament. The melancholic and phlegmatic, being of a cold nature, are found most often in the tribes along the northern frontiers of the Empire. The melancholic are cold and dry and the phlegmatic cold and humid."

Suddenly he changed his tone. "Come with me," he commanded – I was left with no choice.

He led me through his house to a large room opening onto a colonnaded garden, resplendent with a rich variety of flowers, herbs and shrubs. But it was not the garden that drew my attention, it was the contents of the room itself. It was filled with containers of all shapes and sizes and all carefully labelled.

"I use opium, mandragora and hyoscyamus to narcotize severe pain," he said, pointing to each of the containers in turn. "In this I follow the teachings of Hippocrates. But," and here a note of triumph entered his voice, "I have carried forward his understanding of pain. Pain does not come only from outside causes – as when a man is wounded by arrows or swords, or stung by venomous beasts, or burned by fire. No! pain may also arise from the organs within the body and so give warning to the physician that he would be well advised to administer an agreeable remedy. You found no mention of inner pain in the works of Hippocrates or the writings of Celsus?" I admitted that, no, I had not.

Meanwhile, my eyes had been wandering round the shelves. Everything seemed to be in keeping with his Hippocratic protestations until my gaze lighted, first, on a jar labelled "Fox oil" and a moment or two later on another, smaller, container stating "Dried camel brain". Even the Illustrious Galen was not immune to the legacy of folklore.

Hiding my scepticism, I asked what use he found for these preparations.

"I obtain the fox oil by boiling foxes and use it as a bath to ease the aching of painful joints – you have no use for it in Alexandria?" He spoke in all seriousness. I shook my head. "And the dried camel brain, I give in vinegar as a welcome cure for epilepsy – the sacred disease of Hippocrates. And there," he pointed at a glass vessel decorated with gold and containing a concoction resembling nothing so much as a long-forgotten meal, "there you see a favourite remedy for diseases afflicting the skin. It is vipers' flesh specially and most carefully prepared. When required, I shall put it up in pastilles." He went on to explain how the viper owed its excellence to the fact that it shed its skin. When boiled in wine or vinegar, he said, the skin itself was a remedy for toothache and earache, though the rationale for this escaped me – as it did Galen!

It must have been the bemused expression on my face at the sheer quantity of medicines arranged in ordered sequence that prompted his next remark.

"Yes," he said, "drugs are sent to me from Palestine, Syria, Egypt, Pontus, Macedonia, Cappadocia, Spain, Gaul, Africa – from all over the world. Every one I examine meticulously to ensure that it is of the correct variety and age. And, again, before I administer a medicine, I study it closely for though twins may look alike to a stranger, they are easily distinguished by those who know them."

Then, to my amazement, he swept his arm around the shelves: "As you can see, I am running short of many drugs and shall soon have to travel for more!" He stopped; evidently an idea had come unexpectedly upon him. He looked hard at me.

"I cannot leave immediately as the Emperor has entrusted his son to my care and no other physician in Rome is worthy of the responsibility. But," and he looked at me again; he could see in me that quality that so perplexed yet reassured him. "I believe Marcus Aurelius would find you acceptable. I have business at home in Pergamum and on the way I mean to obtain minerals from the copper mines in Cyprus – I have no flowers of zinc for treating weeping malignant ulcers. Also, on my return I intend to visit the Dead Sea to collect a fresh supply of asphalt." This did not surprise me as Galen's reputation for the treatment of gladiatorial wounds owed much to his use of this bituminous substance which he applied with a sponge and set alight. As often as not the bleeding took fright and stopped.

And so it was that a few days later Galen summoned me (there is no other word for it) to attend the Emperor Marcus Aurelius [121–180] with him. The walk from my home to the Tiberian House was short. How Telesphorus had acquired a villa so conveniently close to the Imperial residence would remain his secret, though of one thing I could be sure: the transaction would have been perfectly honourable. The morning was already hot, even for late August – the date is fixed in my mind since Lucius Verus [130–169], co-emperor with Marcus, had earlier that month returned victorious from the east. It was one of life's ironies that he, the supreme commander, had been gaming and sporting in Syria, while Statius Priscus [c.165] had been fighting the battles in Armenia and Avidius Cassius [c.131–169] those beyond the Tigris.

Marcus received me with a natural charm, almost as if we were old friends meeting again after a long absence, though beneath the warmth there lay the austere seriousness of the Stoic philosopher.

I waited for the Emperor to speak while he studied me closely but with no hint of discourtesy.

"You are Paulus Alexandrinus?" he enquired at length.

"Yes," I assured him.

"Your reputation has preceded you. If I am to release my physician," he glanced at Galen who had been standing at his side since my arrival, "from his imperial duties, I must needs replace him with another of comparable worth – and he speaks well of you. Apollonius [c.140] taught me to recognize a man who would treat life seriously and yet remain comfortably at ease. I recognize such a man in you. He also taught me to be immutable at the loss of a child. That was a hard lesson, for I have lost six children, five of them sons. I do not wish that Commodus [160–192] and Annius [162–169] should follow their brothers."

We were about to leave when Marcus stopped me and with a look that I can only describe as quizzically humorous, asked for my opinion on the plague.

"There are some," I answered after a pause in which I struggled to determine the motive underlying the question, "who hold Cassius responsible on account of his sacking of Seleucia after the city had welcomed the Roman army as friends. But that I do not believe since treaties have been violated before without such terrible consequences. Nor do I believe the Christians have brought the pestilence upon us. I agree with the people that it has been sent by the gods – and I do not choose to seek an explanation for their actions."

"Then we are all in agreement!" So saying, he motioned that we might withdraw.

In the middle of October, 166, the two Emperors were awarded a triumph – the first for fifty years – for the victories in the east. But if the eastern frontiers of the Empire were secure, trouble was brewing in the north beyond the Danube. At the turn of the year, two of the tribes invaded Pannonia, not for their customary pleasure in raping and pillaging, but to gain much-needed land. Despite their being rapidly beaten back, Marcus announced that he would go north to discover the situation for himself. This, I was sure, was ill-advised considering the mood of the Roman people. During the winter months the plague had increased in virulence and was carrying off many thousands of citizens, making no distinction between wretched plebeian and noble patrician – except that the most eminent among the latter had statues erected to their memory. The Emperor's presence was urgently required in Rome to maintain the morale of his people.

When the rumour began to spread that the plague was divine retribution – though for what, was never made clear – rather than a mere whim of the gods, the citizens demanded that something should be done, I saw my opportunity and suggested a number of laws and proscriptions on the transport of bodies and the burial of the dead, all of which the Emperors enacted. (I doubt whether Galen would even have thought of these measures as they implied an acceptance of contagion. However, Marcus accepted them on my assurances that Virgil [70–19BC] and other writers had found similar precautions of value.)

Yet the plague continued to wreak destruction and in view of what I had originally said to Marcus, I considered it only right to suggest that he should summon the priests to purify the city. He agreed with an enthusiasm that led me to suspect he had already made the decision. The traditional rites concluded with the celebration by the Emperors of the ancient ceremony of the feast of the gods – this required that statues of the gods be lain on banqueting couches in the city's public places with offerings placed on tables beside them. The celebration continued for seven days with benefit only to the gods. At this Marcus, unintentionally I think, showed me the nature of his concern for humanity.

"Paulus," he said while we were deliberating what further steps he could take, "corruption of the mind is a far greater pestilence than any corruption and change of the air that surrounds us." (This view that disease might originate from a corruption of the air echoed the teachings of Hippocrates which Marcus had doubtless learnt from Galen.) "For this corruption," he continued, referring to the plague, "is a pestilence of men in so far as they are animals; corruption of the mind is a pestilence of men in so far as they are human beings."

That evening as I sat in silent companionship with Telesphorus, I wondered whether the mind was, indeed, of greater importance than the body. I was uncertain whether the Emperor had been speaking literally of human morality or whether he had been inferring that in his philosophy physical disease had its origins in a corruption of the mind. If this were so, and he was right, the search for an understanding of disease must begin with the mind.

COMMENTARY

1) This plague is believed to have been smallpox, though there is always the possibility that it was a compound epidemic. It is likely that the Roman army, which was severely depleted by the disease, was instrumental in bringing it to Rome from the east and in its spread to the distant parts of the Empire. If this was the case, it increases the likelihood that the plague was smallpox rather than a disease of dirt and overcrowding since, if nothing else, the Romans laid great stress on the hygienic well-being of their armies. Any medical benefits thus gained were purely fortuitous.

2) Strict adherence to the doctrine of the humours denied the possibility of disease being spread by contagion – the sole responsible factor was held to be individual susceptibility to humoral change. Yet many veterinarians were well aware of contagion among animals and Virgil wrote of the spread of anthrax in sheep from flock to flock. Nothing could prick the intellectual arrogance of the medical fraternity; anything that did not fit with their theories was discarded.

3) Galen is one of the first of the great characters in medicine. Even his early background would seem to presage this greatness. He was born in Pergamum in 129 the son of a wealthy architect and it is said that his choice of career was determined after his father had been visited in a dream by none other than Asklepios himself. Having begun his medical studies at the age of sixteen, he enjoyed a meteoric rise in popularity owing partly to Imperial patronage and partly to his genius at self-promotion.

4) Galen emphasized that the good physician should combine the practical skills of a healer with the academic skills of logic and ethics attained through the study of medicine. In other words, empiricism in conjunction with the art of thinking and the rule of action.

5) Galen is sometimes accused of having left Rome to escape the plague, but this is unlikely as the epidemic was flourishing in Pergamum just as it was all over the Empire. Another story is that he was fleeing from the hatred of his physician rivals. Both these excuses ring false and would have been completely out of character. There is no reason to doubt the explanation he gave to Paulus.

6) Galen's observation that pain could *originate* in internal organs is both astute and a marked step forward.

7) Galen enhanced the practice of Hippocratic medicine in areas such as diagnosis, prognosis and general bedside manner. He further developed the theory of the four humours by attributing to them personal characteristics; for example, black bile conferred a melancholy characteristic. A sanguine character was another among those he identified. ('Sanguine' is a further example of a word with contradictory meanings [see Chapter 8, Commentary 3] : a sanguine person may be either one who is hotheaded and short-tempered [as in Galen's description] or one who is calm and cheerful.) Galen was one of the first physicians to attempt to identify a life force for which he adopted the name 'pneuma' (see Chapter 9).

SOURCES

1) "The dead were carried away on carts and wagons. At this time, moreover, the emperors exacted the most stringent laws on burying the dead and on tombs; no one was permitted to build a tomb at his country villa [a law still in force today]. And indeed the plague carried off many thousands, including many prominent figures."

An unknown, but reputedly reliable, biographer of Marcus dating from the 2nd century.

2) "In spite of Galen's mistakes and misconceptions, one is astonished at the wealth of accurate detail in his writings. Scholars of later centuries swallowed his descriptions whole – correct and incorrect – not even subjecting them to the scrutiny called for in Galen's principle of discovery by experiment. In actually testing animals he differentiated sensory and motor nerves, elucidated the effects of transecting the spinal cord, examined the physiological actions of the chest cavity, and proved that the heart could continue beating without nerves."

Albert S. Lyons and R. Joseph Petrucelli, *Medicine. An Illustrated History*, 1978

3) Praxiteles and Phidias... were unable to... reach and handle all portions of the material. It is not so, however with nature. Every part of a bone she makes bone, every part of the flesh she makes flesh, and so with fat and all the rest; there is no part she has not touched, elaborated, and embellished.

Galen (129–200/216), *On the Natural Faculties*, Book II, 3

Despite the magnificence of the work produced by these two sculptors, they cannot compete with the work of nature. Praxiteles (4th century BC) sculpted the *Aphrodite of Cnidos* (known, alas, only through Roman copies) and Phidias (5th century BC) was responsible for the Elgin Marbles once on the Parthenon in Athens and for the statue of Zeus at Olympia, one of the Seven Wonders of the Ancient World.

Rome: Marcus Aurelius and Galen – II
(169–177)

Before the year was out, Galen returned to Rome and, whether he wished it or not, I continued to serve the Imperial family. I had certainly gained the confidence of Marcus with my sound medical knowledge and regard for his Stoic philosophy.

Galen, strangely for a man so self-centred and so condemnatory of his fellows, welcomed my assistance, particularly at his anatomy demonstrations. Even so, he could go just so far and no further – he gave me no credit, either in writing or through the spoken word, for a number of accurate observations I made. But at least I was not expected to skin his monkeys for him – he now did this himself after one of his slaves had removed some underlying muscle at the same time. These demonstrations attracted many curious patricians, including Marcus himself.

As far as Galen was concerned, Aristotle's belief that Nature did nothing in vain was the ultimate truth. So, as every anatomical structure must have been designed for a definite purpose, Galen reasoned that if he could identify these structures their purpose would immediately be clear. The first – and only – time I challenged one of his conclusions he told me, in a voice like the wind off a frozen peak:

"The human body is the work of the Creator. He has made even the most inaccessible of its parts to work in harmony, one with another. Each action of the body has its cause. When a cause is out of harmony, there is discord and function is lost – the body is injured or becomes diseased."

That was that. Galen had spoken and there was to be no argument. His technical skill at dissection was impressive and, as he proceeded, seven scribes recorded his descriptions not only of what he found – which was usually accurate – but also his perception of its function –

which was frequently speculative, if not downright fanciful. Speaking anatomically, his greatest deficiency lay with the subjects of his dissections. Only rarely did a human corpse come his way – and even then its value was, as like as not, reduced to the study of its skeleton. But this was of small concern to him. What the Creator had created in the beast, that had He also created in man. So Galen, with supreme indifference, dissected apes [whose right kidneys lie higher than their left], dogs [the disposition of whose livers makes them appear to have five lobes], pigs, sheep and other animals besides, all of whose individual anatomical quirks were solemnly recorded as being human attributes.

On the occasion when I challenged him, he was demonstrating the heart and blood vessels in a goat and expounding on their purpose and that of the blood.

"Blood is created in the liver. Here also the vena cava has its beginning, that it may transport the blood to the right side of the heart. From this side it passes through pores – which I cannot demonstrate as they are too small to be visible to the human eye – into the left ventricle where it becomes charged with pneuma." Galen looked up and paused to assure himself that he had the attention of his audience.

"Why do we breathe?" The question was shot out in a seeming change of direction. No one was inclined to answer. "Because the air enters the lungs where it is partly changed into vital pneuma," he continued. "From the lungs it travels through the pulmonary veins to the left ventricle where the process of conversion to vital pneuma is completed by the heat of the heart. The blood is now redder and thinner than when it was created in the liver. But this change produces sooty vapours which travel back along the pulmonary veins to the lungs and are expelled in the breath."

Galen pointed to the valve [the mitral valve] at the entrance to the left ventricle before proceeding. "The purpose of this structure," he explained, "is to permit the sooty vapours to pass into the pulmonary veins while preventing the blood from doing likewise.

"The blood in the left ventricle is now fully charged with vital pneuma and is propelled by the heart to all parts of the body where it is entirely consumed." Galen moved to the animal's head where I had been busy dissecting the base of its brain. I had displayed the rete mirabile, a network of blood vessels and nerves peculiar to ungulates.

"The rete mirabile has a great purpose." Galen pronounced the statement with all the weight of a line from a Homeric epic. "In the rete mirabile, the vital pneuma is transmuted into psychic pneuma! This flows into the brain and into the nerves. It is psychic pneuma that gives sensation and imparts movement!" It was all so simple and logical, and clearly explained to the Galenic mind why the structures we had dissected had been created.

* * *

In the spring [169], Marcus and Lucius, clad in the military cloak, left Rome for Aquileia [later the site of Venice] where they arrived to find the frontier tribes either pacified or defeated. Instead the threat to Rome came yet again from the plague. The army had suffered badly – indeed, there were those who said it had been destroyed, almost to the point of annihilation.

When Galen received the summons to join the Imperial staff, I decided to keep him company. Although his labours to control the plague were in vain, the presence of the Emperors and that of the greatest physician in the Roman Empire had a steadying effect on the army.

Headquarters were at Carnuntum on the Danube [some twenty miles east of modern Vienna] and during our time there, there were the inevitable minor skirmishes which I mention only because they gave me the opportunity to observe Galen the wound surgeon. His ability was beyond reproach – as I suppose was to be expected of a man who claimed never to have lost a wounded gladiator while working in his younger days at the arena of his native Pergamum. One aspect of his treatment intrigued me: he regarded suppuration – or coction, as he called it – to be part of the natural healing of wounds. He never made it clear whether this was a consequence of a belief in the doctrine of the humours, with the wounded body ridding itself of excess phlegm, or whether it was the fruit of experience. A clue that it might have been the latter came when he asked:

"Have you, Paulus, noticed how the soldier whose wound does not undergo coction and who develops a raging fever usually dies, whereas the one whose wound does undergo coction is more likely to live?"

I had to admit that, no, I had not – which was the truth.

Recrossing the Alps, the Emperors prepared to winter at Aquileia, but it was cold and wet and the plague still held the town in a fearsome grip. Galen advised a return to Rome, particularly as Marcus was not in the best of health, and at the start of the year [169] the Imperial suite set out.

Since he was acutely aware of the importance of extending the Roman conquests beyond the Danube to discourage barbarian aggression, Marcus, on his return, restored the army to fighting strength by recruiting new legions from an assortment of slaves, bandits, provincial mercenaries and (to the annoyance of the people of Rome) gladiators. To finance the undertaking he was compelled to hold a two-month auction of Imperial chattels and personal jewellery and to devalue the currency – the imposition of further taxation would have been perilously unpopular.

Nevertheless, it was October before all the domestic and administrative details were in place and the Imperial party was ready to leave. The campaigning season may have been over, but Marcus had in mind the launching of a mighty offensive to initiate the next.

Galen was ordered to join his staff, but he was loathe to leave his lucrative Roman practice.

"I was able to persuade him, good natured and charitable as he is, to leave me at Rome," he said and I did not need an astrologer to tell me what he would say next. "He was pleased to have you in my stead. I shall meantime continue to supervise the care of Commodus. Now that the boy is his only son [Annius having died], the Emperor would entrust him to no one but myself should he fall ill!"

I chose to ignore the contradiction in what he said and the implied contempt of myself. There was no arguing with the man when he was in one of his boastful moods. In any case, before I could think of a suitable retort, he was lecturing me on the peculiarities of the Emperor's own health – most of which I had discovered on our previous expedition.

"You need not worry overmuch as, indeed, he will soon return," he concluded. If anyone needed the help of an astrologer it was Galen; only if he regarded seven years as soon, would his prediction come true. However, the longer I spent in Marcus's company, the more concerned I became about his health. His physical weakness was even more in evidence than the previous winter and he would often order a review of the legions and scarcely have left his quarters before retiring again. The damp coldness was something he found hard to endure.

"Why," I asked, "will you not return to Rome as last year?"

"There is a saying of Epicurus [341–270BC]," he replied in his customary oblique fashion, "that should help you understand why I choose not to take your advice. He said that pain was neither unbearable nor unending, so long as we remembered its limitations and did not increase it with our imagination. To this I would add only that what we cannot bear takes us away from life; what lasts can be borne! This war is a harsh necessity for the Roman state. It possesses none of the glory of past conquests. You yourself have seen the confidence of our soldiers eroded by the pestilence. I have to remain with them."

Marcus ate only at night and would take nothing during the day except the theriac which, at his request, Galen had compounded for him. Galen's theriac was like none other! He doubled the number of ingredients to one hundred, and instructed that it be taken in honey and wine. It was, he maintained, a remarkable remedy for all internal afflictions, especially those of the stomach. It certainly eased the pains in Marcus's chest and stomach but at the expense of making him drowsy – due, no doubt, to the quantity of opium it contained. Galen was nobody's fool. When he stopped taking the remedy, Marcus was unable to sleep and his pains returned. So it was back to the theriac. This told me how intense the pains must have been, yet Marcus, a Stoic of no mean fortitude, made no complaint.

* * *

I stayed in the north as one of the Imperial suite for two years. On my return to Rome I found Galen immersed in one of his frequent and furious bouts of writing. His commitment to the recording of all medical knowledge verged on the obscene: he shamelessly took as his own whatever extracts from the writings of his predecessors suited his purpose and without any attribution to their source. But he argued that his own discoveries, particularly in regard to the physiology of the nervous system, carried knowledge so far forward that any reference to the past was superfluous – and would, indeed, confuse matters.

When I called on him, he was engaged in describing his pulse lore which he considered to be a cornerstone of the practice of medicine. In all, this required the writing of sixteen books, divided into four groups: the differences between pulses; the causes of pulsation; the diagnoses revealed by the pulses; and the prognoses to be derived from the pulses. (Even he eventually appreciated that this was too much to stomach, and twenty years later he produced a single-volume summary. He insisted on explaining to me the reasoning behind the lore in considerable detail, but rather than use his own words I have chosen to give a short résumé. You will probably find it rather incomprehensible, though to Galen it was, as always, totally logical.)

According to Galen, both the heart and the arteries beat individually but simultaneously. Expansion and contraction of the arteries were distinct active, as opposed to passive, movements. Expansion drew in pneuma derived from the inspiration of atmospheric air (echoes of Erasistratus!) which then became mixed with blood in the heart to become vital pneuma. Contraction helped to expel the sooty vapours. [It was as if the arteries and the lungs worked together towards the same ends.] Consequently, said Galen, the condition of the artery – whether it was hard or soft, for instance – was most important since the pulse was created in the arterial wall and was dependent on vital pneuma.

"The pulse, the arteries, the heart and disease," he had come to the end of his dissertation, "are inextricably linked. Grasp the existence of this relationship and understand the significance of the different manifestations of the pulse and you will be a good physician." (Even if it entailed having to read his sixteen books!) I refrained from telling him – he probably knew, anyway – that Praxagoras [fl. 335BC] about five hundred years before had been aware of the relationship and that it had later been a feature of Alexandrian medicine.

Galen was able to give me a practical demonstration of the value of his pulse lore sooner than either of us expected. He had just finished talking when a messenger arrived from Pitholaus, Commodus's tutor, to say the boy was ill.

"He has come back from a wrestling class with a sore throat and fever," said the tutor in response to Galen's questioning. "I gave him a gargle."

Galen laid his fingers on the boy's wrist. "Commodus has an inflammation. Where is the gargle?"

Pitholaus gave Galen a look of surprised admiration. "I didn't know that inflammation of the tonsils could alter the pulse," he said under his breath, pointing to a flask.

Galen dipped his finger into the solution and tasted it. "Too strong," he said. "Give him instead honey and rosewater."

And on the morning of the third day, the fever had abated.

With the sixteenth book of his pulse lore completed, Galen continued to write or to dictate to his scribes. I had entered his room during a pause for refreshment when he suddenly looked at me and asked in a tone almost of despair:

"What do you make of these followers of Moses and Christ? They live through faith rather than reason. The Christians draw their faith from parables and miracles, and yet some act in the manner of philosophers. Their contempt for death is obvious every day."

As I failed to see where his questioning was leading, I gave a non-committal answer. "They believe that if they are scourged and beheaded, they will rise up into heaven," I said. "No; it is more than a belief, it is a conviction. If they are punished, they will be saved. They go to their execution glorifying their God in the name of their Saviour, even though they know that if they repent, they will be pardoned. I don't understand them."

"And *you* don't understand *me*!" Galen was piqued at what he saw as my obtuseness. "If the beliefs of the Christians take hold, they will undermine the science that is at the foundation of medicine. They believe in miracles, but there can be no such thing in an ordered and stable universe. Our patients are healed through knowledge and understanding, not through miracles! Their recovery is proof, not only of our medical skill but also of the Creator's purpose which allows us to proceed logically in an organized world. If this were not so, chaos would reign and all my work would be in vain!"

What had begun as a mild discourse ended with Galen, passionately angry, pacing up and down banging fist into open palm to emphasize each point of his argument. His scribes had already left when they saw how the situation was developing and at one turn when his back was towards me I, too, slipped from the room.

Galen's reputation, already remarkable for a Greek physician in the Roman Empire, continued to grow. His success with his patients – although not necessarily with the cure of their diseases – was owed in large measure to his practice of explaining the nature of the illness, including the prognosis, and gaining the patient's understanding of the treatment he prescribed.

I had one last opportunity to see and marvel at his skill before I left Rome. At the end of the year [176] it was a sick Marcus who returned with his son. The physicians who accompanied him had diagnosed a violent fever and prescribed rest and thick gruel. Marcus, though, was not satisfied and ordered Galen to be sent for. Galen came but said and did nothing.

"Why do you remain silent?" Marcus enquired.

"These physicians who have been on campaign with you have had the better opportunity to make the correct diagnosis."

"Then, if you will do nothing else, take my pulse."

Galen did so.

"You have no fever," he declared, "merely an upset stomach."

"That's it! That's exactly it!" Marcus exclaimed. "I feel as though I'm weighed down by cold food."

"The usual remedy is peppered wine, but for an Emperor I would recommend also a pad of scarlet wool with ointment of nard applied to the anus."

"My own usual remedy." Marcus's stoic delight at this agreement was evident. "Pitholaus shall apply it."

When this was done, the Emperor had his feet massaged, ordered Sabine wine, sprinkled it with pepper and drank it.

From that day Marcus always referred to Galen as "first among physicians and unique among philosophers".

When Marcus Aurelius died four years later, I felt unaccountably sad. I would never again listen to the words of one of the wisest men, one of the truest friends, I had known. I wandered out of Rome, my footsteps aimless, hoping that Telesphorus would return from whatever adventure he had undertaken and discover me. Perhaps before his death Galen will have unravelled the tangled skein that is medicine. But in my heart I held little hope for, as I looked around and saw the hills of Rome slide into the mist, the words of Marcus returned to haunt me: "Look back at the past, how many changes of dynasties. You can foresee what is to come, for it will be of a totally similar pattern; it is impossible for it to escape the rhythm of the present. So, to study human life over forty years is the same as studying it over ten thousand."

COMMENTARY

1) Much to the relief of the local populations, who had become Roman citizens, Roman military hospitals were built along the frontiers of the Empire. Previously, these people had had to accept the billeting of wounded and sick troops in their homes.

2) At the start of the 20th century, a military hospital was excavated at Carnuntum, Marcus Aurelius's headquarters on the Danube. It was dated to the 1st century AD. In its layout and equipment, it cast all other such buildings in antiquity into the shade. Moreover, not only did the Roman army carry out military engineering works of an extremely high order, but it also undertook civil engineering

tasks such as the construction of sewers, canals, water courses and aqueducts and dredging harbours and draining swamps.

3) The activities of the Roman army ensured the continuing employment of both physicians and surgeons. Loyal service could be rewarded with citizenship – a significant rise in status for foreigners.

4) The extent of public health measures has generally been over-emphasized. Clean water, baths and toilets were certainly a feature of Roman cities, but the benefit to the population was usually minimal as only the wealthiest could enjoy the facilities. In Rome itself the Tiber remained an open sewer and plague and other diseases continued to be endemic.

5) Although Galen's reputation was established during his lifetime, it continued to grow over the centuries owing to the survival of much of his writing whereas the works of later physicians and surgeons, whose names have come down to us, have often been lost. Nevertheless, chance has always to be considered in any study of the history of medicine, and, indeed, in any study of history.

6) Do not be misled by Galen's reference to a Creator. This had no religious significance – he was talking about Aristotle's Nature.

7) Galen claimed never to have lost a wounded gladiator. Believe this if you will. Far more likely he simply selected as his patients only those who showed no inclination to die. Such a practice is not unheard of in modern times.

8) Galen was capable of drawing a logical conclusion from the facts available to him. He had noticed two different types of wound infection – which we recognize as being caused by different types of bacteria. He looked upon suppuration as a good thing since it meant that probably the more lethal wound infection was not going to occur and, though he could not realize this, the suppuration was helping to get rid of any dirt, dead tissue or foreign body, that might have been driven into the wound.

9) Galen and his contemporaries did much to promote the status of physicians within the Roman Empire where the atmosphere was both xenophobic and antagonistic towards the medical profession.

Writers, such as Pliny and Cato, openly derided physicians as the antithesis of all that was noble and good within the Empire. For centuries medical care had been the responsibility of the paterfamilias and materfamilias, but with the development of urban living and the expansion of the Empire, the need for a professional medical service was gradually accepted.

SOURCES

1) "Faced with the sheer size of Galen's output, his multifarious activities, and his relentless desire to be right (and to prove others wrong), it is easy to forget how everything fits together. Hippocrates was indeed Galen's model – some have argued, almost his creation – and much of Galen's activity was aimed at improving on him, at 'perfecting' what he had left unfinished. It was a task that required practical experience, erudition, and thought, and in which the recovery of the sick was proof both of medical skill and of the divine Creator's macrocosmic organisation that allowed one to proceed logically and causally. Galen's patients did not recover through miracles, but through knowledge, understanding, or science."

Vivian Nutton, Roman Medicine, 250BC to AD200. In: *The Western Medical Tradition*, 1995

2) Describing his early years in Alexandria where they exhibited skeletons while teaching, Galen wrote: "Even apart from the classroom, it is possible to see, as I often did, skeletons in graves and in monuments. Sometimes the flooding of the Nile washes bodies from graves buried without much care months before; having been thrown hither and thither, the putrified flesh is stripped off while the skeleton is left intact. We also saw the skeleton of a brigand, killed by a traveller in self-defence, lying on the mountainside just off the road. No one wishing to bury him, rather rejoicing to see him devoured by the birds of prey, the bones had been picked dry and thus left for inspection. If nothing like

this happens to you, you can at least remove the flesh from an ape and study its bones. Naturally you will choose one as similar as possible to man."

The most popular ape was the Barbary ape. The last sentence is a bit of a giveaway. It shows that he appreciated there was a difference between ape and Man, but he was quite prepared to attribute his animal findings to the human anatomy. In his defence it could be argued that, although he knew there were differences, he didn't know which they were as he had not had sufficient experience of dissecting the human body.

Chapter 12

200 — Death of Galen 210/216
Citizenship granted to virtually all inhabitants of the
Empire 212

250 — Aretaeus 2nd or 3rd century

— Empire divided into West and East 284

300 —
— Emperor Constantine granted freedom of worship to
Christians 313
— Oribasius 325–403

350 —

— Magnus of Emesa c.370
— Emperor Theodosius made Christianity official
religion of the Empire 380

400 —
— Rome sacked by Alaric's Goths 410

450 — Rome sacked by Vandals 455

— Fall of Western Roman Empire 475

500 —

— Alexander of Tralles 525–605
— Aetius of Amida 6th century

550 —

— Birth of Muhammed c.570

600 —
— Parthenon consecrated as a Christian church 609

— Death of Muhammed 632
— Paul of Aegina 625–690

650 —

Early Christianity and medicine
(*c*.400–*c*.900)

After the death of Galen the path trod by medicine led into the blackest of nights. The Roman Empire was falling apart. The materialism of its ancient glory may have been maintained by an outward appearance of prosperity, but inwardly its temporal power was crumbling under the spiritual dominion of the Church of Rome. Medicine, too, was subject to that dominion though, held as she was, suspended between the worlds of reality and superstition, she simply bent with the wind. In one regard, however, its resilience was not enough: it became afflicted with an intense respect for the authority of the past which stifled freedom of thought and prevented any serious challenge to its traditional beliefs.

Throughout my existence, the gods had been an intrinsic part of life. They may have squabbled among themselves but, as they had no spiritual or mystical baggage to encumber them, they were on the whole an astute down-to-earth assemblage with a generally reassuring effect on their mortal subjects.

In consequence, I was quite unprepared for the impact of monotheism. It was one thing to be brought up in the knowledge that there may be only one true God and to answer the call when it comes – as had the emperors of the now-divided Roman Empire. But it is quite another to have lived through three thousand years of polytheism and then to hear a man knock at your door saying: "Follow me".

I found myself a stranger in a world whose values were, for me, an uncertain quantity. It was a world in which medicine was in confusion, having lost its sense of direction, and in danger of seeing its doctrines denied. But it was not just medicine, for the entire world was caught in a period of transition between two ages when events were governed by influences outside human control. Man had become aware of his individuality – as distinct from his being one of a tribe – and of his spirituality. He was to be in desperate need of help and guidance in the coming age though, as the ancient prophets had foretold, that help would be forthcoming – but would he make the best use of it? (I am here speaking in astrological terms. The period of transition is from the Age of Aries to that of Pisces at the beginning of the Christian era. As in all astrological periods of transition, new ideas were in conflict with the old; the existing pattern had to be discarded before the design of the new could be accomplished. Crises and uncertainties were inevitable. An 'Age' in this context is a Great Month which lasts approximately two thousand, one hundred and sixty years. These ages progress in the reverse direction to that of your more familiar Zodiacal constellations.)

My footsteps were perhaps not as aimless as I had imagined for, two or three centuries beyond my leaving Rome, I was rejoined at Constantinople by Telesphorus.

"I was waiting for you." He greeted me as though we had parted yesterday which, with his manipulation of time, seemed the truth.

"Master, I did not ensure your arrival here for any good reason. Since yesterday," he gave one of his impish grins, "physicians have been in retreat from the understanding of medicine – such as it was – that Galen had reached. No one has been worth the hurrying of your footsteps. Indeed, I have only stopped you in Byzantium – I still cannot bring myself to call it Constantinople – as being a suitable place for you to take stock.

"Now come. I have gathered some books in your new home. They will give you an insight into the plight of medicine today." So saying, he took my hand and almost bounced along the marbled main street of the city before turning aside to lead me to a villa, secluded behind walls and a veritable forest of trees. Inside, all was prepared for me – the library was more than a mere gathering of books, it was a triumph of bibliological organization.

"I have collected every… " Telesphorus caught my doubting look and began again. "I have collected copies of most of the books written since the death of Galen. I think you will find it instructive to compare them with Galen's own works – and I do have these in their entirety!" And he had – nearly four hundred of them in their varying lengths. There was work here to keep me pleasurably occupied for years.

I began with Galen, amusing myself by identifying the ideas and facts he had adapted from earlier writers; Telesphorus had thoughtfully acquired a score or more of the most important of these ancient works – he had spirited them away from the library in Alexandria when the city began its decline. That task completed I moved on to a study of the more recent volumes in chronological order (in obedience to Telesphorus's injunction!). I learnt nothing new; but what I did find of great interest was the manner in which Galen's work had been presented. He himself had been fairly discursive, not to say rambling, and this gave the later scholars an opportunity to bring together specific topics otherwise scattered throughout his writings. At first, speaking chronologically, these new books were straightforward copies of Galen, interspersed with excerpts from some of the pre-Galenic writers. But as time progressed, they began to omit Galen's philosophical musings and qualifications of his opinions. Instead they presented Galen as dogma. What was particularly disturbing was that this had destroyed Galen's sense of the unity of medicine and had led, in turn, to the separation of theory and practice, an error reinforced by a misunderstanding of Galen's teaching. Galen had indeed emphasized the importance of a philosophical approach to medicine – he either was, or wished to create the impression of being, a Stoic in the mould of Marcus Aurelius – but what he had not implied, as these later scholars had assumed, was that a physician had first to be educated as a philosopher.

In reading these travesties of Galen's writings, I was especially intrigued by a book of Magnus of Emesa [c.370] that typified the extent to which these compilers would go. He had painstakingly worked his way through the entire Galenic corpus and extracted all the comments and observations on the urine. These he had put together as a handbook of the diagnosis of disease by uroscopy. (This book had a greater influence than I suspected at the time. It marked the start of the study of the urine as an integral part of medical practice in the company of bloodletting and the study of the pulse. It even became a popular subject for artists of the Renaissance.)

During my years of study, I scarcely ventured into the city. Telesphorus saw to the management of the household and each day I walked in contemplative solitude in the grounds of the villa which were both extensive and beautiful with their sweeping views across the Bosporus. Sometimes I would wish for company, when Telesphorus would join me and we would pass the hours discussing my studies – usually in terms derogatory of the authors!

My reading completed, Telesphorus and I were, one spring day, seated amidst the glories of a burgeoning land. Yesterday, the world had been shades of grey and black set against a turbulent sky; today the air had a new-found warmth and my garden was freshly green with touches of blue and gold, white and pink – order in disorder. It was the conviction that we were in the presence of my gods, the gods I knew and loved, that made me break the spell Nature had woven around us.

"Telesphorus, my friend, I am saddened by the story these books have to tell. The humoral foundations of our medicine may survive, though I fear Hippocrates would grieve at their condition. Yet the books are only scholars' work; they say nothing about healing in this new Christian world – and this, I know, is at odds with our understanding of disease. Because Galen, in his adherence to Aristotelian philosophy, wrote of a Creator who did nothing without a purpose, many Christians tolerate his ideas since these can be reconciled with their belief in the one God. For that, we must be thankful. And now, Telesphorus, as my work here is done, I shall return to Rome."

"Master, do not go. Your spirit will weep for the city; it is no longer the heart of a mighty empire. Stay here and you will find citizens of every race and from every country who will tell you what you wish to know. Go into the streets and ask!"

"No, Telesphorus. My mind is set. I must see for myself the consequences of this perplexing faith."

* * *

Telesphorus was right. I should never have returned to Rome. The city where I had wandered in the cool breeze of summer evenings lay in ruins, pillaged twice over. The only delight left for me to enjoy in the Forum was the profusion of wild flowers growing along the Via Sacra and amongst the fallen masonry strewn on every side. I scarcely felt surprise when I saw the Pantheon consecrated for Christian worship; but how Telesphorus's heart would have wept at this rejection of his family. I knew now why he had refused to accompany me.

I could find no one prepared to talk with me. As I quickly discovered, evidence of the influence of Christianity pervaded every aspect of medical life. Even to suggest that healing was a strictly medical preserve was to be condemned as a heretic. Had not Christ healed the sick by healing the soul, not the body? It was the soul that was all-important; the body was merely its temporary receptacle.

My mind was in turmoil. The comprehension of disease was no better than in the days of my ancestors and, in certain respects, could not even bear comparison with their ancient logic. For the thousand years since Hippocrates, medicine had been practised with some degree, at least, of practical rationality. But now all that had been swept away in the rising tide of spirituality. The responsibility for disease was laid elsewhere than on earth and, in consequence, its treatment had also to be sought in other realms.

The idea that disease was not sent by the gods but had a cause – whether identifiable or not – had been forgotten. The Christians believed that sickness was visited upon them as punishment for their sins and the sins of their fathers – a favoured site for the Lord's chastisement was the skin as this could be disfiguring and was there for all the world to see. Some fanatics even sought disease, sometimes by deliberate mortification of the flesh, as a test of their sanctity. When I questioned the Christians about their remedies, they could not deny that God had put healing medicines on earth, but they were there, they said, only for those whose faith was weak. "If your faith is strong, God will heal you" was a sentiment I often heard expressed. Yet I fear the faith of all too many was weak, as epidemics of 'plague' [possibly bubonic plague this time, although malaria was rife in Italy] continued to ravage the Mediterranean lands carrying off great numbers of Christians and pagans alike.

Out in the countryside, remote from towns and cities, the Christian faith was less extreme and in places the Roman gods were still worshipped. The choice of healing practices was wide, but in the main relied, as it had for centuries, on folk medicine – as effective or as ineffective as it had ever been. I did, however, encounter the occasional physician who practised a diluted form of humoral medicine, though those of their patients who were Christians would usually follow the consultation with a visit to the nearest church or Christian shrine. When the patient was cured, the Church invariably claimed the credit for the miracle. God would heal, but only when He saw fit to do so. (Remission of chronic diseases was regarded as a cure – and hence as a miracle. And, as I have said before, Nature is a wonderful healer of acute diseases if given a chance – another source of miracles.)

The longer I remained in what had been the Latin Empire, the more despondent I became. One day, Telesphorus, ever my watchful protector, appeared at my side.

"Bal-sarra-uzur, a new city has arisen beside the river Tigris in your own land. There, scholars of a new religion are working to preserve the old medicine. But before we leave I have something instructive to show you. You have already witnessed the baleful influence of the Christian church on medicine; now you shall see how the works of Hippocrates and Galen are being debased by so-say philosopher-physicians." And he led me to a public building where men were studying and talking around a large table. The books they were working on were those of Galen and were familiar to me. But they were not discussing their medical content. They were arguing about the meaning of the words. They believed that if they could interpret them correctly, the eternal truths of man's relationship with his God would be revealed to them. Quite how they came to this belief escaped me, as it did Telesphorus.

COMMENTARY

1) By 364 the Roman Empire had split in half into Eastern and

Western, each ruled by separate emperors. Whilst the Western Empire fell into a state of collapse, the Eastern, centred on Constantinople, upheld the traditions of Hellenic learning.

2) Christianity was established in the Roman Empire by the 4th century and soon controlled all aspects of life including medicine. From the first, Christians believed in an association between illness and sin which meant that God alone could restore health, so long as the afflicted showed remorse through prayer. To emphasize the image of a healing Christ, recoveries were celebrated.

3) Although medicine stagnated for many centuries after the death of Galen, there were still Greek outposts in Italy where Hippocratic medicine was practised and where individual physicians trained their pupils. However, in Byzantium in the Eastern Empire, Galen reigned supreme – or rather, the interpretations of Galen's writings became the supreme authority, and remained so for the best part of fifteen hundred years.

4) Nevertheless, there were a few writers who followed in the tradition of Hippocrates and gave, for the first time, excellent descriptions of diseases. Notable among them was Aretaeus the Cappadocian (2nd or 3rd century, but later than Galen) who described diabetes mellitus, pneumonia, pleurisy, tetanus, asthma and perhaps diphtheria. However, there was no concomitant advance in treatment.

5) The greatest literary activities were the compilations of the writings of previous scholars into ordered accounts of medical practice. Among those who wrote these 'encyclopaedias' were Oribasius (325–403), Aetius of Amida (6th century), Alexander of Tralles (525–605) and Paul of Aegina (625–690). Paul, in particular, although apparently a competent surgeon, admitted that his predecessors had said all there was to say and that he was only a humble scribe. He was, however, being unduly modest as his Book VI gives a highly informative account of Greek surgery dealing with many operations, both simple and complicated which, as far as is known, were still being performed in the 7th century. These compilers were all based in Byzantium, renamed

Constantinople when the Emperor Constantine moved the capital of the Roman Empire there in about 330. Their main accomplishment was to save the ancient Greek texts for posterity.

6) In its early days the Christian church was convinced of the imminence of Christ's Second Coming and in consequence saw no need to bother with such mundane problems as diseases – they would soon be cured for ever. But as time passed and the Second Coming failed to materialize, disease began to be equated with sin. The afflicted had to suffer; their only hope of cure lay in the hands of God, which was, of course, unpredictable. Christians, therefore, saw it as their responsibility to care for the sick, as Christ had done – but since only God could cure, they were relieved of that responsibility! (The influence of both Christianity and Islam on medicine is further considered in Chapter 13.)

SOURCES

1) "The downfall of the Western Empire was mainly due to the degeneration of the Roman stock through mixture with weaker and inferior races. The soldiers who had never known defeat became an easy prey to the invading barbarians of the North, informed with the rugged and primitive virtues which they themselves had once possessed... Degeneration of mind and body, with consequent relaxation of morals, led to mysticism and that respect for the authority of magic and the supernatural which was to pave the way for the bigotry, dogmatism, and mental inertia of the Middle Ages. Under these conditions the physician became more and more of a mercenary parasite and vendor of quack medicines."

Fielding H. Garrison, *An Introduction to the History of Medicine*, 1929

2) "An inhuman calamity! An unseemly sight! A spectacle painful even to the beholder! An incurable malady! Owing to the distortion [contorted arching of the back], become unrecognizable to the dearest friends. Hence the prayer of the spectators – who

previously would not have been reckoned pious, are now become good – that the patient may depart from life, as being a deliverance from the pains and unseemly evils attendant upon it. But neither can the physician, though present and looking on, furnish any assistance as regards life, relief from pain or deformity. For if he should wish to straighten the limbs, he can only do so by cutting and breaking those of a living man. With them, then, who are overpowered by this disease [tetanus], he can merely sympathize. This is the great misfortune of the physician.

Aretaeus the Cappadocian (2nd or 3rd century), *On Tetanus*

Chapter 13

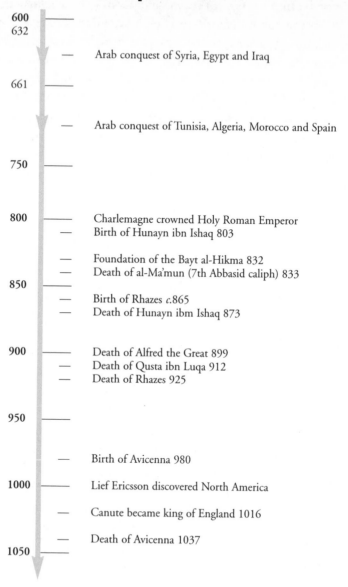

600
632

— Arab conquest of Syria, Egypt and Iraq

661

— Arab conquest of Tunisia, Algeria, Morocco and Spain

750

800 —— Charlemagne crowned Holy Roman Emperor
— Birth of Hunayn ibn Ishaq 803

— Foundation of the Bayt al-Hikma 832
— Death of al-Ma'mun (7th Abbasid caliph) 833
850

— Birth of Rhazes c.865
— Death of Hunayn ibm Ishaq 873

900 — Death of Alfred the Great 899
— Death of Qusta ibn Luqa 912
— Death of Rhazes 925

950

— Birth of Avicenna 980

1000 — Lief Ericsson discovered North America

— Canute became king of England 1016

— Death of Avicenna 1037
1050

Medicine in the world of Islam
(c.900–1037)

The desert air was cold. I pulled the burnous closer about me and shivered. I felt sick; the camel was the one mode of transport I loathed. I hated the uncertain-tempered vicious beasts. Beside me, quite at ease on his animal, Telesphorus kept up an incessant chatter to which I paid no attention as I was more concerned with complaining at my discomfort.

He had chosen, in his perversity, to restore my rapidly declining morale by making the final stage of our journey across apparently trackless desert.

"Bel-shazzar," he said, when we rested to eat before the day. "Marcus Aurelius showed you the nature of the true Stoic philosopher: a man of virtue, of courage and integrity, and above both pleasure and pain. But virtue cannot be learnt from books; it demands practice if it is to be sustained. And," a look more suited to a devil than an offspring of the gods came over his face, "and it has been many years since you suffered physical torment! Endure it as he would have endured it, in silence and without complaint."

Remembering, guiltily, what Marcus had said about pain: "what we cannot bear takes us away from life; what lasts can be borne", I resolved that Telesphorus should hear no more from me.

For day after day we rode on. Sometimes the sand was as smooth as silk, at others it rippled as if the ocean's waves had rested a moment before ebbing home. How I longed for those waves to cool the insufferable, the inescapable, heat. But, sitting on my accursed beast, aching in limbs and back, I kept my thoughts to myself; outwardly, at least, I was a good Stoic. Yet once when I lapsed into sleep and Telesphorus struck my animal into a gallop, I woke, screaming, from dreams of green valleys with cool, crystal waters flowing eternally in their depths; waters that had washed the dust and sand from my eyes, my ears, my mouth, my skin, my very soul.

After many days the desert changed and we passed through a mountainous land where the weather-worn rock towered high above in frantic shapes of brown and grey, where our voices came echoing back. Strange, perfectly formed pyramids that had never known the hand of man kept watch over the dead. What dead I know not, but dead they must have been for no man could live in this terrible world.

As we emerged from cliffs and precipices, the land grew more treacherous still. Leading our camels over smooth black stones shifting uncertainly beneath our feet we entered a wilderness where only the changing shape of the desert floor informed our progress from one area of burning wind-swept desolation to another.

"Telesphorus, how much further must we travel before we reach this newly-risen city?"

"We shall arrive at dawn, Bel-shazzar." I cursed him silently. This was his unvarying answer, and every time he nearly fell from his camel with laughter.

I reined back my beast and allowed Telesphorus to gain on me. Then I gave the animal its head to follow without my guidance. I looked up seeking inspiration, but in vain for the majestic beauty of the heavens was beyond my understanding. In the clear light of dawn the other worlds beyond our own began to disappear. Above us the sky was a vast unfathomable and endless void.

We must have been climbing steadily through the night, for we now found ourselves on a high rocky plateau. Instead of halting to rest through the heat of the day, Telesphorus continued riding. "We are nearly there, Master," he informed me, to my unutterable relief.

Before long we came to the edge of the heights and there in the far distance I could just discover the faint outline of a river with what looked to be a town on its banks. "That is Hit, Master, and the river is the Euphrates! From Hit, we shall take a boat down river to al-Anbar and from there travel the last few miles to Baghdad."

Only a Christian hermit brooding in the wilderness nurturing his immortal soul and dependent on passing travellers for sustenance until his body fell apart, could have been unaware of the changes that had taken place since the Prophet Muhammed had conquered Arabia in the name of Islam. In little more than a hundred years the Arab caliphs had extended his empire from Narbonne to Kabul in a mighty crescent through Spain, north Africa, Palestine, Syria, Mesopotamia, Armenia, Persia and Afghanistan to the Indus. The ancient Persian Empire had been destroyed and the Christian Eastern Roman Empire sat uneasily shrinking along the northern shores of the Mediterranean. The spiritual and cultural vitality of Islam was such that I forgave Telesphorus the nightmare of the journey. My morale was restored.

Nevertheless, with Christian Rome in mind, I reserved my personal judgment until I had gathered evidence of the influence of this new monotheistic religion on medicine. To this end, we travelled slowly and circuitously from al-Anbar, but I saw nothing to give me encouragement. Nothing differed in its essentials from anywhere else in the world outside the great cities. The people, poverty stricken as always, looked after themselves while those who could afford it resorted to a local healer or herbalist; the medicines were still governed by folklore and superstition. Indeed, so little had changed here since the days of my childhood that I felt like nothing so much as a mule condemned to circle the mill endlessly grinding the corn.

I had seen it all before. The jinn that brought disease were the very ones that had brought death to Ebih-Il. The charms to ward them off may not have been the statuettes of Abu; but no matter, if sickness struck the fault lay not with the belief but with the sick man's amulet or incantation which patently lacked the power to overcome the jinn. Disease was still regarded as a divine affliction; good health was the natural state of affairs. (I think you will find the same principle applies in your world – perhaps with even greater force. The technological advances of your age have deluded people into the belief that good health should be theirs by right and if it is denied them, someone is to blame – not that far removed from my jinn? In fact, these advances should have persuaded them that reality is just the opposite.) And so it was that I came to Baghdad, the capital city of the Abbasid caliphate. In the one hundred and fifty years since its foundation it had become the centre of the Islamic world and supported more than a million souls within its walls. I came as a physician from Alexandria because, even though, medically speaking, the city was but a faded shadow of its former greatness, it still preserved a reputation as a centre of Graeco-Roman medicine.

Telesphorus was insistent that unless I visited the Bayt al-Hikma, I would be a ship sailing through Islamic culture without a sight of the lodestar to navigate by.

He was right, of course. The Bayt al-Hikma [established 832] was a worthy successor to Ptolemy's universal library in Alexandria and the true cultural heart of a great Empire. In the years since Caliph al-Ma'mun [?–833] had transformed an idea into a building, travellers had returned with books and medicines from Persia, India and as far afield as China, and scholars had been despatched to discover missing texts. And to preserve the accumulating wisdom within Islamic culture, all was translated into Arabic.

From the manner of their dress, however, I saw that many of the translators were Christians.

"The language of these Christians is Syriac," Telesphorus answered my question. "You have lived too long under the mantle of Christianity to understand why the world of Islam welcomes men of other faiths and of all countries who bring with them their scholarship. Islam seeks knowledge, whatever its source. It was through intolerance that the Christian world descended into the cultural abyss."

"Nevertheless," – it did Telesphorus no harm to be contradicted once in a while – "it is the scholarship of the Christians that enables Islam to save the ancient knowledge!"

The full extent of that scholarship became evident when I began to study the Arabic texts. These were not literal, unthinking translations of the Greek but carefully considered expressions of the sense of the originals, most of which were liberally bespattered with abstruse philosophical commentaries. This was essential if the Arab scholars – highly intelligent men, fluent in Greek, Arabic and Syriac (a sort of half-way house between the other two) – were to grasp the fundamental nature of Greek science.

As I read on, I noticed that passages in the original Greek were missing from the translations. I drew this to the attention of Qusta ibn Luqa [?–910], a Christian. He was an old man and seemed surprised not only at my having identified the missing sections, but also that I, to all appearances a devout Moslem, should question their omission.

"Bel-shazzar," his voice was soft and, after speaking my name, he continued in Greek. "You should know that the passages we omit are offensive to the religion of Islam. But since the Qur'an contains few allusions to medicine, the problems for us are also few and we are able to construct a seamless text so that only… " here he paused and looked at me in the way I had come to recognize. He was one of those intuitively perceptive people who, given in their cup those last few drops of divine understanding, could have read my history, "… only an exceptional scholar would appreciate their absence."

I reassured him that I was not prying into his work which, indeed, he knew I admired, but wished merely to learn whether the scholarship of the Bayt al-Hikma had filtered beyond its walls.

"When I first came here more than forty years ago," he replied, "the answer would have been very little. The traffic in books was all inwards and our responsibility was to make the knowledge accessible to scholars. But it was a time of transition when the flow both of untranslated books and, alas! of our income began to evaporate like the dew in the morning sun. My master, Hunayn ibn Ishaq [808–873], a Nestorian priest and the greatest scholar I have known, realized that unless we continued our studies in a new form, the work of the Bayt al-Hikma – at least insofar as medicine was concerned – would ossify and die and be lost to Islam. In his later years, he completed many texts that were deficient either on account of loss or of the original author's failure, whether from ignorance or simple abandonment, to complete the work. Before he died he wrote an original treatise on the eye which has been much read by physicians.

"I continued in his ways but I have also trodden paths other than those of medicine. I have explored the sciences of astronomy, physics and mathematics and I have written new works which extend the understanding of these subjects." Suddenly Qusta ibn Luqa stopped, conscious that a lack of modesty might seem discourteous.

I urged him to continue. All knowledge, I said, was welcome to me and when it was given me by its originator, it was doubly so.

"When a man has absorbed himself as deeply as did Hunayn and as have I in the writings of others, he is often permitted to discern an inner meaning that perhaps eluded the original writer. We are then able to build upon these revelations.

"Galen remains the authority and because he provides evidence for a divine Creator who determines the order of nature, his work is unquestioningly accepted by the followers of Islam – as it is by those of Christ – and his teachings on humoral medicine are the practice of physicians in the cities of the Empire. At one time, the philosophies of the East, of India and Persia, were popular, but they fell from favour, though some aspects, such as the Indian system of numerals, have persisted."

Qusta ibn Luqa had been studying me intently with a view, I thought, to discovering how far he could trust me. Then, without warning, he changed the subject, coming straight to his point without any of the customary preliminaries.

"You are not an Arab. I doubt you are even a Believer," he began. I said nothing. "Your features are not Arabic, although I cannot define their origins. But with your eyes, it would not surprise me to learn that you came from another world!" He smiled, knowing full well I would neither deny nor confirm his suspicions.

"The name, Bayt al-Hikma is translated into Greek and other non-Semitic tongues as 'House of Wisdom'." Where, I wondered was this leading? I was having difficulty following his train of thought. "But I see you know this already. What you may not know is that, in principle, the wisdom of Islam coincides with the wisdom of the Greeks. It signifies the search for truth wherever it may be found: that which is true is Islamic. (Do not confuse this with: only that which is Islamic is true.) It thus lies within the same conceptual stream as the old Arab tradition which maintains that when a number of possibilities exist, only one can be the absolute truth – though it may, nevertheless, be expressed in a number of different ways – while all the others are absolutely false.

"Medicine's truths are still hidden and, to my mind, none will ever be considered absolute. Both Islam and my own religion stand astride the path that leads towards the understanding of disease" – I saw now why he had been debating whether or not to trust me – "and even were they to be removed, I fear the path would prove endless."

Resigned though I was to an acceptance of this same fear, it still distressed me to hear it expressed by a mortal.

"There is a sect, the Ikhwan al-Safa," he was saying when I had calmed my emotion, "who believe that the study of man's anatomy and physiology holds the key to the wisdom and power of God the Creator. They have established – to their own satisfaction – a correspondence between the anatomy of the human body and the anatomy of the heavens; this, they achieved by means of a numerical symbolism, not by anatomical study.

"I am torn apart like a liver the dogs have been at. I do not know what I believe." It was a long time since I had encountered a man of such intellectual honesty. "I am a Christian. I work with the followers of the Prophet so that the writings of ancient Graeco-Roman scholars may become known to them. And yet I cannot see where it will lead. We are bound by the chains of faith. The Qur'an proscribes the dissection of the human body – as does Christianity. Animals may be dissected, but I am not alone in thinking that the animal anatomy cannot be equated with that of man. Both faiths believe the dead feel pain; and we are agreed that on the Day of Judgement we shall all be summoned before the throne of God to account for the sufferings of the body He has given into our charge. There can be no escape; any desecration of His gift will be there for all to witness. I believe in Christ, but I cannot believe that a loving God would condemn a man to eternal damnation for the loss of an arm in battle or of a limb amputated by a surgeon to save his life. Neither can I believe that a man whose dismembered body was carried before God should also be condemned because another was seeking to understand His miraculous work."

Later, thinking on his words, I wondered how his Christian contemporaries had reconciled their beliefs with the embracing of martyrdom by their early predecessors – a fate that could entail beheading, mutilation in gladiatorial combat and much else besides. Alas! I was denied the opportunity of debating the question with him.

When I next visited the Bayt al-Hikam, Qusta ibn Luqa was dead. His departure from this world coincided with the spread of Arabic learning throughout the Empire, most notably to the Western Caliphate in Spain. Books, texts and manuscripts in Arabic made their way to distant lands by the very trade routes along which they had arrived centuries earlier in their original languages.

If Qusta ibn Luqa had been inclined to despair for the future, maybe because he viewed the world through his books, the Persian physician Rhazes [c.865–925] was fashioned from a mould of a very different design. Although he, too, was widely read and had an exemplary respect for past authority, his first words to me were completely unexpected:

"All that is written in books is worth much less than the experience of a wise physician." My heart warmed to him. Besides, he was one of the kindest of men and his lined old face lit up with a smile as he spoke. Had he not given freely of his time and skill to the more unfortunate of his patients, he could have been the wealthiest of the wealthy physicians of Baghdad.

"We are few, Bel-shazzar, and the sick are many. If we cannot help them directly, we must help them to help themselves." He handed me a book from a little pile at his side; it was *Man la yahduruhu al-tabib* [*Who has no Physician to Attend him*]. "In this I have written down many prescriptions which the poor may have prepared for them. Nevertheless, when a man's health is disturbed, he should first look to his diet before having recourse to drugs – and these should always be as simple as circumstances permit."

I was not surprised at this last caveat since pharmacy and chemistry had become sciences in their own right in the melting-pot of Islamic culture. Treatments were moving rapidly beyond the simple, though numerous, herbals of Dioscorides [fl.60]. When I saw such practices as sublimation, calcination, crystallization and distillation and heard the chemists describe their preparations as alkalis, alcohols, syrups, elixirs and many other strange terms, I had a peculiar (and, I have to admit, not very pleasant) feeling that physicians might be able to cure diseases before they understood them.

We were seated in the large central courtyard of the hospital in Baghdad of which Rhazes was physician-in-charge. The scattered few Christian hospitals I had visited in the West bore no comparison with this magnificent institution. The courtyard was a beautifully laid-out garden with fountains gently playing and trees offering a welcome shade to plants and patients alike.

"We Muslims," – since my encounter with Qusta ibn Luqa I had made no attempt to appear a Muslim. I was simply a Greek physician from Alexandria with no identifiable beliefs. "We Muslim physicians," he repeated, "regard the body to be an extension of the soul. Illnesses that manifest themselves in the body may thus not be of the body itself but of the soul: to heal the body, we must heal the soul. In this we differ from the Christian belief which holds the body in little regard – it is only the temporary abode of the soul." He paused and looked me, wondering whether, in saying this he might have offended me. But I reminded him that my religious beliefs were not strong and did, in any case, take second place to my curiosity to learn about medical practice in the countries I travelled through.

He handed me another book from his little pile.

"This also I have written. Please accept it as a gift. I think the subject will be new to you. I have entitled it *Spiritual Physick* and in it you will read how, in treating disease arising in the soul, we value most highly music, beautiful scenery and agreeable companionship. Such a receipt is balm to the troubled spirit." (This was the beginning of what you now know as psychological and psychosomatic medicine.)

"Forgive me, Bel-shazzar, if I must leave you. I have patients to attend to and students to teach." He rose, gathered up his books and walked slowly across the courtyard into the hospital building.

Rhazes must have been as anxious to talk to me as I was to learn from him. On the next day as I was sitting on the same seat, he walked out of the building and when his attention was drawn to my presence, he went out of his way to join me. We greeted each other warmly.

"You study and practise the medicine of Hippocrates and Galen?" I questioned him. He bowed his head in acknowledgement.

"But is this not in disagreement with Arab-Islamic medicine?"

"Not at all! Not at all! Both believe that men should keep in good health. Where we differ is in our beliefs about the cause of disease. Hippocrates maintained that diseases were natural events with natural causes, but we believe – as do the Christians on this occasion – that disease is a punishment for sin. We also believe it possible that some diseases, perhaps those that arise in the spirit, are sent by the jinn. Where we diverge from the Christians is in attaching no stigma to disease. The Prophet has said, 'Allah sends down no ailment without also sending down for it a cure.' So our task is to seek out, with divine help, the cure that Allah has provided.

"But those who wish to entrust themselves entirely to Allah rather than relying on a physician such as myself as intermediary, there is the *Medicine of the Prophet*. This is a compilation of writings derived from all manner of sources. It began life as a collection of questions on medical matters posed to the Prophet during his lifetime and the answers he gave, as recalled by his followers. As the years passed, it grew to contain anecdotes, aphorisms, folklore, religious dicta and purely common-sense advice. Even aspects of humoral medicine are recommended."

It was some years before we next sat together in that enchanted courtyard, by which time Rhazes's faltering sight had almost completely deserted him. Rumour had it that the failure had started after a brutal beating at the hands of the caliph in punishment for his outspokenness, but he maintained it was simply a matter of advancing years and his intense preoccupation with writing. He had composed more than two hundred works on subjects ranging from alchemy to ethics and from anatomy and physiology [much of which, in view of the proscription on dissection, was an arrangement of earlier writings] to medicine, surgery, obstetrics and beyond.

I suggested I might act as his amanuensis, an offer he readily accepted. Throughout his life he had recorded the smallest detail of every patient he had treated and had insisted that similar notes were kept in his hospital. On his death, I collected all his own notes – which, besides the details of the patients, contained his comments and apposite quotations from other books – and did my best to arrange them in a manageable order. Although I knew they had been for his private use, I took steps to ensure they were made available to all who asked. I called them his *Al-Hawi fi l-tibb* [*The All-Inclusive Work on Medicine*. This massive compendium was translated in the 13th century into Latin as the *Continens*].

(I realize that my attempts at achieving manageability would not have met with modern approval. Ignorance of disease states made any form of organization or classification difficult, if not impossible. Nevertheless, Rhazes's descriptions of smallpox and measles are, unlike so many ancient case histories, instantly recognizable.)

* * *

The last, so it transpired, of the great Arabic physician-compilers, Avicenna [980–1047] by name, had been my friend – though not Telesphorus's – since the days of his precocious youth. His intellect was formidable. As a boy, he had outstripped his teachers; he had mastered the Qur'an at the age of ten; and at twenty-one he had written an encyclopaedia of science. No facet of human knowledge escaped his attention and he was greatly sought after for his legal and political opinions. But it was medicine and philosophy that took pride of place. His weakness was an inability to resist a pretty face and, not for the first time, he had become involved in an intrigue at court. On this occasion, the lady had a high-ranking protector and Avicenna had had to flee for his life. Yet his misfortune was my gain. Until the dust had settled over Isfahan, he sought refuge in my house.

He spent much of his time with me in my library working on his *Canon of Medicine*. In writing this, he based his philosophy on Aristotle and his medicine on Galen, blending the two into a unity that was unmistakably his own. From the practical point of view, his great achievement was his revision of Galen's writings. This he was able to do in a way that had been impossible for the previous commentators whose work I had so admired all those years ago in Constantinople. The *Canon* contained for the first time, an organized, systematic statement of medical knowledge – adorned with Avicenna's own opinions! (I once heard the 18th-century Swiss physiologist, Albrecht von Haller [1707–1777], call this book a 'methodical inanity'!) On one point, however, I was not so sure I agreed with him; this was his insistence on separating surgery from medicine.

"I have seen," he said, "many a good physician who was unable to use a knife as it should be used. A surgeon should, perhaps, be a good physician but a good physician need not be a good surgeon. The talents required for each are different."

I still had my doubts.

"In our country," he continued, "I would recommend the use of the cautery rather than the knife. Wounds heal more favourably in our dry and dusty climate." With this I was inclined to agree. [Avicenna was born in Bukhara in what is now Uzbekistan.]

Before he left my house to return to the court at Isfahan – with a pardon – he made an intriguing observation:

"Conflicts are sometimes not without their benefits. The friction between Islam and Christianity over the possibility that some diseases may be contagious, has drawn physicians together to defend the concept. We now accept that it is true!"

When he had gone Telesphorus, who was glad to see the back of him, remarked: "That man, for all his intelligence, is a rogue." I raised my eyebrows at him. "He is not long for this life. His delight in savouring the pleasures of this world and his obsession with his own intellectual brilliance will bring him to an early grave. But, Master, I ask you how many sick people has he treated? How much of his surgical writings are pure book-learning?"

(I do not know why Telesphorus adopted this stance, though I suspect he may have been jealous of his Greek heritage and was displeased at seeing it usurped, even if only indirectly. On the other hand, it may have been that his long association with a mortal had inculcated in him some of our irrational prejudices! Whatever, despite Telesphorus's scepticism there can be no doubting Avicenna's lasting influence. His *Canon* was still a part of the curriculum in Egypt in the late 19th century. And, as another instance of the resilience of Islamic medicine, you are quite likely to find copies of the *Medicine of the Prophet* on the bookshelves of Islamic households today.)

COMMENTARY

1) Unlike the case in the Christian world, medicine and the role of its practitioners was rarely called into question since Islamic belief did not regard illness as divine punishment for sinning.

2) Once the Islamic world was established, what remained of the Western Roman Empire became progressively isolated and of little consequence, while the Eastern Empire was more concerned with protecting its eastern borders from invasion. Thus political dominance shifted to the Frankish Empire in the north. The teaching of Graeco-Roman medicine (really just Graeco) declined sharply as books, including Galen's, became scarce and the medical world had little contact with its ancient writings.

3) Fortunately, Islam valued scholarship and learning, wherever it came from. So, everything written that could be found anywhere was brought to Baghdad and translated into Arabic. Besides medicine this included science, philosophy and mathematics. The translators were also scholars of no mean ability and not only did they translate, but they also tidied up the works they were translating. One of their remarkable achievements was virtually to create a new language by means of which complex medical, scientific and philosophical concepts and arguments could be presented in Arabic in a clear and precise form. Some of the early translators wrote original medical treatises; for instance, Hunayn ibn Ishaq, one such scholar, also oversaw the translation of at least 129 works by Galen. At first, this scholastic activity was centred on Baghdad but as the Eastern Caliphate began to lose its influence, the Western Caliphate, centred on Cordova, took over.

4) Schools (and libraries) in which medicine was taught were found throughout Islam with the emphasis placed on clinical teaching.

Anatomy, however, was at a disadvantage since dissection was forbidden. This was so as not to interfere with the vital spark that remained in the human body to be reawakened after death and rewarded in paradise.

5) Until the time of Islam, medical care by reputable practitioners had mainly been limited to the rich (the repeated praises heaped on Rhazes for his generosity to the poor suggests that such generosity was uncommon). Popular medicine (folklore and superstition) with the strength of tradition behind it existed side-by-side with humoral medicine which was supported by its association with scholarship and wealthy patronage. Consequently, Arab practitioners used mainly the same methods of treatment as the Greeks. Nevertheless, new medications, such as ambergris, camphor, cloves, myrrh and senna as well as new methods of preparation, for example syrups and elixirs, were introduced. Pharmacy and chemistry were established as sciences with pharmacy becoming a separate profession. In spite of the low standing of surgery (see Source 4) some outstanding physicians practised it and wrote about it.

6) Giving succour to the sick was regarded as good work and would be rewarded in paradise. Even so, Muslims also valued compassion for its own sake.

7) Public heath and hygiene were appalling, as they were throughout the world until the arrival of modern medicine. Poverty, hunger and malnutrition were an inseparable part of life, as were endemic diseases such as dysentery, leprosy, malaria, tuberculosis and typhus; parasitic infections were rampant and eye diseases such as trachoma were common. Where sewers existed, they either couldn't cope or discharged into streams or rivers; needless to say, the rich lived upstream.

8) Hospitals, which were found all over Islam, for example in Cairo, Baghdad, Damascus and Jundisaphur, put even the Roman military valetudinaria to shame. Unfortunately, their value was limited by the vast size of the populations they served.

9) Rhazes was a Galenist in theory, in that he revered learning and

based his knowledge on the books of the authorities, such as Galen. However, he was an independent thinker and a true disciple of Hippocrates in the simplicity of his practice. He was not afraid to rely on his own observations when they disagreed with the past: "all that is written in books is worth much less than the experience of the wise doctor."

10) Avicenna's standing in both Christendom and Islam rivalled that of Galen. Although he may at times have practised medicine (as indicated by his description of diabetes mellitus) his main contribution to medicine was as a compiler and commentator; he cannot be said to have contributed materially to everyday bedside medicine. Regrettably his *Canon* set back the progress of surgery by implying that it was separate from and inferior to medicine, and also by preferring the cautery to the knife. However, the *Canon's* importance lay in its systematization of medicine which it did with a thoroughness that conferred on it an authority that lasted for hundreds of years during which it was endlessly discussed, criticized and commented on. Indeed, until the mid-17th century the curriculum of many Christian universities, including some in the British Isles, was based on the writings of Avicenna.

11) From the time of Avicenna until the end of the 15th century less attention was paid to what medical writers said than the way in which they said it.

SOURCES

1) "While the principal service of Islam to medicine was the preservation of Greek culture, yet the Saracens [another name for Muhammedans] themselves were the originators not only of algebra, chemistry, and geology, but of many of the so-called improvements or refinements of civilization, such as street-lamps, window panes, fireworks, stringed instruments, cultivated fruits, perfumes, spices,… In the intellectual sphere, the monotheism and the dialectic tendencies of Galen and Aristotle appealed strongly to the Muhammedans. Galen's polypharmacy [treatment of a single

condition with a number of different drugs] in particular appealed to these natural chemists, and his haphazard polypragmatism [self-opinionated on just about everything] was moulded by them into iron-clad dogma."

Fielding H. Garrison, *An Introduction to the History of Medicine*, 1929

2) "All believers were entitled to certain governmental benefits which included the protection of orphans, aid to the poor, hospitalization of the sick and asylums for the insane. In the hospitals which grew up under this system, extensive and consistent teaching and facilities for study arose for the first time."

Cecilia C. Mettler, *History of Medicine*, 1947

3) "The eruption of the small-pox is preceded by a continued fever, pain in the back, itching in the nose, and terrors in sleep. These are the more peculiar symptoms of its approach, especially the pain in the back with fever; then also a pricking which the patient feels all over his body; a fullness of the face which at times comes and goes; an inflamed colour and vehement redness in both the cheeks; a redness of both the eyes; a heaviness of the whole body; great uneasiness, the symptoms of which are stretching and yawning; a pain in the throat and chest with a slight difficulty in breathing, and cough; a dryness of the mouth, thick spittle and hoarseness of the voice; pain and heaviness of the head; inquietude, distress of mind, nausea and anxiety; heat of the whole body, and inflamed colour and shining redness, and especially an intense redness of the gums."

Rhazes (*c.*865–925), *On the Symptoms which Indicate the Approaching Eruption of the Small-pox and measles*

4) "Surgery is no longer honoured in our country. In its decadence, it has disappeared almost without trace. There remain some vestiges in the writings of the Ancients, but the transcriptions have corrupted them; error and confusion have over-run them in such a manner as to render them unintelligible and useless. I have

resolved to restore this science to life, and to consecrate this treatise to that purpose."

Albucasis, *Collection*. He was a physician and surgeon who lived in the Western Caliphate (Spain) and was probably born in 936.

Chapters 14 & 15

1020 —— Birth of Constantinus Africanus *c.*1020

— Death of Avicenna 1037

1050 ——

— Battle of Hastings 1066

— Compilation of the Domesday Book 1086
— The Crusades 1095–1270
1100 —— Death of Constantinus Africanus 1097

1150 ——

— Murder of Thomas à Becket 1170
— University of Bologna founded *c.*1180

1200 —— Universities of Oxford and Paris founded *c.*1200

— University of Padua founded 1222

1250 ——

— Baghdad sacked by Mongols. End of
Abbasid Caliphate 1258
— Birth of Mondino de Luzzi 1270

— Death of Roger Bacon 1294
1300 —— Alessandra Gilliani *fl.*1300
— Birth of Boccaccio 1313
— Death of Dante 1321
— Death of Mondino de Luzzi 1326
— Death of Giotto 1337
— Battle of Crecy 1346
1350 —— Black Death reached England 1349

— Death of Boccaccio 1375

1400 —— Death of Chaucer
— Chinese circumnavigated and charted the world 1421–1423

The late Middle Ages
(*c.*1037–*c.*1330)

My humours were in sore disarray. An intellectual movement known as Scholasticism was sweeping through Christendom and appeared set to clarify some aspects, at least, of the nature of disease; but as it took shape I saw it to be no more than a sham, an embellishment of the abstruse and interminable arguments that had so preoccupied philosophers in past centuries. The question now uppermost in men's minds was how to apply the logic of Aristotle to an understanding, not of man and disease, but of the Christian God – illogically, or so it seemed to me, medicine was ignored. When, in a very few centres, it did manage to creep into the curriculum the purpose was not to produce trained physicians but to delve deeper into the relationship between man and God, his Creator.

I was now more convinced than ever that each time man turned a corner in his history or ventured along an untrodden path, he divested himself of some hard-earned fragment of medical knowledge, leaving it to rot in the mire. Fortune smiled only when a scholar passed along the way in later years and rescued the fragment before its message became obliterated for all time.

Since leaving Baghdad my wanderings had once more been utterly aimless and Telesphorus must have found me a sour companion. But while I was continually morose and consumed by misery, he was unfailingly cheerful in his search for the plans devised by the gods for the benefit – or otherwise – of mankind.

"Master, you know you cannot influence Nature's great design," he spoke with sympathy for my plight as we made our way between Arles and Aix in the spring of the year. "Remember Rhazes, and when your soul is sick, seek the healing balm of serenity in all that is beautiful around you."

But even the scent of that most beautiful of lands could not ease my burden.

"Look at me! You ask me to seek peace in beauty!" My words came more sharply than I intended and I was relieved when Telesphorus took no offence. Indeed, I doubt that he noticed, so eager was he to chide me for my faults.

"Balthasar, are you both blind and deaf?" He had me by the hand and pulled me round to face him; his strength never ceased to surprise me. "You have stubbornly refused to make a home in France, rather you have chosen to walk – to walk! not even to ride like the nobleman you are! – to walk from town to town in the hope of meeting another Galen, another Hippocrates. No, Balthasar! such hopes are forlorn if you insist on walking with your eyes shuttered and your ears blocked – they are forlorn anyway," he muttered under his breath but just loud enough for me to hear. "You must look at people to see where they come from. You must talk to them to learn what they have to say.

"In your search for a king you have ignored the peasant. Have you been completely oblivious of the physicians who come to France after studying in the south of Italy? They have learnt from ancient commentaries on Galen and, for the most part, are good practical exponents of the art."

I looked blankly at him. "Where have they studied?" I asked in disbelief.

"Salerno. There, there is a school where the monks have studied at the excellent library of Monte Cassino."

"Then we must go to Salerno!" In the twinkling of an eye my vitality returned and I could not act quickly enough. I sent Telesphorus to buy the best horses the district could offer and away we went. I was borne by a Pegasus of the new millennium.

The old Roman health resort of Salerno was not greatly impressive and its school, in size, could not compare with the intellectual emporia of France. Where it excelled was in cultural vibrancy. And nowhere else in the world were healers taught in the same manner. When I questioned the monks about the source of their knowledge, the name that kept recurring was Constantinus – called Africanus since he came from Tunisia. And where might I find him? I asked. At Monte Cassino, where he had recently retired to continue his literary work.

Perched high on a precipitous mountain top, the monastery of Monte Cassino had been designed on the lines of an impregnable fortress. Secure from the worldly exchanges far below them, the monks pursued their labours in uninterrupted calm.

Telesphorus insisted that he came with me when I visited Constantinus [c.1020–1097] in his cell. The reason, he said, was to meet the man and learn from him, but in reality it was to prepare himself for my reaction to what I was about to discover. Surrounded by books, Constantinus was solemnly translating the Arabic translations of Galen and Hippocrates, and the opinions of their Arabic commentators, into Latin. It was unbelievable! I had been through all this before; it was as if medicine was merely an exercise in the art of translation. Somehow I managed to retain a civil tongue in my head and discuss intelligently some obscure Hippocratic argument – much to the amazement of Constantinus.

"Telesphorus, this is absurd! We are no further forward than when Galen was alive – and he has been dead now some eight hundred years." I was furious with Telesphorus, with Constantinus, with Salerno, with the entire world and everything on it.

"Am I to believe that an understanding of disease will come only when Galen and Hippocrates have been translated into every tongue at Babel? That cannot be so, and foolish also is the man who thinks it can be reached through philosophy alone!"

"Oh, Balthasar, Balthasar!" Telesphorus was grinning with delight. "Anger sits better on you than misery. The monk wishes to talk with you again tomorrow – his work goes beyond translation and I think you will approve of his achievements."

I had my doubts, but the next day we returned to Constantinus's cell. As our conversation proceeded, it was soon apparent that Telesphorus's forecast had been correct.

"Galen's writings were obscure and confused," Constantinus began. "The commentaries of later writers sometimes clarified an argument, but more often added to the confusion. It requires a very perceptive mind to unravel Galen's reasoning. When his texts were translated into Arabic, not only did they encounter a new language but also an alien culture and a new style of thought. Consequently the translators were compelled to reinterpret Galen's ideas and most did so with remarkable competence." (I chose to overlook the man's remarkable condescension!)

"Now it has become our turn to make the true medicine of the ancients accessible to our students by translating the Arabic texts into Latin. We have allowed ourselves more licence than those who made the Arabic translations as our culture is more advanced and we have a few hundred years more learning to draw on. We have, you might say, 'opened up' Galen to an extent that has been impossible hitherto.

"To show you what I mean, this is a translation I have prepared of Johannicius's *Questions on Medicine*."

Constantinus handed me a book entitled *Liber ysagogarum*. I looked at it and then at him; I was totally perplexed.

"Are you perhaps an Arabic scholar yourself?" he asked.

When I answered that I was, he picked up an old book from among those lying on a table.

"You recognize it now, I see." He could hardly have missed my expression as I found myself given a copy of Hunayn ibn Ishaq's *Al-Masa'il fi l-tibb* [*Questions of Medicine*].

"We know Hunayn as Johannicius but, by whatever name, his writings hold the key to the understanding of Galen. So, after passing through a Nestorian Christian, a Tunisian monk and several hundred years (an inconsequentiality to the Lord) Galen's work has come alive, and the essence of his philosophy can at last be given practical expression.

"As you are a physician familiar with the old concepts of Hippocratic and Galenic medicine, this new understanding will be of value to you and, moreover, you will be able to spread the knowledge on your travels."

In the next hour my eyes and ears were opened and many obscurities that had plagued me over the centuries were cleared away. Constantinus was an excellent teacher. First, he explained how, as time went on, the Hippocratic waters had become muddied and even Galen had failed to clear them. "Now, through Johannicius, I have reached the truth.

"Good health is wholly in the power of pairs of what I have termed non-naturals: the sleeping and the waking states; movement and repose; food and drink; fullness and excretion; and finally the passions and the emotions. If these non-naturals do not receive their due attention, the body grows sick. A consideration of imminent changes in the needs of the body – whether on account of changes in climate, forthcoming exertion and the like – allows a man to adjust the non-naturals and so prevent a disruption of the humours."

* * *

Despite Constantinus's insight into the works of Galen, I remained unaware of any progress in the understanding of disease that could be put to practical use. The poor still suffered from diseases their folk-healers were unable to cure, and the rich still endured the ministrations of their physicians who only added to the sufferings inflicted by disease.

Universities and hospitals sprang up across Europe and, as they were founded, I enrolled in one university after another, but invariably I was one of a mere handful of students studying medicine. At every one we were subjected to the same Aristotelian philosophy of the logical progression from universal causes to specific effects. We were taught how matter was created, how it was changed, and how it obeyed the universal laws. From this we were supposed to see how it applied to mankind. (Every generation has to make use, as best it can, of the information available to it. Your data, too, sometimes prove wide of the mark – and who knows how much more will prove false in years to come?)

The Christian Church had shifted its ground and now believed that at the Day of Judgement all mankind would stand before the throne of God, where those who had been mutilated or become dust and ashes would be made whole again. Whether this was its motivation or not, the Church had sanctioned dissections – provided the body was that of an executed felon and his remains given a decent Christian burial. Even so, dissections were occasional affairs – once a month, once a year or less, maybe – attended with considerable pomp and ceremony, and of more religious than medical benefit.

These anatomies were presided over by the Magister, resplendent in his doctoral robes and seated above the proceedings on an often ornately carved canopied throne. He was attended by a prosector and a medical student, also in academic dress. The student's duty was to read from the Magister's favourite anatomical text to indicate to the prosector what he was supposed to be exposing. Rather than explain the different organs and structures in anatomical terms, the Magister, in his commentaries, related them to the philosophy of Galen and the one Creator – thus the 'truths' revealed were acceptable to the Christian Church.

When I was attending the more secularly inclined university at Padua we once had the unusual experience of having a female corpse for dissection. This attracted a large audience of fifty or more citizens anxious to discover the mysteries of the female body. The Magister (whose name I forget) decided that I should read the anatomical text. His chosen authority was Aretaeus [fl.2nd–3rd century] (almost a contemporary of Galen!) who, in his opinion, was the greatest physician since Hippocrates. The demonstration took place in a church and as soon as the Magister was enthroned, I began:

"In the middle of the flanks of women lies the womb, a female viscus, closely resembling an animal; for it is moved of itself hither and thither in the flanks, also upwards in a direct line to below the cartilage of the thorax, and also obliquely to the right or left, either to the liver or spleen; and it likewise is subjected to prolapsus downwards, and, in a word, it is altogether erratic."

As I recited in solemn, measured tones pausing, when I caught his eye, to allow the Magister to deliver a commentary, the prosector manhandled the uterus in a vain attempt to demonstrate its supposed motions.

"It delights also," I continued, "in fragrant smells, and advances towards them; and it has an aversion to foetid smells, and flees from them; and on the whole, the womb is like an animal within an animal."

For three days this highly imaginative litany continued. At the start, only those standing closest could have caught sight of the organs as they were displayed and by the end even the prosector was unable to define the putrefying muscles. If nothing else, here was proof indeed that the human body was but the temporary residence of man's immortal soul!

To describe most of these anatomies as farcical would be to do them greater justice than they deserved, though a notable exception were those of Mondino de Luzzi [1270–1326]. He employed, as assistant prosector, Alessandra Gilliani [*fl.*1300] who, to the amazement of all, had the skill to dissect out the blood vessels to their smallest divisions without damage. She then prepared them for Mondino's demonstration by filling them with coloured liquids that hardened, allowing her to paint the arteries and veins in their natural colours.

In Spain, they were still translating as if the future of the world depended on it. Over the years, though, I had met a handful of Spanish physicians – Christians, Moors, Jews, alike – who achieved recognition through their writings; the Arabic influence was, not unexpectedly, predominant. Their scholarship was of a high level and they continued to bring yet more order and a deeper comprehension to the ancient works than had previous translators. In this sense medicine was moving forward. But in the treatment and understanding of disease, in the healing of the sick, there was little change. In the Christian world, much compassion was extended to the poor in the monasteries and in the hospitals (which, for the most part, were run by religious orders anyway), but this was for the good of their eternal souls rather than the comfort of their suffering bodies.

The one faint glimpse of encouragement was the appearance of works translated into the vernacular. These were mainly surgical treatises – as if to drive home the widening gulf between the 'academic' discipline of medicine and the despised barbarity that was surgery. Even so, the books that circulated frequently described the most intricate operations; their wealth of beautifully drawn instruments reminded me of those with which Avicenna had decorated his books – though not, if Telesphorus was correct, employed on patients. Regrettably, reality was not reflected in their pages. Few operations were performed and happy the patient who did not journey to oblivion on a tide of his own blood or endure the lingering agony of a festering death.

"Telesphorus," I said, "I have reached a moment of decision. For how many centuries have we travelled together and for how many more did I travel alone before you came to me as a companion beyond imagined worth?" Dear Telesphorus, I truly loved him and he was not averse to occasional flattery – even though he was never quite sure how to react.

"Telesphorus," I continued, "there is nothing but night along this endless road named Medicine. The straight and ancient road from Greece and Rome is now a rutted, dusty, treacherous track. What is medicine now?" I asked, rhetorically. "It is yet another illusion. It is no more than a magic sleight of hand." I paused waiting for him to accuse me of inconsistency, but he remained silent. Anger and frustration were rising within me. "All the innumerable books – most of them of interminable length and full of false philosophy – have for centuries been merely the amulets, charms and incantations of the 'learned' physician! They might as well wear them around their necks as read them for all the good they do the sick!" I had never been so venomously inclined towards my brother practitioners.

"I have lost all hope. At the next turning I shall strike out along a different path in search of understanding."

"Yes, Master," was his only response. He refused to discuss my intention. His unspoken disapproval was so vehement that I should have heeded it. I did not. I blundered on, stubbornly believing I was in the right; that I would find the understanding of disease along a different route.

COMMENTARY

1) The frustration experienced by Balthasar reminds us just how little progress had been made in medicine up to that time. This

demonstrates how important it is to ensure that we have a clear understanding of progression/regression – medicine did not progress at a constant rate through the ages.

2) Scholasticism flourished between the 12th (some say 9th) and early 15th centuries. The Scholastics rediscovered the Arabic writers, and through them, Aristotelian philosophy. Just like their predecessors, the philosophers of ancient Alexandra (see Chapter 9), the Scholastics much preferred disputation to the seeking of objective evidence. However, they found it necessary to establish supreme authorities in the various fields to support their arguments. In the medical field, the philosophical dogmatism of Aristotle and Avicenna suited the purpose admirably. The Scholastics wrote on a vast number of moot medical questions of no real significance and a great length. Such questions were, for instance, whether fever could coincide with apoplexy, whether a small head was better than a large one, whether the heart or the flesh was the organ of touch; all these were taken from passages in the works of their authorities but completely out of context. Their works were often written in the form of question and answer. But in a world that was building up to the Renaissance, the methods of Scholasticism eventually had to give way to personal investigation.

3) Salerno was often referred to as the 'urbe graece' thus acknowledging its reputation as a seat of learning in the West. Many subjects were taught at the University but medicine was the prime concern. Students and patients came from many different countries to profit from the standard of medical learning and practice. On leaving, the patients were given a guide-book on the maintenance of good health – the *Regimen Sanitatis Salernitanum* (see Source 3, below).

4) Not everyone shares Balthasar's opinion of Constantinus, though most agree that his translations had a lasting influence. Typical of the criticisms are that his translations of the Arabic texts were inaccurate and rendered into bad Latin – that may be so, but the charge of bad Latin has been levelled at many other translators of

his era. He has also been accused of having had a negligible knowledge of medicine.

5) Constantinus's interpretation of Galen's philosophy and views on good health led in the coming centuries to countless books of advice on how to restore and preserve health. Although many of these appeared, at first glance, to deal only with diet, this was not the case. To the writers (and their predecessors), the word 'diet' referred to a person's entire way of life.

6) By this time the view that the divine oversaw the temporal in all matters pertaining to humanity had become a deeply entrenched belief of the Christian Church. Illness remained a manifestation of sin – from which it followed that redemption outweighed medical intervention. Physicians were of far less importance than the clergy, since the soul must be saved at all costs. Furthermore, the Lateran Council of 1215 completed the subordination of physicians by ruling that all practitioners of medicine must be appointed by the Church. This also had the aim of curtailing the practice of Jewish doctors. The Council, likewise, forbade clerics from being involved in any medical procedure that required the shedding of blood (many physicians were also doctors of divinity!). This was not an attack on surgery as has been suggested, but a means of curtailing clerics from taking part in the more demeaning (as they saw it) vocational aspects of medicine. In 1482 Pope Sixtus IV clarified the position of dissection by acknowledging that it could be permitted so long as the body was that of a convicted criminal and that it received a Christian burial.

7) Bleeding, purging and the familiar methods of folk medicine still were the best that people could hope for, although prayer and all the hocus pocus of amulets, religious reliquaries and the like took pride of place. Earthly problems, such as war, plague, economic and political anarchy, left people feeling powerless to help themselves.

8) Despite Albucasis's best endeavours (see Chapter 13, Source 4) surgeons were no longer aware of Graeco-Roman surgical achievements. Faith was enough and so surgery was limited to the

simplest of procedures such as tooth extraction and to the obviously necessary such as amputation.

9) Besides Alessandra Gilliani, there was another woman who helped with the teaching of anatomy by developing wax models of dissected specimens coloured to resemble the original. She was Anna Morandi Mahzolini of Bologna; although her precise dates are unknown, she lived around the same period.

SOURCES

1) "Thus began the period of Monastic medicine, in which, along with a praiseworthy zeal for preserving the remains of ancient literature and the traditions of a rational praxis [example], there grew up a cult of faith-healing or theurgic therapy, an implicit belief in the miraculous healing power of the saints and of holy relics. Supernatural aid came to be more esteemed as the medical art showed itself to be powerless, particularly in the time of the great epidemics. Western medicine, unlike that of Byzantium and Islam, went into eclipse and its practice became as rudimentary and stereotyped as that of primitive man."

Fielding H. Garrison, *An Introduction to the History of Medicine*, 1929

2) "As Arabic culture was gradually transplanted from Spain and the African coast to Sicily and Salerno, the hygienic conditions of Italy slowly began to improve, but no significant alterations in pathologic theory occurred until the revival of dissection at Bologna. This revival itself was an outgrowth of the awakened consciousness on the part of the Bolognese to the necessity of establishing the structural alteration attendant upon disease."

Cecilia C. Mettler, *History of Medicine*, 1947

3) "If you lack medical men, let these three things be your medicine: good humour, rest and sobriety."

Regimen Sanitatis Salernitanum, 1260–1300

Boccaccio and the Black Death
(*c.*1330–1348)

"For, as the last degree of joy brings with it sorrow, so misery has ever its sequel of happiness." Giovanni Boccaccio [1313–1375] would have been pleased that I should borrow his words, even though he was now victim to the former state while I rejoiced in the latter. He knew I had not stolen Fiammetta [*d.*1348] from him – their ways had parted some months before our chance encounter in the square of San Lorenzo. Our eyes had responded and, with hands clasped, we had climbed the steps into the church. There, in the cool midday twilight lit only by the candles of the penitents, Fiammetta kissed me.

Firm in my resolve to find a different path, I had returned to Naples from Spain. Telesphorus, however, had declined to accompany me.

"If you wish to believe that understanding lies in strange places, you will discover only falsehoods." He was still resentful and not to be placated. Nevertheless, he gave the distinct impression that, had he wished, he could have explained the fixation with the ancients that so disturbed me. On the morning of my departure, I decided to confront him.

"You know why medicine remains chained to the past, yet you refuse to tell me. Why?" I demanded.

"The time has not yet come." He was taking delight in infuriating me. "You see only the outward signs of the philosophers' thoughts while their profound concerns lie beyond your present comprehension." At that moment I could have dismembered him. "But Balthasar, be patient." He saw that I was in no mood for his goading, however playfully intended, and laid a sympathetic hand on my arm.

"Master, if I were permitted to open your eyes to the future, even for the briefest moment, I would willingly do so. But you are mortal –

an unusual example, I admit," he giggled. "And so you must endure the uncertainties of a mortal's existence.

"Farewell! and do not forget that the real treasures of the world you inhabit arrive unannounced and in the most unexpected places." And with that typically enigmatic remark he slapped the hindquarters of my horse and I was off like the wind for Naples. "But you will not find the understanding you seek where you are going." His final words reached my ears as faintly as a receding echo.

In that first moment in the church of San Lorenzo, all memory of the past was expelled from my mind. The centre of my universe was Fiammetta – I could no more think of her as Maria as I could believe the Vicar of Christ had converted to Islam; if Boccaccio's mistress was now mine, why should I feel shame at loving her by the name he had given her?

I had long known that the deliberate pursuit of happiness was always destined to fail even before the chase had begun. But happiness came with Fiammetta at the dawn of each new day. To be loved by this most beautiful of creatures was Paradise enough. When we had quite exhausted the pleasures of Naples, we journeyed leisurely northwards through her father's kingdom and on into the Papal States until at length we came to Assisi. Our route had been determined by Fiammetta's delight in the sanctity of the multitude of churches and abbeys that dominated the landscape. Even greater was the inner peace she drew from contemplation of the paintings ornamenting every last space within these temples – which I sensed were witness more to the vanity of man than the glory of God.

Assisi was her chosen destination but before we entered the town, she took me by the hand and led me through the woods to the Porziuncola [the little chapel that witnessed the birth of the Franciscan order]. There we spent the night on our knees praying, each in our own way. There, too, I think I was as close to the Christian God as I had ever come, or was ever likely to come again. But my prayers were haunted by the Saint's dying verses recorded in his *Canticle of the Creatures*: "Praise to you, my Lord, for our sister Death, for no one living can escape her." I wept at the irony of these words.

The next morning we roused ourselves – for we had both slumbered during our vigil – and walked the league [about two and one-third English miles] into town. Rising before us, in complete contrast to the humble Porziuncola, was the monumental fortress of the double basilica dedicated to St Francis [1182–1226] – not that such an edifice would have found the remotest flicker of favour with the Saint who, both by word and example, had preached the gospel of Holy Poverty. His spirit had even to endure the 'ungodly' embellishments of the greatest artists of the day.

The storm clouds, which had threatened before we left the little chapel, opened with sudden fury as we reached the San Pietro gate. Dampened, we found shelter of a kind under its archway. The outburst was the first of the autumn and, consequently, of more than a little intensity. Knowing Fiammetta's purpose in Assisi, I wondered whether the wind and the rain were a signal of St Francis's displeasure or merely an indication that in death he had become resigned to man's follies and was welcoming us by bringing a freshness to the air and rinsing the alleys of their filth.

"When I was a child," Fiammetta began, "my father brought many artists of talent under his patronage. My favourite was one as ill-favoured as his paintings were beautiful. Giotto [c.1267–1337] was kind to me; he made me laugh and, had his artistic genius deserted him, his ready wit would have secured him a place as my father's jester. I loved him with a child's adoration; when he left us, I wept for days." There was an undeniable catch in her voice as she spoke of him.

"Even before his death, it was said he had transformed the art of painting. Now we shall see how true that is!"

As swiftly as it had begun, the rain ceased, remembered only by the vapour lazily rising from the cobbles and rooftops. The sun, blazing from a newly-washed sky, accompanied us to the doors of the church. For some moments we stood silently within the lower basilica waiting for our sight to return. Gradually the form of the building took shape until at last I was able to see its decorations emerge from the gloom in all their exquisite beauty. I had quite expected Fiammetta to take me first to the paintings of her favourite but instead she played on my emotions, leading me to the right transept and Cimabue's [*c.*1240–*c.*1302] Madonna with its sad St Francis at Her side. When I had admired this to her satisfaction she walked me slowly round the paintings of Martini [*c.*1284–1344] and the two Lorenzetti brothers [Pietro, *c.*1280–*c.*1348; Ambrogio, *fl.*1320] drawing my attention in particular to Martini's much stronger depiction of the Saint. When next she stopped, it was before scenes of the Nativity and life of Christ. Unable to control her sobbing, she clung to me.

"These are by my old friend," she managed to say. "Are they not truly wonderful?"

Indeed they were. By comparison, the paintings we had already seen were flat and lifeless though, if I could trust my artistic sense, the work of Cimabue had been a brave attempt to break with tradition. Giotto had succeeded where his master had failed. His figures were so imbued with life I could almost feel their breath upon my face.

"There are more." Fiammetta, tears still in her eyes, led the way to the upper basilica. Here, in frescos of unbelievable spiritual power and movement, Giotto had recreated the life of St Francis within a world of delightful simplicity. In these paintings he had surpassed the Giotto of the lower basilica: never before had life been expressed with such truthfulness and sensitivity.

For many days we returned to the church, lost in wonder at both painter and subjects. On our last visit Fiammetta was in a strange, other-worldly mood.

"These paintings of Giotto's will have a greater influence on your life, dear Paul, than you can possibly imagine. They will prove to be one of the means whereby you are drawn closer to your goal." She turned towards me with a look that penetrated my innermost being. She seemed not to be herself – and then, intuitively, I knew Telesphorus was speaking through her. But what was he telling me? Belabour my mind though I would, it was beyond my understanding. How could an artist influence medicine. I might ask the question now; the answer lay in the future.

Before the winds of winter came we returned to Naples by roads still easily passable. Our villa, a mile or two outside the city, had been given to Fiammetta by her father and here we rested from our travels. On summer days when we chose not to seek entertainment in the city, we would spend our afternoons in the walled garden, the beauty of which reminded me of a corner of my estate in Constantinople. Days spent with Fiammetta in that heaven on earth were enchantment indeed.

Strolling together hand-in-hand in the balm of a summer twilight, I said something that I must have said in different ways almost every day.

"This garden is blest," I murmured. "Whatever the season, whatever the weather; in rain, wind, or sun it shows a different aspect. But it is always beautiful; it never ceases to please and delight. It is Paradise on earth!"

Her response surprised me. Instead of squeezing my hand in silent agreement and drawing closer to me, she said simply and in a matter of fact tone:

"There are flies, even in Paradise."

Although I banished from my mind the unwelcome sense of foreboding that this conjured up, her words returned to haunt me before another year was passed.

It was spring again. Each year at about this time I returned to Salerno. Despite my misgiving at the direction orthodox medicine seemed to be taking – if, indeed, it had not already entered a dead-end – I was resolved to keep a watchful eye on its travails. I was away for three weeks.

On my return I could not escape the fearful disaster that had overtaken the land. Terror crowded the streets of Naples and when I arrived home, it was to find the servants fled save for Fiammetta's young handmaid whose bare arms were disfigured by ugly livid blotches. Bidding me not to touch her, she hurried ahead to Fiammetta's bedroom.

"Yes, my beloved, there *are* flies in Paradise! Come, let me hold you that we may leave this world together."

I fell to my knees at the bedside and took her in my arms.

With her dying breath, Fiammetta kissed me.

* * *

Fiammetta had been Boccaccio's inspiration, both in his life and in his work. I knew, from reports received from Florence, that he loved her still and continued to live in the belief that one day she would tire of her current lover and return to him. Since it was eminently possible, given the present state of the country, that word of her death would never reach him, I resolved to travel to Florence with the news that Fiammetta was lost to both of us for ever.

I gathered a bodyguard of the soundest fighting men left in Naples and ensured their loyalty: money is the answer to many things. We carried our needs with us and rode across country by uncommon tracks. At night we made camp in the open and far from human habitation. I strictly forbade the men to come close to other people.

The journey was one of unmitigated horror. Even in the remotest regions we encountered citizens who had fled their homes, their possessions, and their families in the hope that God would not pursue them with His wrath but intended to destroy only those who remained within the city walls. Their mistaken belief was everywhere in evidence in the foul pollution that assailed the senses.

Free from the pestilence, we were admitted to Florence. My enquiries, however, elicited the fact that Boccaccio was living at Corbignano, a short distance outside. Much to my relief, and with all possible speed, we abandoned the city.

The Boccaccio I found at Corbignano was not the Boccaccio who had left Naples seven years previously. A deep melancholy had settled on him and when he learnt of Fiammetta's death he shut himself in his room and wept unceasingly for three days. When he emerged he had purged himself of his grief and, knowing now that Fiammetta was truly beyond his recall, he seemed to have prepared himself to face reality once again.

Although we had little in common he urged me to stay. He wished to talk, not only about Fiammetta – he felt he had seven lost years to regain and showed no jealousy when I recounted their joys and delights. I, too, was happy to hear him speak about the Fiammetta I had never known. Our talk released my numbed emotions and I was able to view the world, not with an uncomprehending vision, but as it was – and it was worse, far worse, than I had feared.

Boccaccio was insistent on describing for me the ravages of the pestilence now sweeping with devastating fury throughout Europe. It was as if he was driven to rehearse a story he was intending to use in another place. His tale, indeed, left nothing to my imagination.

The deadly pestilence had, he said, originated some years earlier in the East from where it had pursued its relentless progress into the West, consuming uncountable lives along the way. Whether it had been brought upon mankind by the influence of celestial bodies or had been sent by God in His just wrath as punishment for their sins was of little consequence in the presence of its mighty destructive power.

"We took every precaution that came to mind to prevent the disease from entering Florence." Boccaccio spoke as lucidly as he wrote. "We appointed officials to clean the city and we refused entry to all who were sick. Those who believed the pestilence to be a visitation from God, addressed their humble supplications to Him in the churches and in processions through the city. But it was all to no avail and in the spring the pestilence breached the city's defences in all its horror."

What, I asked, were its manifestations, for all I had seen had been its awesome consequences.

"They are not as they were in the East, where a sudden bleeding from the nose was a sure sign of impending death [the pneumonic form]. In European countries, in men and women alike, swellings appear in the groin or armpits – these are about the size of an egg or an apple; some larger, some smaller; the people call them gavoccioli [buboes]. They soon spread indiscriminately to all parts of the body. After a while the illness begins to change form with the appearance of black spots or livid marks, often on the arm or thigh, some few and large, some minute and numerous. Both swellings and spots are invariable tokens of approaching death."

He stopped abruptly and for a minute or two sat gazing inwardly. Fiammetta was in his thoughts as she was in mine. Pouring some wine, he waved a request that I did the same. "And how do the physicians treat the disease?" I enquired. He gave a start, almost spilling the wine, gathered his thoughts and continued.

"Nothing influences the disease, neither the art of the physician nor the virtues of physic. Whether it is in the nature of the illness to defy treatment or whether the physicians are at fault, being in ignorance of its source and thus failing to apply the correct remedy, I know not. Besides, many, both men and women practise without the least knowledge of medicine. Few recover and many of those who die, do so within three days of the appearance of their symptoms and in most cases without fever or any other manifestation!

"The pestilence is deadly beyond belief. It is conveyed from the sick to the healthy merely by speech or association. Its virulence is such that should a healthy person touch the clothes of the sick or anything that has been used by them, they seem to contract the disease. The energy of the contagion is startling.

"Those who remain alive," he said, "shun, each in their own way, all contact with the sick and their belongings. Some think that to live temperately and avoid all excess is the best means of preserving their health. They have banded together and formed communities in houses free of the sickness.   Others take their pleasure in song and merriment, indulging the satisfaction of every appetite.

"Between these two," Boccaccio continued – I was as fascinated by this tale of human misery as if by a cobra poised to strike – "are those who keep to a middle course. They walk abroad carrying flowers or fragrant herbs or spices which they frequently raise to their noses, believing it an excellent thing to give comfort to their brains with such perfumes as an antidote to the stench emitted by the dead and dying. But whatever the course of action adopted, many die.

"The world is changing, my friend. Life will never be the same again." Boccaccio's voice was hesitant with emotion. His happiness had been destroyed and now that Fiammetta was dead he was deprived even of hope. But it was not his personal world he was mourning; it was the life of all mankind on this earth.

"In consequence of the dearth of servants and the neglect of the sick, the previously unthinkable is happening," he continued his story.

"No woman, however fastidious, fair or well-born she may be, shrinks, when sick, from the ministrations of a man whether young or old. She does not scruple to expose to him every part of her body with no more shame than if he were a woman, and submits to whatever necessity her disease demands. This has resulted, among those who recover, in a loss of modesty. Citizens who have heard of this – let alone those who have witnessed its occurrence – are struck dumb with amazement. The effect, which is not to be wondered at with death ever present night and day, is that practices contrary to their former conduct have taken root among the survivors.

"How many families of historic fame, of vast ancestral lands, of proverbial wealth, now have none to continue the succession!" A note of despairing sadness entered his voice. "How many brave men, how many fair ladies, how many gallant youths, whom any physician, were he Galen, Hippocrates or Aesculapius himself, would have pronounced in the soundest of health, breakfasted with their kinsfolk, comrades and friends in the morning and, when the evening came, supped with their forefathers in the next world!"

Boccaccio sank back in his chair, exhausted from the emotions aroused by the telling of the tale, and entered his own other world of lost love and creative fantasy. He spoke not another word in my presence.

COMMENTARY

1) Giovanni Boccaccio (1313–1375) was the author of, inter alia, the *Decameron,* a collection of one hundred tales purporting to have been told in ten days during the plague in Florence. The book, completed in about 1353 and often regarded as the first novel, influenced such writers as Chaucer, Edmund Spenser and Shakespeare.

2) Fiametta was Boccaccio's affectionate name for his mistress, Maria d'Aquino, natural daughter of Robert the Wise, King of Naples, whom he first met in Naples in 1336. She was the inspiration for much of his earlier work before she found a new protector.

3) 'Black Death' is a relatively modern term. It first appeared in 1820 in a story written by Mrs Markham (Elizabeth Penrose, née Cartwright [1780–1837]. She was a writer of stories for the young.) There is no reference to the 'Black Death' in the 14th and 15th centuries.

4) The extent of the plague is unknown owing to the lack of records. In the absence of official birth and death registers the historian can only estimate. *Bills of Mortality*, dating from the end of the 16th century, were English parish records of deaths and baptisms. They began to be supplanted by civil *Registries of Births, Deaths, and Marriages* in the 19th century. The same century saw the start of population censuses.

5) Paul Balthasar's instinct proved correct. Boccaccio's account of the Black Death in Florence was to appear in the introductory paragraphs of the stories of the first day of the *Decameron*. It is perhaps of interest that in his written description Boccaccio states that the pestilence (bubonic plague) raged from March to July. The flea that spreads the disease does so through its bite, but only when the plague bacilli (*Yersinia pestis*) form a blockage with fibrinous matter in its gut. A blocked flea makes repeated attempts to feed on blood, but since it cannot get the blood to pass the blockage, it regurgitates masses of plague bacilli into the bite wound. Curiously, the blockage clears at temperatures above 27ºC (80ºF); consequently epidemics of plague subside spontaneously when the ambient temperature exceeds this level. Buboes are the painfully enlarged lymph nodes in the groin and armpit. The emerods that afflicted the Philistines after they had stolen the ark of the covenant from the Israelites could well have been the buboes of plague (I Samuel, 5, v.12).

6) The pandemic that was the Black Death began in Central Asia and spread first to China and India before reaching Europe (the Crimea) in 1346. A year later it struck Sicily and then early in 1348 it was in Genoa, Marseilles, Venice, Pisa, and Florence. By the summer it had reached Paris and in 1349 England and nearly every country in Europe was involved. The mortality rate was

horrendous though contemporary estimates, such as those of Boccaccio (which exceeded the total population of Florence), were usually wildly exaggerated. A more realistic estimate would probably be that one-third of the population of Europe (about thirty million) were killed – some one-and-a-half to two million in England. The Black Death was generally believed to be either a response to astrological events or a divine punishment for sin.

7) Pneumonic plague may be a primary infection resulting from close contact with an infected person, but it is more usually secondary to bubonic or septicaemic (bacilli in the bloodstream) infection. The buboes are excruciatingly painful.

8) The practice of holding sweet smelling flowers and herbs to the nose to mitigate the stench and perhaps to ward off infections generally persisted for many years. In London during the Black Death some physicians wore a leather cover-all outfit with a beak-like projection in front of the nose containing spices or other aromatic substances. Flowers, in particular, were supposed to 'dry' the inhaled air since moistness (in the humoral sense) was believed to be associated with predisposition to the plague.

SOURCES

1) "The condition of the lower, and, perhaps, in great measure of the middle ranks, of the people showed even worse and more deplorable; for, deluded by hope or constrained by poverty, they stayed in their quarters, in their houses, where they sickened by thousands a day, and, being without service or help of any kind, were, so to speak, irredeemably devoted to the death which overtook them. Many died daily or nightly in the public streets; of many others, who died at home, the departure was hardly observed by their neighbours, until the stench of their putrefying bodies carried the tidings; and what with their corpses and the corpses of others who died on every hand the whole place was a sepulchre."

Giovanni Boccaccio (1313–1375), *Decameron*

2) "The social and economic consequences of such gigantic losses must have been very far reaching. Indeed the Black Death was conventionally seen by historians as the decisive point in the decline of the feudal system in Western Europe.... Yet nowadays specialists tend to argue that many of the changes were visible before 1347... This means that the Black Death was the accelerator of existing processes rather than their originator. At all events, serfs were increasingly commuting their labour dues for money rents, thereby creating a more mobile, and less dependent, labour force.... Above all, in a labour market deprived at a stroke of manpower, wages were sure to rise with rising demand. The money economy was expanded; social barriers were threatened."

Norman Davies, *Europe: A History*, 1996

3) "Meanwhile the king sent proclamation into all the counties that reapers and other labourers should not take more than they had been accustomed to take, under penalty appointed by statute. But the labourers were so lifted up and obstinate that they would not listen to the King's command, but if anyone wished to have them he had to give them what they wanted, and either lose his fruit and crops, or satisfy the lofty and covetous wishes of the workmen. And when it was known to the King that they had not observed his command and had given greater wages to the labourers, he levied heavy fines upon abbots, priors, knights, greater and lesser, and other great folk and small folk of the land of the realm."

Henry Knighton (a contemporary writer), *Chronicles*

Chapter 16

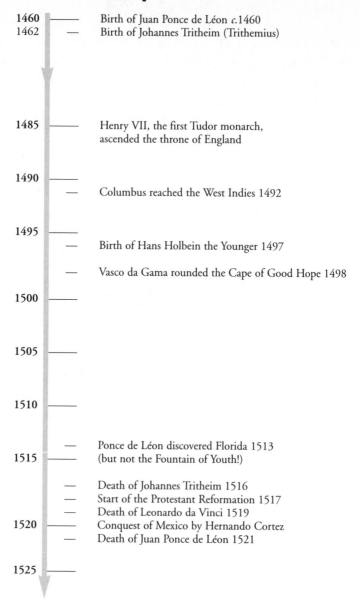

| 1460 | Birth of Juan Ponce de Léon *c.*1460 |
| 1462 | Birth of Johannes Tritheim (Trithemius) |

| 1485 | Henry VII, the first Tudor monarch, ascended the throne of England |

| 1490 | |
| | Columbus reached the West Indies 1492 |

1495	
	Birth of Hans Holbein the Younger 1497
	Vasco da Gama rounded the Cape of Good Hope 1498

| 1500 | |

| 1505 | |

| 1510 | |

| | Ponce de Léon discovered Florida 1513 |
| 1515 | (but not the Fountain of Youth!) |

	Death of Johannes Tritheim 1516
	Start of the Protestant Reformation 1517
	Death of Leonardo da Vinci 1519
1520	Conquest of Mexico by Hernando Cortez
	Death of Juan Ponce de Léon 1521

| 1525 | |

Alchemy
(1348–1516)

Boccaccio was right. The world *would* never be the same again. By the time the pestilence had run its course that terrible summer, upward of one hundred thousand citizens of Florence were supping with their forefathers [Boccaccio's somewhat excessive estimate!]. Many had lain putrefying in the streets before their mortal bodies had been thrown with less ceremony than would have been accorded a goat, into a common trench. At every church, pits were dug down to the water level and the poor who had died in the night were bundled up and thrown in. The next morning, earth was shovelled over them; later others were cast on top with another layer of earth, just as one would make lasagne with layers of pasta and cheese. (I have to admit that I borrowed this metaphor from Boccaccio.) For three more years the plague flowed and ebbed throughout Europe with the same mournful consequences, sparing few cities, few countrysides. And that was just the beginning.

Death was the ever-present spectre. A second Flood was confidently predicted. Comets and meteors were interpreted as signs of God's wrath. Every event that seemed to contradict nature was a call to mankind to repent and atone for his sins. And God did not stop at warning; He punished. He constantly sent new epidemics of plague, both bubonic and pneumonic, to destroy the cities and lay waste the land. The unknown took a hand in the shape of new, terrifying, diseases. People were taken with the English sweat and other strange fevers. The dancing mania added to the horror as those caught in its grip defied their fate to the last moment as they sank exhausted into death.

And there was famine. Starving, panic-stricken peasants abandoned their homes, compelled by some incomprehensible drive to wander, to escape to a better land. Unable to find it, they formed themselves into marauding bands to plunder and ravage wherever the spirit took them, until eventually their excesses were put down with a cruelty that surpassed their own.

The fear of death permeated every aspect of life, not as an intellectual curiosity about the hereafter, but as a real, morbid state of mind. Christianity may have preached the defeat of Death, in the sense of death being the gateway to a new (and better) life, but it could not conquer the fear of extinction which took outward shape in a powerful imagery. Death was seen as the reaper with his sickle, the hunter with his bow and arrow, and, in company with War, Rebellion and Famine, as one of the four horsemen of the Apocalypse. The unrepentant newly dead were accompanied by Death, the piper, in a ghastly dance across the graves and burial pits from which arose the decomposed corpses still wearing the clothes appropriate their estate. The dead were robbed of the peace promised them in the requiem mass.

Whenever an epidemic of plague or pestilence was feared or entered a parish, this dance of Death was painted on the walls of churches and cemeteries – not just as a warning call to repentance, decency and morality, but also in the hope of foiling the power of Death through his image. [A fine example may still be seen in the Church of La Chaise-Dieu in the Haute Loire.]

Yet, distant and objective observer though I was of a society in decay, as the years passed I detected a more subtle upheaval. In memory's eye, I was back with Giotto's frescos in Assisi seeing again art announcing change, but now with a greater certainty. No longer was the message conveyed by the dance contained in a pictorial sermon. Instead, the artists, such as Hans Holbein [1497-1543], allowed their pictures to speak for themselves by showing how Death surprised man in the midst of life. "Death," these pictures said, "may come with violence and destruction or be welcomed as friend and liberator; man himself, by the way he shapes his life, makes the choice." They were plainly indicating that in the intellectual movement, the Renaissance, now in progress, Christian man was displacing his God by planting himself firmly at the centre of the world – and, in so doing, lessening his confrontation with matters not of this sphere.

The scientific discoveries of the time seemed only to make matters worse. The hidden was being illuminated but, by contrast, the only mystery that really concerned the people – the mystery of existence – was being plunged ever deeper into darkness. And their superstitious natures were being fanned by the visions of St John the Divine recorded in the Book of Revelations and thundered abroad by every vagabond prophet who could read. I could make little sense of this apparent paradox: religious and social confusion on the one hand, and a freeing of the intellect to permit a cultural flowering on the other.

I travelled the length and breadth of Italy in search of an answer; on the purely material plane this could be found in the economic, social and political conditions that now prevailed in the north of Italy. Yet this was not the entire story; there was something more and that something was analogous to the wisdom that comes with the years as the body grows old. And the most noticeable change was in the people's outlook on life. I experienced it also north of the Alps, modified only insofar as the humours of these peoples differed from those of their more sensual southern neighbours. I even wondered whether I, too, was experiencing this same change in my state of mind.

Medicine was, at first, unaffected by the intellectual upheaval – though I knew in the end escape would be impossible. But until this time came, the sick continued to rely on what worked for them – whether this required the services of a herbalist, a uroscopist, an astrologer, a magician, an apothecary, an alchemist or a physician. If the affliction was one of exquisite pain and the patient knew its cause, he might call upon a drawer of teeth, a cutter for stone or a coucher for cataract. But the most fortunate were those blessed with a woman of the house who could draw upon the experience of her mother and her mother before her.

Since the followers of traditional humoral and Galenic teachings were stumbling along in a trackless desert, I decided to take a closer look at alchemy. As always, when the main road fails, man takes to alternative pathways.

* * *

The next morning I awoke to find Telesphorus standing at my bedhead.

"Yes, Master, I know what is in your mind and I have returned to see that you come to no harm. Although Gerber [*fl.*776] gave the material aspects of alchemy a semblance of respectability some seven centuries ago, its well-nigh impenetrable symbolism hides many secrets that may, to the uninitiated, be spiritually harmful. You may think that my return implies a measure of approval of your action, but you would be wrong – as I shall show you. You, Paul Balthasar, are pursuing alchemy believing the discovery of the philosophers' stone is the route to both wealth and a medicine to cure all mankind's ills – a panacea, in fact. But remember my father's words: Panacea will always be sought by man, but she will be forever inaccessible.

"I, however, know that in one of its many aspects, alchemy will overturn the past and open a new sphere of medical knowledge – if not of understanding. You must appreciate that alchemy is a turbulent conglomeration of matters chemical, mystical, and theological with its roots grasping through undercurrents of astrology and magic. So, I must acquaint you with its past. For, if a man had only the experience of his own lifetime to call upon, his knowledge would be commensurate with the shortness of his existence."

Telesphorus beamed at me, his eyes twinkling with delight. "I learnt that at school on Mount Olympus!" It was a long while since I had seen him so pleased with himself.

"But for now, let us eat and prepare ourselves for the day. Then I shall walk with you through the woods and meadows and take you back to school."

* * *

"Whatever view you take of alchemy, it is submerged in symbolism," was Telesphorus's not very encouraging start. It also warned me that he was about to deliver a lecture in truly magisterial manner.

"Although al-kimia is the Arabic origin of the name, alchemy extends back through Greece to Egypt." By his tone I knew I was correct about his intentions. "In its purest form it was concerned with the transmutation of the lower nature into the higher or Divine nature; it represented man's desire to achieve union with God. But this very soon became inextricably entangled with his baser struggle to wrest from Nature her most closely guarded secrets. The ancient Chaldeans believed that there were spirits in all things and that these could be extracted by fire. They named the spirits according to their origin: collectively they were regarded as the soul of the world – the source of life. This is why, Balthasar, their furnaces are so important to the alchemists of today.

"Astrology was next to complicate the issue by postulating that the seven planets – the sun, moon, Mars, Mercury, Jupiter, Saturn and Venus – corresponded to the seven days of the week and to the seven metals – gold, silver, iron, quicksilver, tin, lead and copper. These metals were all believed to be, in essence, the same as one another and to be generated in the very bowels of the earth. Here they ripened into gold, the purest and noblest of them all. The alchemists deceived themselves into thinking they could speed the process.

"They considered mercury to be the closest to gold, lacking only a certain something to give it the required colour and solidity. The missing something was thought to be related to sulphur and, indeed, the Arabic name for the philosophers' stone – al-kibrit al-ahmar – may be translated as red sulphur.

"Through some rather tortuous thinking, they next decided that by transmuting base metals into gold they could also discover an elixir of life, a cure for all ills and the guarantor of immortality. They called this their aurum potabile, their golden cordial."

I hid my face in my hands and sighed at the folly of mankind.

"Ah! I see the possibility of eternal youth for everyman fills you with pity – or is it horror?" Telesphorus was genuine in his sympathy. "But let me reassure you. It will never come to pass."

By now our walk had returned us to my home and as we entered, Telesphorus, ever sensitive to my wishes, led me to my room.

Gradually my ears closed to his words and his voice grew more and more distant. My world became silent.

I had fallen asleep. My mind could absorb no more.

I awoke as dawn was breaking. I never cease to marvel at the beauty Nature can unfold when she chooses. I watched, spellbound, as her colours deftly changed in hue and brightness as night's lingering clouds caught the rays of the rising sun and sped them back to earth. When next I looked, all was gone and there in the sky the sun reigned supreme.

Turning from the window, I saw that Telesphorus had entered the room and been watching the miracle as entranced as I.

"Good morning, Master," he said softly. "I sense your mood is well suited to the story I shall tell today.

"You know," he continued, "that one of the prizes sought by world-blinded alchemists is not to be won: Panacea will never return. Their quest for the elixir of life, for the immortality to allow them to enjoy to the full the fruits of their labours, also is doomed to everlasting failure."

As the sun climbed towards its zenith, we began our walk in the welcome shade of the woods. At each step the scent of plants trodden, unavoidably, under foot rose to please our senses.

"But, Balthasar," he adopted once again his magisterial tone, "nothing, it seems, can awaken your race from its dream of perpetual youth enriched with the knowledge of maturity!" And he proceeded to pour out a deplorably long list of instances of mankind's credulity. My attention returned when he arrived at his last, and most recent, example.

"… And then, a year or two after he had taken Puerto Rico, Juan Ponce de Léon [c.1460–1521] mounted an expedition to find the Fountain of Youth in the New World. He was mightily upset at failing to do so."

The lesson concluded, we completed our walk in comparative silence, rejoicing in small things: the wild cyclamen nestling in clumps between the rocks, our feet idly kicking fir cones along the path. I was as close to happiness as I could come. "Tomorrow," he announced, as we bade each other goodnight, "tomorrow I shall take you to the laboratory of Johannes Tritheim [1462–1516] where you shall witness a marvel more magnificent than the transmutation of base metal into gold: the creation of life itself!" And before I could gather myself, he had disappeared into his room and closed the door. I heard the bolt pushed to.

* * *

We opened the heavy oak door to Trithemius's dungeon-like cell to be assaulted by a fearsome stench compared to which the reek of putrid flesh was as the odour of sweet violets. Feeling our way down the treacherous steps we saw its source. Bent over his furnace, a filthy leather apron wrapped around his waist, the alchemist was pumping away with his bellows at the flames beneath a steaming iron cauldron. Constantly glancing up at an hour-glass, suspended from a long iron peg driven into the overhanging chimney breast, he ensured the safe passage of every grain of sand. Behind him, his long clay pipe rested on a three-legged stool. The only light seemed to come from the furnace itself – the windows were encrusted with grime and what little light did penetrate was obstructed by piles of books filling the deep embrasures. All around were littered the instruments and symbols of his calling.

Trithemius ignored us until the last grain of sand had fallen through. Then he coughed, a deep bubbling cough rising from the very bases of his lungs, and turned his bloodshot eyes towards us. He gave no greeting and we responded in like fashion.

"Man's struggle to create life has been recorded in myth and legend." The intensity of the sound emerging from the alchemist's plump round body was spellbinding. "He has attempted to awaken the dead and to make new life to spring from the decay of corpses. It is said that many centuries ago a Jew created stags from cucumbers and roebuck from gourds. But no one has created life in human form." Trithemius paused and peered into the stinking cauldron. "Until now!

"Within this cauldron," his voice reverberated within the stone walls, "there lies a work of God, a miracle; the food to nourish the human life I shall create. It is the arcana sanguinis humani. It is the food that has eluded all my predecessors." (Being 'a work of God' the nature of the arcana is destined to remain mysterious and a secret until the end of time.)

At this point Trithemius acknowledged our presence, not out of courtesy but because he wished the recognition of his genius. Like two obedient children we uttered a few appropriate words in Latin which seemed to give him pleasure.

"Hitherto they, myself included, have implanted human semen into a member of the cucumber family putrefying in the natural heat of horse dung. After forty days in a glass retort, the material begins to stir and to take the shape of a transparent embryo. No man has progressed beyond this, because no man has possessed the food of further life. Now, I have it at my disposal!" Trithemius was exultant.

He said nothing more until the sand had once again run through the glass. He stood, unmoving, gazing at the cauldron.

"You have no children?" He raised his head and spoke directly and curtly at me.

"No," I answered, "although I have known many women."

"Then you are of no use. Why did you come? Your assistant," indicating Telesphorus, "had said you wished to assist me in my greatest experiment."

Telesphorus had once again taken a hand in determining the course of my life.

"Trithemius, I cannot have made my meaning plain." Telesphorus, ever the tactful soother of irate emotions, spoke for the first time. "I had hoped you might allow my Master to observe this greatest of all alchemical experiments and to encourage and reinforce the spiritual power you will conjure up."

"Tonight I am host to two couples who have undertaken to obey my instructions and to lie together as the dawn begins to break." Trithemius was mollified and eager for my 'spiritual' help. "When the sounds of their coupling have ceased you, my renowned physician, shall collect the material I require – though when your assistant told me of your great talents I had intended to dismiss one of the men and use you as a giver of seed. Evidently, your seed lacks sufficient life force." He was not an expert in veiling his insults.

Nevertheless, I agreed to do as he wished and the next morning I visited the two bedrooms and removed the semen from inside the women. I took both portions to the adjoining chapel where Trithemius awaited. He was standing by a table at the chancel steps bathed in the early morning light. On the table were two glass retorts, the sides of which were translucent, with the vapours rising from the ugly glutinous masses at their bottoms.

Trithemius took the semen from me and introduced one portion into each retort.

"My method of gathering the semen is unique." His voice was hushed; even he was overawed by his surroundings and the enormity of what he was attempting. "Moreover, I have added a human afterbirth to the dung to create the most natural conditions for success – and success is ensured by the perfection of the astrological aspects at this moment. It will be many years before all the conjunctions are again favourable."

During our stay, we were treated in a more civilized manner than I had expected. Trithemius's house was comfortably furnished and we were well attended by his servants. He himself sometimes appeared at table looking clean and presentable in his clerical garb, but mostly he occupied his days in the sordid surroundings of his laboratory where he was pleased that I should watch and, sometimes, help.

Toward the end of the forty days of waiting – during which time we neither of us entered the chapel – he grew agitated. This increased until, unable to concentrate on his work, he confided in me.

"As a man of God, I am disturbed by the consequences should I succeed. I am thinking of Maimonides [1135–1204], the only man to have created a homunculus. Although his experiment was re-creation and not creation, my dilemma is the same as his.

"With the promise that he would bring him back to life and with his agreement, Maimonides cut up the living body of his pupil, Menasse. The pieces, he sprinkled with the perfume of the 'plant of life', the 'balsam of immortality' and an extract of the 'flower of the

strength of life' and let them lie under a glass vessel. On the fourth day
he saw that the tissues had begun to melt and to rearrange themselves.

"After five months he could recognize the human form; after six
months nerves and blood vessels became apparent; and in the seventh
month he saw the first movements. Then, he realized the catastrophe
that would result as soon as people saw the revitalized corpse: they
would worship him and thereby lose their reverence for God. In the
eighth month Menasse smiled at him.

"In utter desperation, Maimonides weighed his promise to bring his
pupil back to life against his duty to preserve humanity from
incalculable disaster. He laid his conflict before a meeting of wise men
who decided that, for the honour of God, Maimonides must break his
oath and take the life of a being created under such unusual
circumstances. This he did.

"Balthasar, do I continue?" Trithemius was in mental agony, but my
curiosity outweighed my sense.

"Trithemius," I said, "you shall pursue the experiment to its
conclusion. Should it succeed, then let us face the consequences."
(Observe how I reacted like one of your 'pure' scientists searching for
his Holy Grail with no thought of a practical application and a total
disregard of the consequences should he be successful.)

"I have two days until I must begin feeding my creations." He
looked searchingly into my face, as if seeking irresolution on my part.
"You, Balthasar, have given me the strength to carry my work to its
conclusion. I shall pray for us both. May God have mercy on us!"

The two days passed and at dawn on the third we entered the
chapel. Life was stirring in both retorts; it was of a pale colour in one
and of a darker in the other. Trithemius carefully introduced a small
quantity of arcana sanguinis humani into each retort reading, as he did
so, a long incantation from a book produced from under his apron. For
forty more days he repeated the ritual, and each day we watched the life
assume increasingly recognizable human shape.

On the forty-first day, a thunderstorm (obligatory, are they not, in
situations of this nature?) was raging as we approached the chancel,
lightning filled the chapel and the two retorts shattered. There was no

noise apart from the instantaneous clap of thunder; gently the glass sides fell away to the table top, leaving two perfectly formed human figures standing in their places. Both were female, of the height that would be expected of a new-born, but both were unmistakably fully mature adults in miniature. One was fair skinned; one was dark.

Trithemius gazed at his creations in silence, unable to believe what he had done. Then, as the significance of it penetrated his mind, he fell to his knees and began to whimper. It was the sound of man suddenly made mad.

For the next hour, I stood transfixed as the figures slowly grew to adult size. "You have committed a mortal sin. It is given only to the gods to create life." I could swear I heard one of the creatures speak. "Man cannot meddle in the work of the gods and escape unscathed!" At these words Trithemius ceased his whimpering as he slumped to the ground.

* * *

The fire had started from Trithemius's untended furnace and spread throughout the buildings despite the desperate efforts of the servants and the rain which lashed down furiously all day. The chapel was completely burnt out; only a shell remained and everything within it was destroyed beyond recognition.

Telesphorus had rescued me before the fire had taken a hold.

"Bal-sarra-uzur, what you experienced with Trithemius was only an illusion. Man is a strange and susceptible creature. When his convictions are strong enough, what he wants – what he expects – to see, he will see." Was I imagining it or did I really hear him say, "Maybe, though, your illusion will be a future reality"?

COMMENTARY

1) One form of the dancing mania may have been due to the use of grain, especially rye, contaminated with the ergot fungus. Inevitably, it led to waves of hysterical imitation. A condition

known as the English sweat remains unidentified, though it may have been influenza. It died out almost as soon as it began. However, famine was rife and roughly once in each generation epidemics were associated with famine. (Malnutrition = vulnerability to infections.) These 'famine fevers' dominated epidemics of infectious disease until 1348 when epidemics of plague took over. Later, in the 17th century, smallpox and typhus (spotted fever) were the dominating epidemics.

2) Women with their 'defective soul' were regarded as physically, intellectually and morally inferior to men (see Chapter 8). Aristotle has a lot to answer for in this regard as his view of women had both scientific and cultural implications right up to the late 19th century. However, throughout history women, in the absence of anything better, have looked after the health and well-being of their families and have passed their knowledge on to succeeding generations. This role probably reached its high-point in the 17th century when upper class women saw it as their duty to care for their tenants and local villagers. But with the coming of the 18th century the number of university-qualified male doctors increased and were employed by the wealthy, not only in the towns but to a growing extent in the country. Consequently, upper-class women forgot the medical aspects of their household skills and with the changing social climate they lost the drive for charitable work. Thus the care of the middle and lower classes lay in the hands of their own kind and those of quacks and the Mrs Sarah Gamps (Charles Dickens: *Martin Chuzzlewit*) of that world.

3) "Although al-kimia is the Arabic origin of the name, alchemy extends back through Greece to Egypt. In its purest form it was concerned with the transmutation of the lower nature into the higher or Divine nature; it represented man's desire to achieve union with God. But this very soon became inextricably entangled with his baser struggle to wrest from Nature her most closely guarded secrets." This quotation from the text is important if the true nature of alchemy is to be appreciated (see also Source 2, below). The origin of the Arabic word, kimia, is obscure but

possibly derives from the Greek chemeia which is taken to mean Egypt or 'the art of the Egyptians'. Alchemy is usually described in dictionaries as the forerunner or infant stage of chemistry, followed by such comments as its main pursuits being the transmutation of other metals into gold and the search for the elixir of life. That may be so, but only in respect of man's 'baser struggle'. Side-by-side with the pursuit of alchemy the Arabs, from about the 8th century, were developing practical chemistry and pharmacy with the introduction of new methods and techniques, new chemicals and new drugs.

4) What Juan Ponce de Léon discovered was not the legendary Fountain of Youth but Florida! The amusing irony of this today should not be lost. His expedition nonetheless demonstrated the influence exerted by the legend of the fountain on the practical affairs of those days. The search for perpetual youth – or, at least, for rejuvenation – still continues with people throwing their money away on the likes of specific sera, monkey glands, transplantation of human testicles and various imaginative potions and injections.

5) The account of Trithemius's alchemical attempt to create human life is all based on historical evidence, except for the final human addition to his experimental technique and the success of the experiment.

6) The extension of the concept of the homunculus into modern times (for instance, in-vitro fertilization, cloning, the freezing of embryos and, most recently [2004], the development of parthenogenetic mice) is the ultimate achievement of the Renaissance and entirely negates all spiritual values surrounding the mystery of life. Man has now well and truly displaced God from the centre of the universe. Does it also prove there is no God?

SOURCES

1) "The printed versions of the *Dance of Death* follow the original format, which is a serial representation in which the living and the

dead mingle in an energetic procession painted on a wall, perhaps of a churchyard or some other burial place. The *Dance of Death* was characteristic of the early modern death ritual in two ways: first, the living appeared in the order of their social rank, that is, emperors and kings followed by nobles, the gentry, the people and so on; second, the dead were displayed as part of an instruction to the living about the nature of death. Viewers took the dance of the living and the dead to refer to their own mortality."
Nigel Llewellyn, *The Art of Death*, 1991

2) "The marriage of sulphur and quicksilver, sun and moon, king and queen, is alchemy's central symbol, and in the light of its meaning we can clearly distinguish between alchemy and mysticism.... The starting point of mysticism is that the soul has alienated itself from God through turning itself towards the world and that it must be reunited with Him.... Alchemy on the other hand takes the standpoint that through the loss of his primordial 'Adamic' state, man is rent with inward discord, and can only regain his full being when the two powers whose strife has robbed him of his strength have been reconciled with each other.... The marriage of the soul's masculine and feminine forces ultimately opens out onto the marriage of Spirit and soul... which is none other than the mystical marriage. Thus the two states overlap: the realization of psychic plenitude leads to the soul's giving itself to the Spirit, and the alchemical symbols have, correspondingly, more than one meaning: the sun and the moon can denote the two powers of the soul which are termed sulphur and quicksilver; at the same time they are images of the Spirit and the soul.... Closely connected with the symbolism of marriage is the symbolism of death: according to some representations of the 'chemical marriage' the king and queen are killed at their wedding and buried together, thence to rise up rejuvenated."
Titus Burckhardt, *Alchemy*, 1967

3) "If *Romeo and Juliet* were the only plays of Shakespeare's that had

come down to us, and... we were called upon to answer the question: 'Is the symbolism of *Romeo and Juliet* mystical or alchemical?', there would be a strong case for replying that it is alchemical, the more so in that the two lovers are as it were transmuted into gold after their deaths, for Romeo's father says: 'I will raise her statue in pure gold', (v, 3, 298) and Juliet's father replies: 'As rich shall Romeo by his lady lie.' (v, 3, 302) Moreover, the strife between the two powers of the soul would seem to be adequately represented by the enmity between the houses of Montagu and Capulet, an enmity which is at the end transformed into friendship."

Martin Lings, *The Secret of Shakespeare,* 1996

Chapter 17

1460	
—	Birth of Desiderius Erasmus *c.*1466
—	Death of Johann Gutenberg 1468
1470	
—	Birth of Sylvius (Jacques Dubois) 1478
1480	
—	Battle of Bosworth Field 1485
1490	
—	Birth of Paracelsus 1493
—	Birth of Jan Calcar 1499
1500	Birth of Charles V of Spain
—	Birth of Johannes Oporinus 1507
1510	
—	Battle of Flodden Field 1513
—	Birth of Vesalius 1516
1520	Conquest of Mexico by Hernando Cortez
—	Birth of Gabriele Fallopio 1523
—	Birth of Philip II of Spain 1527
1530	
—	Conquest of Peru by Francisco Pizarro 1532
—	Death of Desiderius Erasmus 1536
1540	
—	Death of Paracelsus 1541
—	Vesalius's *Fabrica* published 1543
—	Death of Jan Calcar 1546
1550	
—	Death of Sylvius 1555
—	Death of Charles V of Spain 1558
1560	
—	Death of Gabriele Fallopio 1562
—	Death of Vesalius; birth of Shakespeare 1564
—	Death of Johannes Oporinus 1568
1570	
—	St Bartholomew's Day massacre in France 1572
1580	
—	University of Edinburgh founded 1585
—	Defeat of the Spanish Armada 1588
1590	Death of the surgeon Ambroise Paré
—	Death of Philip II of Spain 1598
1600	English East India Company founded

The shackles of medieval medicine are broken

(Second quarter of 16th century)

For a while during his adolescent years, Paracelsus [1493–1541] had been apprenticed to Trithemius. Subsequently he, too, made use of arcana sanguinis humani in his attempts to create a homunculus, not in the least deterred by his old master's fate. If Paracelsus is to be believed – and there is, admittedly, little reason to do so – his father, a respectable, educated physician, taught him medicine, botany, natural philosophy, and mineralogy and mining. The fact that the first determined his choice of career and the last the direction it would take, is evidence only of the atmosphere in which he was raised and not of the reality of an education.

In our wanderings throughout Europe the paths of Paracelsus and myself never crossed. If they had, I doubt that we would have suited each other, for he was a braggart and arrogant to the point of insanity, preaching the unintelligible with an astounding degree of incoherence. Nevertheless, he acquired a considerable number of eminent (and intelligent) men as his patients. Although I knew of his reputation during his lifetime, it was not until a year or so after his death that I learned of his spectacular influence on the course of medicine.

At a time when the printing houses of Europe were vying with one another over the quality of their typography, that of Herbst in Basle excelled thanks to the work of Joannes Oporinus [1507–1568]. This man was no ordinary printer for he was professor of Greek at the University and had, on occasion, been Paracelsus's amanuensis. His reputation was such that when Vesalius [1514–1564] was seeking a printer for his monumental text on anatomy, he chose Oporinus. There was, however, a problem: the woodcuts were in Padua and the printing house was on the other side of the Alps in Basle. The difficulty was resolved by Oporinus's agreeing to oversee their transport strapped to the sides of mules. As I had already been in Padua for some years while Vesalius dissected and Jan Calcar [1499–1546] prepared his exquisite illustrations, I took the opportunity to move on.

Knowing the cargo of our little caravan to be beyond price, we were in a state of almost constant agitation lest one of the animals should lose its footing among the clouds and disappear over a precipice; but I believe we were in the greater danger of that hazard ourselves. Since all I know about Paracelsus I learnt from Oporinus, I shall record the story as he related it to me during that treacherous journey:

* * *

Paracelsus (Oporinus began), Paracelsus – I shall call him that, even though he did not assume the name until some years later – left Trithemius with his head full of an avalanche of magic, mysticism and chemistry. His obsession with the alchemical belief that the seven metals were generated in the bowels of the earth led him to the mining school run by the Függers at Huttenberg and then to Sigismund Függer's mine at Schwaz, where he investigated the chemical properties of various metallic substances. (He also produced a meticulously observed account of the diseases prevalent among the miners. This could be regarded as the first work on occupational medicine and was probably the only rational thing he wrote.)

The urge to be a physician had already taken hold of him and his reticence about where he had studied made me suspect that at the start he had simply relied on the knowledge gained from being his father's son and from his astute observation of the world around him. He was constantly on the move, never staying in one place for long because, as he said, "A physician must be a traveller, since he must enquire of the world." And enquire he most certainly did, not of authority but of the people – for preference gypsies, keepers of bath houses, fortune tellers, executioners and his drinking companions in the more disreputable taverns. In this manner he acquired considerable expertise in folk-medicine and a good grasp of what would succeed and what would fail.

Frequently, those he attended were cured when other physicians had despaired.

His contempt for authority, both past and present, was formidable and he had the temerity to write and lecture in German, not in Latin – something no one aspiring to even a modicum of learning would contemplate. Through the good offices of Erasmus, [*c.*1466–1536] one of his distinguished patients, he was appointed physician to the city of Basle, a position carrying with it the responsibility of lecturing to the medical faculty. On the first occasion he was, as usual when lecturing, half-drunk – the complete state he reserved for his visits to the sick – and began, I remember, by announcing, in German, that he would ignore the teachings of Hippocrates and Galen and would instead demonstrate the truths of disease from his own experience. To emphasize the point, he cast a book of Galen's writings and Avicenna's *Canon* onto a students' bonfire booming, as he did so, with typical modesty:

"The buckles of my shoes know more of medicine than both of these venerable physicians together! All the universities and all the authorities in the world know less than the hairs of my beard!"

This was greeted with shouts and raucous applause as his beard was sparse in the extreme and he was, indeed, reputed to be a eunuch.

Unabashed, he continued:

"I am the true monarch of medicine. You will follow me. You, Avicenna; you, Galen; you, Rhazes. You will follow me, you messieurs of Paris, of Montpellier, you meinen Herren of Cologne, of Vienna, and all, however many you may be; you who inhabit the isles of the sea; you Italians, Dalmatians, Athenians; you Greek, you Arab, you Jew, follow me, your king!"

I stood with the crowd, recording his words.

"The humours of Hippocrates and Galen do not cause disease. They do not exist! – but if they did… " the contempt in his voice invited challenge; he waited. There was only silence. His audience was stunned; that any man should have the gall even to harbour such heretical thoughts, let alone proclaim them publicly "…if they did, they would be the consequences and not the causes of disease.

"A crowd of physicians rise up against me," he roared – and that, at least, was indisputable. "They give you the names: bile, melancholy, phlegm and blood. But who has seen bile in Nature? How can phlegm resemble one of the elements? How does blood resemble air? You say *this* is a vice of the blood, and *that* of the liver; but what, I pray you, has given you the eyes of a lynx that you know so well that the blood or the liver is the cause when you are utterly ignorant of the nature of the blood?

"Instead of saying *this* is due to bile, *that* to melancholy, we should say *this* is due to arsenic, *that* to alum and, also, *this* is under the influence of Saturn, *that* of Mars. Thus you can see that half the disease comes from the earth and half from the heavens. Again, you say that the disease is due to the blood – but the blood is no more than wood, and just as there are many kinds of wood, so there are many kinds of blood. And just as the heavens send the trees to sleep in winter and wake them in summer, so the blood similarly changes with the seasons.

"From this it follows that a physician should say that this disease is turpentine, that is mountain celery, the other is hellebore, and not this is phlegm, that is rheum, a coryza, a catarrh. Those names have no medical foundation."

(If you regard Oporinus's tale as showing how Paracelsus employed destructive criticism so that he could then indulge in ridicule, we might admire him for his defiance and questioning of ancient authority. But alas! since he firmly believed that disease did originate partly in the stars, and since he plumbed the depths of absurdity with his doctrines, I have abbreviated Oporinus's account which fully occupied a week of our journey.)

I was compelled by a sense of duty to record all that Paracelsus said, despite my conviction that most of it was worthless (Oporinus continued). He had concocted three important doctrines – the entities, the archaeus and the tartarian or calculous origins of disease. But, since consistency was not one of his virtues, each of these could be the sole cause of disease, depending on which suited his fancy. He stated that since there were five entities (to which, true to his inconsistent reasoning, he gave Latin names), and since all diseases were produced by them, there must be five phlegms, five hydropathies, five jaundices, five fevers, five cancers and five of every disease known to man.

The archaeus was the invention of a Benedictine monk some fifty years previously. It was not so much the soul as a form of deity that lived at the entrance to the stomach from where it directed and, by chemical means, regulated the bodily functions. Death came with its loss.

But, when the mood took him, the very same diseases could be produced only by tartar. Every moisture on earth had, so he said, a substance within it that was prone to coagulate. Wine, on keeping, coagulates and the clot separates and adheres to the side of the vessel. Water contains a tartar which separates on boiling and adheres to the side of the kettle. Urine contains a tartar which separates as stones in the kidney or bladder. Bile contains a tartar which separates to form gallstones. Blood contains a tartar which separates as a blood clot.

Paracelsus passed like a destructive hurricane through medical authority, denying the demigods of the past and contradicting his illustrious contemporaries, whatever they said. The apothecaries and the herbalists, already in conflict with the alchemists, also felt the sting of his influence. At the moment when new and exotic botanicals were flooding in from the Americas, the alchemists decided they had more chance of finding a medical remedy among the residues in their retorts than of turning base metal into gold. Into the fray stepped Paracelsus, his philosophy resting on chemical principles first set out by that same Benedictine monk who had conjured up the archaeus. There were apparently three primary substances, but they were philosophical substances rather than chemical elements: philosophical sulphur, philosophical mercury and philosophical salt (this last being the state of equilibrium between the other two). They were operated by the spiritual force of the archaeus. (Make of this what you will.)

He was a fervent advocate of tinctures amongst which he favoured his *Lilium Paracelsi*, a concoction prepared from alloys of antimony and iron, antimony and tin and antimony and copper.

When I worked with him he always kept several preparations stewing on his furnaces – for example, a sublimate of oil of arsenic, a mixture of saffron and iron or his marvellous Opodeloch, a plaster. I cannot recall him ever giving any recommendations about diet or hygiene. To his credit, though, he was bitterly opposed to polypharmacy. [The treatment of a single condition with many drugs.]

His popularity among those who sought his help was due in no small measure to his ability to tell them what they wanted to hear. To the religious, he declared that his system was based on Holy Scripture – the Bible was the key to his theory of disease, which was founded on the Apocalypse. He proclaimed himself to be a man who submitted without a second thought to the Divine Will; who identified himself with the celestial intelligencies; who possessed the philosophers' stone; who could cure every ill and who could prolong his life at will, and all because he possessed the tincture which had been used by Adam and the Patriarchs before the Deluge to prolong their lives for eight or nine centuries.

To the sceptic, he professed the grossest pantheism. To the credulous, he posed as a magician (for magic is a highly refined area of knowledge): he had received letters from Galen and had visited Avicenna at the Gates of Hell. He duped them with his accounts of drinkable gold, the philosophers' stone, the quintessence, the mithridate and whatever else entered his mind at the given moment.

* * *

"Eventually, having been driven from city to city by his ungovernable delight in irritating authority," Oporinus came to the end of his tale, "Paracelsus was offered the ecclesiastical protection of Archbishop Ernst of Salzburg. He accepted, but a few months later he was killed in a drunken brawl. As the prophet Jeremiah truly said, 'Can the Aethiopian change his skin, or the leopard his spots?' "

Oporinus walked on in silence with an arm laid thoughtfully across the neck of one of the animals.

"You know," he said, as if the idea had just come to him, "had it not been for Paracelsus we would not be making this journey today."

I looked at him in amazement. What possible connection could there be between that unscrupulous charlatan and these invaluable woodcuts?

"For all that his teachings were unmitigated claptrap," Oporinus was responding to my incredulity in his own way, "he left the world a different place from the one he had entered. Although he would never forgive me for saying so, his studies on chemistry, concealed by the cloak of alchemy, have expanded the scope of medical therapy. Since his death, many physicians have been persuaded of the absurdities of alchemy and have turned to chemicals in a more reasoned – though not necessarily effective – manner. No, wait!" He thought I was about to interrupt at the seeming irrelevance of his words, but my reaction had quite another cause. At last I realized what Telesphorus had meant when he said that alchemy – though, more precisely, an alchemist – would open a new sphere of medical knowledge.

"Paracelsus has had a two-fold effect on medicine – intellectual and practical. If I had begun with the intellectual, I should probably have had difficulty convincing you. So, I deliberately drew your attention to his practical influence on pharmacy – of which I imagine you are already aware – in the hope of thus making you receptive to the abstruseness of the intellectual influence.

"The teachings of Hippocrates, Aristotle and Galen were – and, to many, still are – regarded as divinely inspired and containing the full sum of medical knowledge. Consequently nothing remains to be discovered. That is why scholars have been searching for original Greek texts, to prepare fresh translations uncluttered by the detritus and distortions of the intervening ages. These ancient texts hold the key to the eternal truths. The only path to progress lies in their rediscovery and reinterpretation. Until Paracelsus arrived to trouble the waters!

"He may have failed, in his own eyes, to make the walls of authority fall down flat by his relentless trumpeting, but his questioning and ridiculing of the teachings of the great have created a breach ready for storming. Ridicule, you know, is a wonderful weapon for it creates a vulnerability to serious attack. Although he died as ignominiously as he had lived, he was not struck down by the heavens for his iniquity, and this gave strength to others themselves to challenge the received truth.

Without Paracelsus before him, Vesalius would never have dared to publish his anatomical discoveries – and we would not be travelling this road."

When we had reached Basle and the woodcuts had been safely entrusted to the printing house, I lodged with Oporinus. He was a most knowledgeable and agreeable companion who needed little urging to talk.

"What I was saying about Paracelsus liberating the medical mind accounts only in part for the existence of Vesalius's anatomy. The intense intellectual energy investing all aspects of human activity today has taken longer to reach medicine than some other spheres. But the scholars in these spheres had, in their time, also accepted the books of antiquity as their supreme authority and had neither the desire nor the means to improve upon them. Until, that is, something awoke them to the arrival, in a changing world, of the truly scientific spirit that seeks to acquire knowledge by observation and experiment and then its critical evaluation. In the military field that something was gunpowder. In art, it was a less explosive occurrence," he grinned. "It had started with Giotto who painted his saints as real people and not in the stylized Gothic form." At last, it seemed, I was to learn how an artist could have an influence on medicine.

"On our journey, I was speaking as a Greek scholar and amanuensis to Paracelsus. Now, I shall talk as a typographer and, in my own way, an artist. The freeing of the intellect combined with two other driving forces has unleashed the scientific spirit of medicine in the shape of this book by Vesalius and Calcar.

"In the past, anatomic dissections were necessarily demonstrations, since anatomists had little or no idea how they should record their work pictorially. Thus their drawings were symbolic, fulfilling spiritual needs rather than the requirements of realism. And, after Galen, the anatomy seen and recorded at dissections was unalterably Galen's.

"You, Balthasar, I believe followed Vesalius for five years while he dissected and Calcar drew. We both know that Calcar's woodcuts are lifelike representations of the structures Vesalius demonstrated to his audiences. Yet Galenists still maintain that the drawings are inaccurate.

Sylvius [1478–1555] even tried to make Vesalius recant some of his teachings – and this despite his own valuable service to anatomy by ridding it of mongrel Arabic terms and returning to the Latin of ancient writers such as Celsus [which is still the familiar terminology]. Vesalius had been a student under Sylvius in Paris, and it is ironic that the Latin nomenclature helped give much-needed precision to his demonstrations and Calcar's drawings.

"This, the ability to represent accurately what is seen during dissection, is the first of the driving forces I mentioned; the second is the ability to disseminate that information. I believe it to be true that without our artists and without our printing houses – and without the heretical Paracelsus – anatomy might never have freed itself from ancient authority. Anatomists would continue to see what Galen had said they would see."

"So," I questioned, "once Giotto had broken free from the spell of Gothic art, anatomists could give a true representation of their dissections?"

"No, not immediately," Oporinus answered. "In my imagination I see Giotto holding open the gate through which Masaccio [1401–1428] would pass a hundred years later. Giotto brought painting to life and Masaccio gave it space – his vision of reality was a function of his mind as well as of his eye; his vision of space was his intellectual vision of reality."

"All in keeping with the spirit of the times." I felt some comment was called for, although I was not entirely sure what he meant.

"Yes, particularly as the vision was not entirely of his own creation," Oporinus continued, apparently oblivious to my incomprehension. "Brunelleschi [1377–1446] had slipped through a nearby 'gate' in Florence a few years previously. In his work as an architect, he had conceived the principle of perspective for the rational distribution of architectural elements in space. Masaccio had the genius to see how this could be applied to painting: he used the laws of perspective to create the conditions for perfect unity of time and place, thus eliminating all inessentials." This was indeed the artist in Oporinus talking!

"Once Masaccio had shown the way, artists began to pour through Giotto's 'gate' to explore the new world before them. Artistic activity was equated with science – based either on geometry and mathematics, which gave a logical explanation of the structure of the universe, or on the direct methodological study of nature. The artists studied, drew and painted the human body; but without a knowledge of its structure, they could not achieve a true representation. So they began to dissect for themselves whenever the opportunity offered and to draw what they saw unencumbered by Galenic preconceptions of the anatomy they would uncover.

"When a great anatomist, like Vesalius, works with a great artist, like Calcar, the repercussions will resound down the ages. You, Paolo, a physician, will say that the palm should be awarded to Vesalius, but I, speaking as an artist, would award it to Calcar for, without him and Giotto and Masaccio before him, Vesalius's dissections would have suffered the same fate as that of all his predecessors. Furthermore – and I now speak as a typographer – I would award the palm to Gutenberg [c.1400–1468] who showed how it was possible to print from moveable metal type. Without him, both your Vesalius and my Calcar would still be dependent on books prepared laboriously in manuscript.

* * *

While artists had poured through Giotto's 'gate', anatomists more slowly climbed the 'stile' provided by Vesalius. Galen's intellectual hold continued to dominate the mind despite the evidence of the senses. Before anatomists dared to publish a discovery that contradicted his word, they felt impelled to secure their position by repeated and emphatic demonstrations before witnesses of unimpeachable honesty.

Shortly after his book, *De Humani Corporis Fabrica*, was published, Vesalius travelled round the universities of Europe in an attempt to convert his critics – his enemies, he called them – by demonstrating the new anatomy. When he returned to Padua, his reception was so venomous in its intensity that, in utter disgust, he burnt all his notebooks and accepted the appointment (almost a sinecure) of court physician to the Holy Roman Emperor, Charles V [1500–1558] and, subsequently, to Charles's son, Philip II of Spain [1527–1598]. He was content with this life for twenty years until the day he received a copy of a text by Fallopio [1523–1562] – one of his former students and now occupying his old chair of anatomy at Padua – in which many of his own errors had been corrected. And, as he soon learnt, other former students were making discoveries that had escaped him. Anatomy was no dead subject; the time had come for him to return to the dissecting table.

But it was not to be.

Telesphorus appeared, as if from nowhere, with the news that Vesalius had died in a shipwreck on his way back from the Holy Land.

"You know," Telesphorus said, "it was the man's anatomical honesty that I admire most. Can you remember what he said to you on one occasion when he had finished discussing the Emperor's health?"

I could indeed. "When I first dissected the heart," he had said, "I could find no evidence of the pores between the ventricles that Galen had described so graphically. Yet I was reluctant to deny their existence as how else were we to explain the flow of blood. I simply wrote of my wonderment at a God who could give us an invisible passage for the blood. But, when I revised the book in later years, I knew there were no pores and I said so in quite explicit terms. Do you wonder that the Galenists hate me?"

I believe he knew that by his confidence in rejecting the pores to which Galen had ascribed an otherwise inexplicable function, he had revealed the existence of yet another new world lying beyond his chosen one of anatomy.

COMMENTARY

1) The invention of printing by Gutenberg is one of those developments in history that it is almost impossible to quantify or assess accurately. The fact that printing allowed the dissemination of knowledge along lines never before seen makes it one of mankind's greatest inventions. Material from all subjects could

now be printed relatively cheaply and generally free of the confines of earlier methods of production.

2) Theophrastus Phillipus Aureolus Bombastus von Hohenheim was one of the few characters who had no doubt about their contribution to medical history. Such was his confidence in what he did that he named himself Paracelsus (which, translated, means 'Surpassing Celsus'). His fundamental conviction was that Nature was above all else the sovereign power and so long as one accepted this, then healing was possible. To support the power of nature he developed a natural philosophy based on chemical principles. Paracelsus was particularly controversial in his contempt for academics, past and present. In a sense, he might be said to have had a modern approach; for instance, he claimed that when studying urine the old method of uroscopy was grossly out of date in the light of chemical analysis.

3) How much of Paracelsus's success as a physician depended on the alcoholic content of his tinctures, such as his *Lilium Paracelsi*, is your decision! The fact that antimony is a dangerous poison did not dim his enthusiasm for the metal one little bit. In 1566 in France the use of antimony as a drug was prohibited and continued so for about a hundred years until Louis XIV was apparently cured of typhoid fever with a huge dose of antimony administered by a quack. During the prohibition era, enthusiasts for the metal found they could get round the ban by drinking white wine out of cups made of antimony. (Antimony-based drugs were popular for reducing fevers.)

4) Much of Paracelsus's writings are extremely difficult to understand today though they probably made some sort of sense to the alchemists of his own times. Even so his vocabulary is so obscure that one of his followers wrote a *Dictionarium Paracelsicum* to help contemporary readers understand what he was talking about. Apart from his writings on miners' occupational diseases, Paracelsus noted the relationship between cretinism and endemic goitre; he also described diabetes mellitus and if, in his description, sugar is substituted for salt, that description is reasonably

comprehensible (see Source 1, below). An important contribution to pharmacy was his emphasis on the importance of chemical as opposed to herbal treatments.

5) The Benedictine monk who invented the archaeus is an elusive character. He may have been Johann Estchenreuter of Erfurt who wrote under the name of Basil Valentine. At all events his complicated and confusing theory was adopted by Paracelsus.

6) The Renaissance (which in art may be said to date back to Giotto [see Chapter 15]) permitted a new-found wonder of the human body. Artists and sculptors alike not only marvelled at the external form but openly argued the case for a knowledge of anatomy if they were to represent it accurately. By the mid-15th century artists were expected to follow courses in anatomy and many also dissected privately.

7) Calcar's illustrations could well have been described as incomparable except for the fact that the anatomical drawings made by Leonardo da Vinci (1452–1519) in his notebooks between fifty and sixty years earlier are artistically superior. Although Galenic elements appear in the earlier of these, the later ones are more detailed and realistic and are accompanied by extensive notes. Regrettably, Leonardo drew for himself and did not publish (although a planned Galenic anatomical atlas never came to fruition). His notebooks inexplicably disappeared from view until the end of the 19th century and the beginning of the 20th when they re-emerged in the Royal Library at Windsor, the Ambrosian Library in Milan and the Institut de France.

8) The publication of Vesalius's *Fabrica* set anatomy and the anatomists free. Hitherto unknown structures were dissected out and named, often after their discoverers; for instance, the Fallopian tubes, the Sylvian fissure (this was the same Galenist Sylvius – otherwise Jacques Dubois – who had taught Vesalius), Scarpa's fascia, Bartholin's gland, Stensen's duct, Wharton's duct, the circle of Willis, the Eustachian tube. Today Latin proper names, often descriptive, are internationally agreed for all structures although a few discoverers are still remembered unofficially; one of these is

Bartolomeo Eustachio (*c*.1500–1574) yet he was not even the first to discover the auditory tube – that priority really belongs to Giovanni Ingrassia (1510–1580), but somehow the Ingrassian tube doesn't have quite the same ring!

9) The reverence with which the three greats of the ancient world – Hippocrates, Aristotle and Galen – were held is almost beyond belief. But think on this: Averroës (1126–1198) asserted that Aristotle's doctrine was "the perfection of truth, and his understanding attained the utmost limit of human ability; so that it might be truly said of him that he was created and given to the world by Divine Providence that we might see in him how much it is possible for a man to know." There were dons in the late 19th century at the University of Oxford who might well have said – and believed – those very words!

SOURCES

1) "Diabetes is due to a dry salt dissolved and divided by the ingress of a sharp salt in the midst of the principal parts. This salt is lasting, permanent and fixed. Signs: Thirst of a chronic kind, pain in the back (which for the most part begins in the neck) swelling of both feet, much urine, yellow and very red, rapid pulse and pains in the thigh, that is in the hip. Cure by anodynes: salt divided alone is curative."

Paracelsus's description of diabetes mellitus, *Dritter Theil Der Bücher und Schrifften des Edlen Hochgelehrten und Bewehrten Philosophi und Medici....*

2) "Paracelsianism seemed superstitious [to 19th- and 20th-century historians] while Galenic medicine was at least rational, even if it was not always 'scientific'. However, in the 16th century, magic and witchcraft were believed in, both at government and legal levels as well as in villages. Religion could be the subject of intense belief, debates and wars. What to us may appear non-rational was central to the consciousness of early modern Europe. It makes,

therefore, no sense to emphasise and approve of only those pieces of Paracelsus' work which by hindsight seem to contribute to the formation of modern science and medicine."

Andrew Wear, Medicine in early modern Europe, *The Western Medical Tradition*, 1995

3) "Vesalius could be said to have been a true Galenic anatomist in the wider sense of following Galen's advice to see for himself (and he certainly kept to many of Galen's physiological theories and to their teleological conclusions), but Vesalius presented himself as a critic of Galen's and trumpeted aloud Galen's errors. He made an immense impact on the discipline of anatomy.... Around 1539 Vesalius became more critical of Galenic anatomy. His increasing knowledge of human anatomy and of Galen's anatomical writings led him to the crucial realisation that Galen had dissected only animals and that animal anatomy could not substitute for human anatomy."

Andrew Wear, Medicine in early modern Europe, *The Western Medical Tradition*, 1995

Chapters 18 & 19

1578	Birth of William Harvey
1590	
	Birth of René Descartes 1596
1600	
	Dutch East India Company founded 1602
	Death of Andrea Cesalpino 1603
	Death of Pope Clement VII 1605
	Gunpowder Plot 1605
	Birth of Giovanni Borelli 1608
1610	
	John Napier invented logarithms 1614
	Death of William Shakespeare 1616
	Pilgrim Fathers sailed for New England 1618
	Death of Heironymus Fabricius 1619
1620	
	Birth of Thomas Sydenham 1624
	Birth of Queen Christina of Sweden 1626
	Birth of Robert Boyle 1627
	Harvey's *De Motu Cordis* published 1628
	Birth of Marcello Malpighi 1628
1630	
	Birth of Antonj van Leeuwenhoek 1632
1640	
	Start of the English Civil War 1642
	Battle of Marston Moor 1644
	Battle of Naseby 1645
	Execution of Charles I 1649
1650	Death of René Descartes
	Oliver Cromwell became Lord Protector 1653
	Deaths of William Harvey and Jean Riolan 1657
1660	Royal Society founded
	Great Plague of London 1665
	Great Fire of London 1666
	Death of Rembrandt 1669
1670	
	Deaths of Leeuwenhoek and Molière 1673
	Death of Giovanni Borelli 1679
1680	
	Birth of Giovanni Battista Morgagni 1682
	Deaths of Sydenham and Théophile Bonet 1689
1690	
	Death of Robert Boyle 1691
	Death of Marcello Malpighi 1694

Discovery that the blood circulates and a mechanistic philosophy

(Second half of 16th – first half of 17th century)

It was not what he had discovered, but how he had arrived there that the old man was remembering for his questioner.

"I thought the blood must move in a circle when I noticed that the valves in the veins of so many parts of the body were so placed as to give free passage of blood towards the heart, but to oppose its passage in the opposite direction," was William Harvey's [1578–1657] response to Robert Boyle's [1627–1691] opening question.

For a moment, in my mind's eye, I was back with Vesalius a hundred years ago, listening to his friend, Giambattista Canano [1515–1579] from Ferrara, describe the membranes – as he called them – in the veins which, he said, prevented the backward flow of blood. Vesalius, though, believed the membranes were there simply to strengthen the veins, and this belief was generally accepted as it did not compromise Galenic thinking.

In the years between, I had travelled leisurely around the universities of Europe watching anatomists reap where Vesalius had sown. They explored the depths of the body and various were the tubes, ducts and canals named in honour of their discoverers. I have no doubt that my presence at the right university at the right time was not fortuitous but due to Telesphorus's guiding hand. He led me first to Amatus Lusitanus [1511–1568] who spoke of ostiola (or little doors) in the veins that prevented the return of blood – just like those in the heart, a point that Canano had also made.

But Galen was still a power in the land. Indeed, Vesalius's convincing demonstration that the pores between the ventricles did not exist was attributed by some to their natural disappearance after death and by others to a change in man's anatomy since Galen! It was this baleful influence that was preventing men's minds from realizing the functional implications of the new anatomy.

This was all too apparent when Telesphorus decided we should make another visit to Padua where the chair of anatomy was occupied by Heironymus Fabricius [1533–1619]. I arrived bearing a letter of introduction purporting to be from Andrea Cesalpino [1519–1603] who had recently published his speculation – not supported by any experimental evidence – that in systole the heart sent blood into the aorta and pulmonary artery and, in diastole, received it back again through the venae cavae and pulmonary veins (the opposite to received opinion). The letter was, in fact, one of the concoctions Telesphorus had devised as a means of 'giving me a recent past', and they were invariably effective.

Fabricius glanced at the letter, saw it was from Pope Clement's [1536–1603] personal physician and embraced me warmly.

"Come, Paolo, you have arrived opportunely. You shall be of the first to bear witness to a discovery that thrusts anatomy into a new field. We anatomists must now go beyond a description of what we find and determine the *function* of anatomical structures and the *purpose* of that function. For Nature does nothing without a purpose."

His flow of words was uninterrupted while, taking me by the arm, he walked me to the anatomy theatre he had had built at his own expense. I knew it to be large but I did not expect to find its interior windowless. Fabricius dissected by the light of candles, demonstrating as he did so to the students crowding the balconies rising perpendicularly above him.

While he dissected he continued to talk, as much for my benefit as for that of the students. It was the same old story: Galen teaches that arterial blood carries the vital pneuma to every part of the body where it is almost completely consumed; it does not return to the heart; it is the carrier of life. Venous blood ebbs and flows to meet the needs of the tissues for nourishment. (The variations on this theme down the ages are almost as numerous as the anatomists themselves!)

Fabricius directed his assistant to throw the candlelight more clearly on the vein in the leg he had been dissecting. He had laid it open.

"Here you see my ostiola within the vein. They quite evidently hinder the outward flow of blood. They do not impede its inward flow. This is their function. But what is the purpose of that function?" He looked up and around. No one was prepared to offer an answer.

"No? Then I shall have to tell you. These ostiola function like the floodgates that obstruct the flow of water in the sluices of a mill. Their purpose is to prevent the blood from flooding the extremities of the body. Galen said that an attractive force served this purpose. But I have shown it to be a visible anatomical structure!"

Fabricius had thus opened the way to a mechanistic, as opposed to a Galenic, physiological explanation. Nevertheless, it was one that was quite acceptable to Galenic authority as it contradicted none of Galen's basic assumptions. Even so he waited twenty-nine years before publishing his 'discovery'. However, during those years Saloman Alberti [*fl.*1585] had published his *Tres Orationes* in which he had illustrated the valvulis, as he called them, and had drawn attention to their one-way action.

I shook myself free of my daydreaming to hear Harvey explain to Boyle how he had learnt of the existence of the venous valves.

"I spent the first two years of the century in Padua, studying medicine and anatomy under Fabricius. It was he who inspired me to devote my mind to function and purpose rather than structure. And he it was, too, who impressed on me the importance of the valves. Both in Padua and on my return to London, I made frequent dissections of human and animal bodies. Observing the heart in the living animal was fraught with difficulty owing to the rapidity of the movement which in many animals remained visible but for the wink of an eye and the length of a lightning flash. I answered this by studying the slow-moving hearts of cold-blooded animals and of dying dogs and pigs.

"In none of these dissections was it possible to show the pores that Galen supposed to lie between the ventricles. Moreover, I was unable to find evidence for the existence of vital pneuma or psychic pneuma. I tell you that when philosophers and physicians discuss the role of these spirits in the workings of the body, they are making an unworthy attempt to veil their ignorance."

He paused for a moment or two while he gathered himself to continue with the matter in hand.

"I also read widely and was assiduous in confirming or confuting the anatomical findings of others. Of particular relevance to your questions, Dr Boyle," Harvey looked up from the notes he held on his lap and nodded at Dr Boyle, "I repeated the experiments of Colombo [1516–1559] on the passage of blood through the lungs and confirmed that it was so."

"But," Boyle interrupted, "what made you reject your old teacher's explanation of the purpose of the valves? After all, you were – you are – a respected member of the medical fraternity. You had already been Lumleian lecturer at the College of Physicians for thirteen years and three times one of the Censors of the College when you published *De Motu Cordis*. And yet you must have known your work would have a harmful effect on the traditional medicine of which you were a part."

On the table at Harvey's side were his old lecture notes and a copy of *De Motu Cordis* (*Exercitatio Anatomica de Motu Cordis et Sanguinis in Animalibus* to give it its full title), to both of which he had referred from time to time. He picked up the book.

"If you turn to chapter eight you will see that I have kept faith with Aristotle." He leant across the table and handed the opened book to Boyle. "I shall return to that example in due time, but throughout I have been true to his philosophy. There is nothing revolutionary about my work."

I had been watching his face as he spoke and those last words were sincere and without a taint of false modesty.

"You will also see that in my lecture notes," he pushed these across the table, "I referred to the venous membranes as valves, not as ostiola, as Fabricius would have done. By naming them thus, the idea that they closed completely, or almost so, is established in the mind. I believe it was this matter of nomenclature that prevented Fabricius from discovering their true purpose. His book contains a drawing of the opened heart to show the cusps of the aortic valve which he likened to the ostiola of the veins – the sole obvious difference being that the aortic valve has three cusps whereas the venous valves have only two or one. He knew the aortic valve permitted flow in one direction only, yet the similarity of purpose of the venous valves escaped him."

Harvey laid his left palm flat on the table. The veins on the back of the old man's hand stood out quite clearly. He pressed on one of them with the index finger of his right hand and ran the nail of the thumb back along the vein towards his wrist. The vein collapsed, leaving a hollow channel until it reached a valve. When he removed his index finger the vein refilled.

"A very simple demonstration that the venous valves prevent the backward flow of blood. In my original experiments, though, I used the forearm with a tourniquet to distend the veins, as you will see illustrated in the book. I first wrapped a length of cloth tightly around the arm above the elbow to stop the flow of blood in the arteries, then I loosened it sufficiently to restore arterial flow, but not the flow in the veins. These swelled up, so demonstrating to me that a connection must exist between the two in the extremities.

"I was greatly impressed also by the abundance of these valves. Surely, I reasoned, if in some places the valves did not act with perfect accuracy, their greater number plainly served to prevent the passage of blood from the centre. Moreover, the existence of valves in the jugular veins, also preventing flow backwards from the centre, was contrary to Fabricius's idea of their purpose. And, let me add, there are no valves in the arteries save at their exits from the heart."

"So, a year or two after you had prepared your notes for the Lumleian lectures on anatomy you had already decided that the blood moved with a circular motion?" Boyle enquired. "And yet you added nothing about your discovery for another eight or so years, although you made many other additions to the notebook."

"I believe you would have done the same." Harvey's answer was plainly matter-of-fact. "The content of the lectures was so arranged that the full course took six years to complete. At first, I had only the evidence of the valves to present; the physiological argument to replace the old teaching was still inadequate. Then, when I had gathered a sufficiency of evidence, I was writing my book and there was no need to insert more than a brief mention in the notebook for the next occasion when I should deliver that lecture. Nor did I trouble to correct statements that I believed were now erroneous."

Harvey leant back in his chair and closed his eyes. His notes slid to the floor.

"There is not much more to tell," he overcame his weariness and continued. "After many dissections on the living, I saw clearly that the symmetry and magnitude of the ventricles of the heart and of the vessels entering and leaving it were too large for their supposed purpose. Nature, who does nothing in vain, would not have needlessly given them such a large size. How was I to explain this unless the purpose was to transmit blood in great quantity – far greater than the small amount hitherto supposed to originate from the liver. Furthermore, my investigations led me to observe that this great quantity was transmitted in so short a time.

"Thus I have written," and he pointed across the table to *De Motu Cordis* lying in Boyle's hands. "Privately I began to think that the blood might have a certain movement, as it were, in a circle.

"So, Dr Boyle, I shall draw together the strings of our conversation, if you will pass me my book." He opened it, found the page he wanted and began reading.

" 'By reason and experiment I have shown that, by the beat of the ventricles, blood flows through the lungs and heart and is pumped to the whole body. There it passes through pores in the flesh' " (shades of Galen, I thought, this is the one flaw in his argument that he should have to conjure up 'pores' to account for what he cannot explain) " 'into veins through which it returns from everywhere in the periphery to the centre – from the smaller veins into the larger ones, finally coming to the vena cava and right atrium.

" 'This occurs in such an amount, with such an outflow through the arteries, and such a reflux through the veins, that it cannot be supplied by the food consumed. It is also much more than is needed for nourishment. We must therefore conclude that the blood in the animal body moves around in a circle continuously, and that the purpose of the heart is to accomplish this by pumping. This is the only reason for the motion and beat of the heart.' "

He closed the book, replaced it on the table, patted it lovingly and begged to take his leave. As he stood up, I was struck once again by how short a man he was.

When he had seen Harvey into the care of his servant, Boyle returned.

"Harvey, as you know, has not been without his critics. The most vehement of his attackers has been the Parisian, Jean Riolan [1577–1657] – as you might expect of the man." Boyle was happy to talk about Harvey and I made a willing listener. "Riolan sees Harvey's proof that the blood is in circular motion as a threat to his reputation and practice which is strongly founded in Galenic medicine; you would have to travel a great distance to find a more ardent disciple. Having been, with reluctance, compelled to accept the existence of a circulation, he now states that the heart pumps no more than a drop or two with each beat. Then, having estimated how many drops are pumped in the hour, he has calculated that there can only be two or three circulations each day. To explain Harvey's findings, he has resorted to the popular refuge of the intellectually destitute Galenists: changes after death! As the heart of the dying animal slows, the blood accumulates and the heart appears to pump these greater quantities. This compromise allows him to continue teaching a Galenic form of physiology according to which he can still argue that blood is produced by the liver.

"For reasons, perhaps on account of some obscure French logic, Riolan also objects to Harvey's concept of two circulations. So, in the letters he is writing to the Frenchman, Harvey is delighting in pointing out that there are, in fact, three circulations, the third being… " Boyle searched through the papers on his table, found what he wanted and began reading: "… 'a very short circulation, namely from the left ventricle to the right, driving a portion of the blood round through the coronary arteries and veins, which are distributed with their small branches through the walls and septum of the heart.' These are notes of a conversation I had with Harvey concerning his reply to Riolan," he added in explanation.

"The undeniable truth of Harvey's work is founded on

experimentation and observation and not on what is to be found in books. He refuses to accept what others have written until he has confirmed it for himself. Even so," Boyle hesitated a moment and looked at me, as if assessing how I might respond – it was the look I had come to know well over the years – "even so Harvey is unwilling to let go of the past. Despite his contention that the heart is merely a pump, he believes it to be driven by the pulsative power of the soul; he rejects completely the mechanical and chemical concepts of nature that are gaining in popularity today. Truly, if any man may be said to stand at a crossroads, it is William Harvey!"

Boyle was showing me out of his lodgings when an idea seemed to come to him. "Should you wish to know more about the mechanistic concept," he said, "I would advise you to visit Descartes – he is somewhere in the Low Countries. His philosophical approach is, however, quite the reverse of Harvey's. While Harvey draws his conclusions from meticulous observations, Descartes first constructs a clear picture in his mind and then verifies, or not, this mental concept by experimental observation. But beware, for he is inclined to select only those facts which fit his theories!"

On which encouraging note we bade each other farewell.

* * *

"So, Paolo Balthasar, you have come from England?" was René Descartes's [1596–1650] abrupt greeting; he treasured his privacy and preferred not to receive visitors. "From London? And did you meet William Harvey?"

"Yes," I replied. Before I could continue, Descartes was talking again. That, he enjoyed when he could expound his own philosophies.

"I agree with him that the blood moves around the body in a circular manner, but not with his explanation of the driving force of the heart, since this is not in tune with mechanistic principles. You must understand that the body is a machine which is fired by the innate heat of the heart. This heat vaporizes the blood and causes the heart to expand and to drive particles of blood into the arteries."

We were sitting in the scrubbed cleanliness of his Dutch home in the quietly dignified city of Amsterdam and, probably owing to the warmth – for he was averse to cold – I was finding it difficult to concentrate sufficiently to follow his thesis.

"You are perplexed?" he enquired. "Then let me take you through my philosophy of the body's functions.

"At the beginning, you must free your mind from the notions of humours, elements and qualities so beloved of the ancients. Instead, accept that the body is governed by mechanistic laws. It, like the world we live in, is matter in motion."

Descartes's reputation as a mathematician was already well known to me. His excessive love of the subject was, perhaps, not surprising, as it was the only science that could be depended on with certainty – and Descartes was determined to apply it to every aspect of learning or, seemingly, to die in the attempt. In some instances, he succeeded, in others he failed. But, watching and listening to the man, I knew why his philosophy of life was doomed to be unworkable – it was his denial of human emotions, spirituality, of the essential quality that makes a human being a human being, call it what you will.

"Now," and he rose and began pacing up and down. "Now, matter and mind both emanate from the same divine source and operate along parallel lines, but they are unrelated." He spoke those last words with dramatic emphasis.

I then realized how he had managed to escape the wrath of the theologians for so long: he had been careful to write nothing that could be construed as in direct contradiction to the first chapter of Genesis. Alas! the heresy seekers had eventually decided that he was using science as a cover for an attack on religion and had proceeded to denounce him as an enemy of the Christian faith. Fortunately, the Estates General in the Low Countries had refused to surrender him to Papal authority – as was their practice for all who enjoyed their hospitality – and he was able to continue his work.

"The soul," he proceeded to explain, "which is situated in the pineal gland in the brain, can call forth no movement unless all the bodily organs which are needed for that movement are properly disposed.

Nevertheless, when the body already has all its organs properly arranged for a particular movement, it has no need of the soul to carry this out. Hence all movement except those which we know to depend upon thought ought not to be attributed to the soul, but to the mere disposition of organs."

He spoke, as he wrote, with deliberate obfuscation – to blind his enemies with science, as you might say. I think I saw what he was getting at. At least it was better than his belief that the nerves were hollow tubes designed to transmit the juice of animal spirit to all parts of the body and that they contained valves. (Did he, I wonder, copy this idea of valves from Harvey's work?) Nevertheless, in his beliefs about movement you can discern a parallel with your voluntary [central and peripheral] and involuntary [autonomic] nervous systems.

I visited him frequently endeavouring to comprehend his physiological ideas. But they were entangled in Galenic thinking and he remained essentially a Galenist to the end – an end which was not very far away.

One day as summer was mellowing into autumn, he announced he would be leaving for Sweden. He had been invited by Queen Christina [1626–1689] to initiate her into the mysteries of higher mathematics and philosophy. It was destined to be his last journey, as that strange queen had a habit of conversing in her unheated library in the early hours of the morning. Descartes caught a chill at the end of January and died early in February from a congestion of the lungs.

COMMENTARY

1) William Harvey was the product of a medical education in Padua, the outstanding university of the day. The holders of the Chair of Anatomy at the University had included such men as Vesalius, and Fabricius who taught Harvey anatomy and medicine, and later would include Malpighi, Morgagni and Valsalva. It would have been well-nigh impossible for a motivated student not to have been influenced by the academic excellence of the place. Harvey returned to England a man inspired. There was no English

university at the time that could have provided a similar education.

2) Harvey guessed that something like the capillaries must exist, but he could only speculate on the presence of 'pores in the flesh'. He lacked the one instrument that would have allowed him to see the networks that connect the arterioles with the venules – the microscope. Some one hundred and thirty years were to pass before Malphigi was able to complete the circle (see Chapter 19).

3) With the gradual acceptance that the blood circulated to all parts of the body, it was logical that the idea of transfusion of both drugs and blood itself should be considered. Blood transfusion had been written about and actually practised (with lethal results) on one or two occasions since the mid-15th century. But now Harvey's work had provided what seemed to be a sound basis for the undertaking. Between 1657 and 1669 Robert Boyle, Christopher Wren (1632–1723) – better known as the architect of St Paul's Cathedral – and Richard Lower (1631–1691) experimented with the transfusion of blood and the intravenous injection of drugs. The subject was written about by a number of other experimenters but any attempt to put theory into practice met with such dismal results that the whole idea went into hibernation until the 20th century.

4) In his experiments Harvey had shown that the purpose of respiration was to change venous blood into arterial blood, but how this happened remained a mystery. A little later, Giovanni Borelli (1608–1679) stated, as a result of some experiments on the mechanics of inspiration and expiration, that air was vital to life. Nevertheless, another hundred years or so were to pass before the nature of the gaseous exchange was elucidated.

5) The patronage of the wealthy was still something to be enjoyed and once his ground-breaking work had been completed, Harvey entered the service of the Earl of Arundel. Foreign travel as personal physician to the Earl gave him the opportunity to visit European universities and so spread the message that the blood really did circulate and did not behave in a Galenical fashion.

6) Even though his concept of the physiology of the circulation may

have been worthless, Descartes's analogy of the workings of the body with those of a machine was valuable – and probably inevitable in an age of mechanical invention – in that it undermined the thinking that the bodily functions were driven by the soul (or souls). In succeeding generations the analogy shifted to whatever was the popular science of the time – from mechanics, through chemistry to the electronics of today. The difference from Descartes is that in later years these analogies were validated experimentally. The body is a union of them all, with probably sciences yet to be discovered.

SOURCES

1) "The *crux* of Harvey's argument – that the actual quantity and velocity of the blood, as computed by him, make it physically impossible for it to do otherwise than return to the heart by the venous route – was the first application of the idea of measurement in any biologic investigation and, had he chosen to express this discovery in the language of algebra (by using the symbol of inequality), it would long since have taken its proper place as an application of mathematical physics to medicine. The importance of Harvey's work, then, is not so much the discovery of the circulation of the blood as its quantitative or mathematical demonstration. With this start, physiology became a dynamic science."
Fielding H. Garrison, *An Introduction to the History of Medicine*, 1929

2) " 'The new physics had also raised the question of the nature of matter, and thus what determines the physical processes of nature. More and more people argued in favour of a mechanistic view of nature. But the more mechanistic the physical world was seen to be, the more pressing became the question of the relationship between body and soul. Until the seventeenth century, the soul had commonly been considered as a sort of "breath of life" that pervaded all living creatures. The original meaning of the words

"soul" and "spirit" is, in fact "breath" and "breathing".... Even Descartes could not deny that there is a constant interaction between mind and body. As long as the mind is in the body, he believed, it is linked to the brain through a special brain organ which he called the pineal gland, where a constant interaction takes place between "spirit" and "matter" '. "
Jostein Gaarder, *Sophie's World*, 1996

3) "When Descartes started out, there was an urgent need for a system that would place the mind before the heart and would let intelligence play the rôle it ought to play in shaping our daily existence. But in the end, his system led to the unrelenting one-sidedness of so many modern experiments in which there is no longer any room for the ordinary human emotions. And when that happens, man ceases to be a human being and becomes a cog in a machine. "
Hendrik Willem van Loon, *Van Loon's Lives*, 1943

Beginning of microscopic anatomy
(Second half of 17th century)

There is a garden in Bologna – I hope it is still there, restored to its former glory by some loving hand – lying close under the city wall. The house is invisible from the arbour where I spend my days, alone with my thoughts.

I have lived here for some time now and have adopted the life of a recluse. My sole pleasure is to tend my herb garden and prepare medicines which Telesphorus distributes to the sick poor. I seek, not to sustain the therapeutic authority of Galenism which flags in the face of competition from Paracelsian chemical remedies (often given as Christian charity – to the intense annoyance of the commercial herbalists), but to ensure a fair balance of choice for the people of Bologna. My herbals, being a part of the tried and tested traditions of the land, are especially popular with travellers from the countryside.

The garden is surrounded by an ancient wall – that of the city forming one boundary only – with every nook and crevice adorned with the colour of its sweet-scented occupant. Above the entrance is a horse's head carved in stone, an ancient Roman spur to all that grows within to be fruitful. And carved above the door to my physic garden is an open rose surmounted by two buds, a device to protect the secrets of the herbalists' art. I shall not betray those secrets, except to say that my garden is a confusion of scents, with first one and then another predominating as I wander, dreaming, along the paths, sometimes adding to the intensity of the odours as a careless foot crushes an errant plant thrusting up between the flagstones.

I think that in those years I was at the lowest ebb of my life. I was beyond despair; I was trembling on the borders of madness, and that would never do as, to their considerable displeasure, it would cheat the gods of their full payment. It is said that a man is closer to his god in a garden than anywhere else on earth. This I knew and had experienced many times. But in Bologna, I was strangely unsettled. Yes, I was at peace among my flowers and they brought me comfort, but not the comfort of a human embrace. Were my gods, then, slipping away from me? (I still believed in my ancient gods, the gods of Nature. I could not wholly accept those that seemed to me to be the creations of the human mind.)

At this moment in my misery, Telesphorus appeared, bringing refreshment to lull me into sleep through the heat of the afternoon.

"Telesphorus." I paused while he sat himself cross-legged on the warm grass. "You know I do not ask why things happen to me. I have long learnt to accept that what the gods choose to do with me is inevitable and unalterable. But tell me why I feel my mind is about to break." I had difficulty controlling the agony in my voice.

Telesphorus leant forward and took my hand. I felt a surge of spiritual strength pass from his small body to mine. "You must keep faith, Bal-sarra-uzur, for regrettably Trithemius's experiment has disturbed the ordered pattern of events."

"But I also feel a sense of disillusion over the advancement taking place in our learning." Although I knew Telesphorus was aware of all that troubled me, I felt a desperate need to unburden my soul. "Vesalius and Harvey may have added immeasurably to our understanding of anatomy and of the manner in which the body functions. But have they brought us any closer to the achievement of most importance to me, to an understanding of disease itself? I wonder. The more that is revealed, the further the truth recedes. And I am alarmed by the present influence of Descartes's materialism."

The grip on my hand increased and I felt a delicious languor creep through my body. I heard Telesphorus speak as if in a dream.

"My father understood the extent of the suffering you would have to endure and he permitted me, should your mind be close to disintegration, to grant you a glimpse of the future. But you will forget my words as though they were never spoken until the events have taken place; then you will remember with gratitude my telling you.

"Medicine," he spoke as if gathering knowledge directly from another world, "stands at the brink of great scientific advancement. As it moves on, many different paths are to be revealed, so varied and extensive is the knowledge waiting to be acquired. As you – indeed, as any man – will be unable to walk along every one, I shall lead you to those that will increase man's understanding of disease."

* * *

When I awoke the next day, I felt as though a crushing weight had been lifted from me. I was also not a little surprised to learn that a professor from the university wished to visit me. Accordingly, I sent a messenger with a note to say that, as I was weak from my illness and should not be leaving my house for a while, I should be pleased to receive him at any time.

I have no hesitation in saying that Marcello Malpighi [1628–1694] was one of the kindest and most sympathetic of men it had ever been my privilege to meet. The gentleness in his character was evident in every look and gesture, yet there was a touch of sadness in his eye as though he despaired of mankind. He was a modest man – too modest for his own good, was Telesphorus's opinion. Although he suffered from ill-informed criticism, he bore his critics, who in later years included some of his former pupils, no animosity. The reason for the attacks on his studies was due to their being concerned with structures seen through the magnifying lenses of the new-fangled microscope: such detailed scientific knowledge was regarded as useless when compared with the practical knowledge required for the cure of patients – a cry as old as Socrates [c.469–399BC].

Malpighi held my hand; his grasp was firm while he looked closely at me.

"Yes," he said, "you have indeed been ill and, I would hazard, on the verge of death." Would that I had, and been carried beyond! "But you are restored to health and that pleases me. Might I enquire – as one physician of another – the nature of your sickness?"

I doubt if there was another human being I would have told, but Malpighi inspired confidence; despite this being our first meeting, it seemed I had known him long and intimately.

"I was plunged into a deep melancholia, the circumstances of which are too painful to recall. But why did you wish to see me?"

"Among the many rumours attending your arrival in the city and your known desire not to enter into society, was one that you had come from London. Was that so?"

"Yes."

"And you did speak with the Englishman, William Harvey?"

"That is true."

"Then you know there was one crucial hiatus in his demonstration of the circulation of the blood. Because he saw no connecting channels, he was compelled to postulate the existence of pores in the lungs and tissues to account for the continuous flow from arteries to veins. He could not see them. I have seen them!"

His words conveyed the joy of intellectual achievement, not of triumphant boasting. My expression must surely have made him fearful of a return of my insanity.

"You do not believe I can be speaking the truth?" He answered my amazement.

"No! No! I believe you. What I cannot believe is how such a miracle is possible."

"Then you shall accompany me to my laboratory as soon as you are fully recovered and see for yourself."

Suddenly my weakness left me and I was eager to see this wonder without delay. Together we walked to the university.

The preparations for the demonstration were soon completed.

"While the heart is still beating," he was lucid in his description as he bent over my shoulder, pointing to what I should note, "you can see the movements of the blood in the vessels in the opposite directions, so that the fact of its circulation is clearly laid bare. This, you will more readily observe in the mesentery and other larger veins in the abdomen. Thus the blood cascades in minute streams through the arteries into the different cells. The stream repeatedly divides, loses its red colour and, carried round in a sinuous manner, is poured out on all sides until it approaches the walls of the absorbing branches of the veins."

Malpighi stood back. The hedgehog had died.

"The eye can see no more in the opened living animal," he said as I turned to face him. "So, you might argue, the blood itself has escaped into an empty space and has been gathered up again by the mouth of a gaping vessel and by the structure of the walls. But I would answer that the movement of the blood is tortuous, scattered in all directions, and is united again at a definite point.

"For this argument to be resolved, you must come over here." He led me to another bench where lay the dried lung of a frog. He handed me a more powerful microscope lens.

"The redness of the blood is preserved to a very great extent in minute tracks, which are vessels joined together in ring-like fashion. Such is the meandering about of these vessels as they proceed from the artery on this side, and to the vein on the other, that they no longer keep to a straight direction. Instead, the continuations of the two vessels appear to make up a network. This network not only occupies the whole area but extends to the walls and is attached to the outgoing vessels – I can show this more abundantly, but with more difficulty in the oblong lung of the tortoise.

"Hence," he went on, greatly pleased at my interest, "hence, it is evident that the blood flows away along tortuous vessels and is not poured into spaces. It is always contained within tubules and its dispersion is due to the multiple winding of the vessels.

"When I made these discoveries, I wrote of them to Borelli [1608–1679]. He is a mathematician, you know, and he considers physiology to be a branch of physics. He will be intrigued by some of the other things I have seen. Were you aware that the lungs are not of a muscular consistency? No? They are made up of a multitude of extremely thin-walled compartments which are connected to the final minute filaments of the bronchi. And I have seen fat globules in the blood vessels which resemble nothing so much as rosaries of red coral."

"Did you invent this instrument yourself?" I was intensely curious about this invention which had turned speculation into reality.

"No. Magnifying lenses have been in use both singly and in combination for some years. You have to look to Leeuwenhoek

[1632–1723] with his beautifully ground lenses if you wish to discover the real creator of the science of microscopy."

Throughout the years that followed, I maintained a correspondence with Malpighi and his letters contained detailed descriptions, accompanied by the most delicate drawings, of the minutest components of innumerable organs and tissues. The last letter I received was, though, unutterably sad.

"I live," he wrote, "if it can be called life, in idleness without other aim than to distract my grief. A chance fire in my house in the last month has burned what little I had, my manuscript notes, my microscopes and lenses – only one was saved and this, with a small sum of money, was stolen a short time afterwards. I must recognize in this the voice of heaven, the more that to my old ills there are added particular pains which fetter me close so that nothing remains to me but to study and enjoy as best I can the work of others."

* * *

I doubt whether that study would have given him much enjoyment. The advancement of science through the microscope failed to impress the physicians. Indeed, those who dealt with the sick saw little or no profit in any of the wealth of new anatomical and physiological discoveries. They were far more concerned with gaining experience through the exercise of their own observational skills.

"Paolo, I think we should journey to England again." Telesphorus's thoughts about my travels and destinations were less suggestions, more decisions already taken. "I believe you should meet a great exponent of the art of bedside medicine before it is too late. He is, as the English would say, a martyr to the gout and it seems likely to kill him."

And so I found myself once more in Robert Boyle's lodgings in London, alone this time, with one of his closest friends, Thomas Sydenham [1624–1689]. It was autumn and his gout was in abeyance. He was a man of pleasing appearance, unassumingly dressed as befitted a one-time soldier who, as a youth, had been a captain in the Parliamentary army during the English Civil War. Hoping to get our conversation off on the right foot, I began by asking which books he would recommend in order to acquire medical knowledge.

"Peruse Don Quixote," was the revealing answer.

He smiled. "Let me explain. I have, myself, been very careful to write nothing but what was the product of faithful observation and neither suffered myself to be deceived by idle speculation, nor have deceived others by obtruding anything upon them but downright matter of fact. And, furthermore, symptoms should be recorded with the same minuteness and accuracy as is observed by a painter painting a portrait."

He went on to show me his writings on a number of diseases. Those I remember best were on gout (which was agonizingly informed from his own experience), the measles, an epidemic cough with fever (this you would recognize to be influenza) and scarlet fever. I was able to read them within the space of a few minutes, so concise and masterful was his style and containing all that a physician would require to make the diagnosis and prescribe the treatment. They also made plain that, since each patient was a unique human being, the manifestations of a given disease might vary from person to person. He was truly a physician in the direct line from Hippocrates.

I returned the papers. "I am fascinated. You mention the manifest qualities of the air as being responsible for the epidemic cough, and scarlet fever attacking mostly children and at the end of the summer; while gout, when regular, comes on at the end of January or the beginning of February. Your observations would indicate that climate and weather govern some aspects of disease."

"Many things influence the occurrence of disease," Sydenham responded. "As you say, the adequacy and foulness of the air and the seasons mark out the occurrence of many fevers. But health or ill-health depends on much else besides. The physician must heed the sufficiency and quality of what is eaten, the exercise that is taken, also rest and sleep, the calmness or perturbation of the mind, and the state of the bowels and the passing of the urine. All are to be considered by the observant physician."

He fell into a moment's contemplation. Raising his head, he

continued:

"But of one thing I can assure you, the stars neither cause diseases nor influence their natural courses. Do not believe those who tell you otherwise!"

"And treatment?" I enquired.

"I generally follow the practice of my fellow physicians, except in two notable respects. I give quinquina or the Jesuits powder for the malarial fevers – though it finds no favour with many. And it is not always necessary to treat with medicines; in many instances I look to my patients' safety and to my own reputation most effectively by doing nothing at all!"

Did I detect a lingering echo of my first master, Imhotep?

COMMENTARY

1) Herbalism has been an essential component of medicine from earliest times. However, from the late 15th century onwards it enjoyed a revival with not only the arrival of plants from newly discovered lands and the rediscovery of classical formulae in ancient texts, but also the introduction of chemical substances. Preparations based on herbs alone were known as 'simples' while compound mixtures were termed 'galenicals'.

2) Although Antonj van Leeuwenhoek has come down as the inventor of the microscope, this is not strictly true. Priority probably rests with Zacharias Janssen who described a compound microscope in about 1590 (this gave a magnification of no more than ten times); among a number of other contenders for the distinction is Galileo Galilei (1564–1642). Leeuwenhoek's microscope would be unrecognizable as such today: the viewing took place on a horizontal plane as opposed to the familiar vertical. A small lens was firmly clamped between two vertically mounted brass plates while the specimen was mounted on a pointed holder opposite. Focusing was achieved by the use of screw adjustments which could move the specimen in two directions. He preferred one lens to two, since the use of two only compounded the optical

distortions of the lenses, inevitable at this time unless, perhaps, ground by Leeuwenhoek himself; his microscopes could give a magnification of x 270. Despite Malpighi having shown that significant information could be gathered, about a hundred years were to pass before the microscope found its place in pathology.

3) The 'fat globules' seen by Malpighi were, in fact, the column-like formations or rouleaux that red blood cells assume under certain conditions. The red cells, themselves, had been discovered six or seven years earlier by the Dutch physician Jan Swammerdam (1637–1680). Although he never practised, he was an excellent experimental physiologist, studying the movements of the heart, the lungs and the muscles. In 1677 he devised a method of wax injection of the blood vessels.

4) Malpighi died in Rome of an apoplectic fit and his post-mortem was carried out by Giorgio Baglivi (1669–?1707) who had attended him in his last illness. Baglivi's report began with a brief history and an account of the treatment which included blood-letting, cupping over the shoulder blades, powders applied to the soles of the feet and several other spiritous and specific remedies – pretty much the treatment of the time. The part of the report covering the findings in the brain are given in Source 1, below.

5) Sydenham was not at all impressed with the recent scientific and medical discoveries, such as the fact that the blood circulated, since he did not consider them to be of medical value; observation and experience were what mattered. Neither did he see any practical value in microscopical findings; he was concerned only with the anatomy he could see with his own eyes and how it related to the patient's state of health. His remarks on health and ill-health show that he was indeed the 'English Hippocrates' – his mind-set was little different! Reluctance to use the microscope was common amongst physicians. All too often new ideas and new technologies failed to gain acceptance – a major achievement was not always seen as such.

SOURCES

1) "When I open'd his Head, I found, in the Cavity of the right Ventricle of the Brain, an extravasation of about 2 Pints of black clotted Blood, which was the Cause of his Apoplexy and his Death. In the left Ventricle we found about an Ounce and a half of yellowish Water, with a small Quantity of little Grains of Sand mix'd with it. The Blood Vessels of the Brain were dilated and broke on all Hands. The whole Compass of the *dura mater* adhered tenaciously and praeternaturally to the *Cranium*. And this is the sum of what I observ'd in Dissecting his Corps, *Dec. 7, 1694.*"

Giorgio Baglevi's report of his post-mortem examination of Malpighi, *The Practice of Physick*, 1704

2) "We cannot in any better manner glorify the Lord and Creator of the universe than that in all things, how small soever they appear to our naked eyes, but which have yet received the gift of life and power of increase, we contemplate the display of his omnificence and perfections with the utmost admiration."

Antonj van Leeuwenhoek. *The Select Works of Anthony van Leeuwenhoek*, 1798. Translated by Samuel Hoole

3) "The sad list of symptoms begins with chills and shivers; these are followed immediately by heat, disquietude, thirst, and the other concomitants of fever. One or two days after this (sometimes sooner) the patient is attacked by severe pains in the joints.... This pain changes its place from time to time, takes the joints in turns, and affects the one that it attacks last with redness and swelling. Sometimes during the first days the fever and the above-named symptoms go hand in hand; the fever, however, gradually goes off whilst the pain only remains; sometimes, however, it grows worse. The febrile matter has, in that case, been transferred to the joints."

Thomas Sydenham, *The Works of Thomas Sydenham*, 1848–1850. From his description of rheumatic fever.

4) "However, in the eighteenth century Thomas Sydenham was given much of the credit for the transformation in the medical perception of disease. Sydenham... practised largely amongst the poor in London after the Restoration of Charles II in 1660 and this together with his radical wish to improve medicine for the benefit of all, led him to study epidemic fevers rather than individual patients and their constitutions. As a follower of [Francis] Bacon [1561–1626] he was concerned to make general histories of diseases, collected from individual cases, which would allow diseases to be classified like plants. He wrote 'it is necessary that all diseases be reduced to definate [*sic*] and certain species, and that, with the same care which we see exhibited by botanists in their phytologies'. In his belief that diseases were real entities (or collections of symptoms) and could be classified into groups, Sydenham looks forward to the nosological systems of the eighteenth century."

Andrew Wear, Medicine in early modern Europe, *The Western Medical Tradition*, 1995

Chapter 20

1710 ——

— George I became king 1714
— Jacobite rebellion 1715

1720 ——

— Birth of Leopold Auenbrugger 1722
— Deaths of Christopher Wren and Antonio Valsalva 1723

1730 ——

1740 —— Frederick II (The Great) became king of Prussia

— Battle of Dettingen 1743
— Battle of Culloden 1746

1750 —— Death of Johann Sebastian Bach

— Birth of Jean Nicolas Corvisart 1755
— Birth of Wolfgang Amadeus Mozart 1756

1760 ——

— Morgagni's *De Sedibus* published 1761
— Catherine II (The Great) became Czarina 1762

— Birth of Napoleon Bonaparte 1769

1770 ——

— Birth of Marie-François-Xavier Bichat and
death of Giovanni Morgagni 1771
— Oxygen discovered by Joseph Priestley 1774
— Start of American War of Independence 1775

1780 ——

— Birth of René-Théophile-Xavier Laennec 1781
— Death of Samuel Johnson 1784
— Birth of John Forbes 1787
— Start of the French Revolution 1789

1790 ——

— France became a Republic; battle of Valmy 1792

— Birth of John Keats 1795
— Battle of the Nile 1798

1800 ——

— Death of Marie-François-Xavier Bichat 1802

223

Birth of pathology
(18th century)

Malpighi was dead, from a haemorrhage into the brain, when I returned to Bologna. He had lived on, plagued by vomiting, bilious stools and kidney stones, for ten unhappy years after the fire. As I received no reply to my letters I had, at length, stopped writing.

With the changing times I was finding it increasingly difficult to keep a home in any one city for too long and I did not take kindly to Telesphorus's subtle alterations to my appearance to create the illusion of increasing age. Sometimes, though, when I returned after a relatively brief span, I could do so as my own son. On these occasions Telesphorus would have retained the property and always, by some miracle, would have both house and garden prepared for my homecoming, unchanged as though they had never been deserted.

I strolled, at ease with myself, in the garden rejoicing in the myriad of scents, cupping a bloom here and there between the fingers of my hand or simply gazing in wonderment at each well-remembered and treasured plant. The tour of inspection completed and old acquaintances renewed, I made my way to the arbour where I settled myself in delicious comfort and let my mind wander.

My visit to Sydenham had persuaded me that if medicine were finally to shake itself free of the past, the physician had to heed discoveries in anatomy and physiology and adapt them for practical use at the bedside. But this he was unlikely to do until he could grasp their relevance to diagnosis and choice of treatment. In the meantime, he would continue to rely on what the patient – and the patient's friends and relatives – told him; he would feel the pulse, smell and taste the urine and treat the symptomatic manifestations with greatly misplaced enthusiasm. What else could he do when he had no concept of the effects of the disease on the body – on its inner structure and functioning?

Over our evening meal, I discussed these thoughts with Telesphorus. He was not impressed.

"You should have learnt by now that you cannot have ideas foreign to the time you are inhabiting." He spoke kindly despite the implied rebuke. "But insofar as morbid anatomy – which is what you are talking about – is concerned, a start has already been made by the Swiss, Théophile Bonet [1620–1689]. When he was physician to the Duc de Longueville [*fl*.1670] he grew so bored he began to fill his time by collecting all the post-mortem records he could find. In the end he gathered some three thousand. But, alas! the published collection, known as the *Sepulchretum*, was irredeemably flawed because Bonet had uncritically accepted the opinions of the original authors... " Telesphorus broke off his story as we both burst into gales of laughter at his wit. (Telesphorus, speaking in French, had been making a play on Bonet's name: "opiner du bonnet" can be translated as "to go along with the opinion of others".) When we recovered, I had a niggling feeling of guilt as Bonet had clearly been making a genuine attempt to move medicine forward. Telesphorus merely gave a not entirely convincing display of contrition. Wiping the tears from his eyes, he continued:

"The knowledge was not yet there for Bonet to group the cases adequately, but even so he failed to use his own initiative. Consequently, the book lacks any semblance of order and is no more than a list of little practical worth.

"So." There was something about the tone of his voice that boded ill for me. "So, I want you to return yet again to Padua."

I tried to remonstrate that my home in Bologna was one I had come to love more dearly than any for many a year, but Telesphorus was not to be argued with.

* * *

The tradition of the Italian school of anatomists was long and influential, and nowhere more so than at Padua. When I met the current professor, I was left in no doubt that Telesphorus had, yet again, been right in bringing me to the city. Giovanni Morgagni [1682–1771] had been taught by a previous occupant of the Chair, Antonio Valsalva [1666–1723] who, in turn, had been a pupil of Malpighi. Valsalva's chosen pleasure had been to study the correlation between anatomy and physiology and how this might be disturbed in the presence of disease. He had sown the seed that was to germinate in the work of Morgagni.

I came to know Morgagni as well as I did any mortal man, and if I closed my eyes I could for the moment imagine that time had stood still and that I was once again talking with Malpighi. In appearance, the two men resembled each other not at all, but kindness and understanding spoke in the voices of both. Morgagni was an excellent teacher and it was his sympathetic relationship with his students that led, indirectly, to his great achievement.

"I had been in Padua for nearly thirty years before I started writing the letters that were to become my book." This had recently been published and he was explaining to me how it had come to be written. "The idea took shape while discussing the deficiencies of Bonet's *Sepulchretum* with a student. Whether he suggested that I should improve upon the work or whether I decided that, as the task needed doing, I should do it myself, I can no longer recall – remember I am in my eightieth year and am going back twenty years. But whichever was the case, I undertook to record the circumstances and findings of all my post-mortems from then onwards. For some reason – which again escapes me – we agreed on a total of seventy letters, which were to be returned to me. You, Paolo, now hold in your hands a book that I hope will contribute to the well-being of mankind."

I have always had a love of books, not only for the written words they contain, but also for the feel of them. It is a sensation approaching the sensual; it is as if the spirit of the author is made manifest without the need to read the words. One of my deepest regrets has been my inability to build a library of all the books that have passed through my hands. Every collection I have attempted has either been dispersed or destroyed – most frequently the latter.

And now, holding Morgagni's book [*De Sedibus*] – or should I say books, as it was in two volumes – I felt I was touching his very soul. I asked leave to sit and turn the pages.

"Indeed, yes, my friend," he said, "but first let me explain how it is arranged. The volumes contain my accounts of nearly six hundred and forty dissections. In addition I have included the patient's symptoms and the mode of their dying, so that with all the details assembled, I have been able to relate the symptoms during life with my findings after death. Mostly I have been able to identify the diseased organ responsible for the symptomatic manifestations.

"You will see that diseases are often represented many times. It is always possible to learn something new and the more frequent the dissections, the more reliable are the conclusions likely to be. As I say to my students: 'Those who have dissected or inspected many bodies, have at least learnt to doubt; while others, who are ignorant of anatomy and do not take the trouble to attend to it, are in no doubt at all.'

"Now, Paolo, I must leave. I have other work to attend to, but you are welcome to stay."

And so I remained in his room for the rest of the day. I was already familiar with some of the cases as he had shown me a number of the letters, but what I was not prepared for was their organized presentation in the book. The five 'books' into which the whole was divided were categorized: cerebral disorders; respiratory and cardiac conditions; disorders of digestion and the genito-urinary tract; fevers, tumours, traumatic and surgical conditions; and miscellaneous states together with further deliberations on previous cases. Cross-references abounded and Morgagni never failed to give credit to other writers whose work he cited as adding to the authority of a point he was making.

As I leafed through, I soon noticed there was even more information than he had suggested. He had included personal details about the patients: apart from their age and whether or not they were married, he had recorded the illnesses they had suffered previously, the nature of their occupation and, with Hippocratic percipience, any apparently relevant details about the weather and climate. And, on occasion, he had paid attention to the sicknesses that had affected other members of the family.

The skill with which he had identified the salient features, both in life and in death, was masterful. One case I particularly remember since the impression it left on my memory was of the old order giving way to the new.

An epidemic in Padua one winter had spread "especially in some convents of nuns. In one of them all who had contracted it had died. It was obvious that there was nothing contagious as none attending the sick had contracted the disease and even some who had been most careful to keep away from them had contracted it – but not without a particular cause and disposition in almost every one." Those particular causes had included injury to the chest and "infirmity of the powers of the thorax and lungs, such as occur in those of decrepit age".

"Although three different physicians had attended, not one of the sick could be saved; yet many ascribed the deaths to the unknown nature of the disorder rather than the intensity." (Evidently the cloak of superstition had not been shaken from the people's backs.)

On the death of the tenth patient, a virgin aged forty-two years who every winter had had a violent cough, Morgagni said: "Come let the body be dissected; it is certain to be in the nature of the disease that the lungs shall appear to have the substance of the liver." And so it proved.

As I read on, I realized that now, for the first time, physicians would be able to form a definite picture in their minds of what was happening inside the body. The origin of the symptoms described by the patient would have anatomical meaning which, if interpreted intelligently would help to guide the choice of treatment. In these seventy letters, Morgagni had sounded the death knell of humoral medicine. No longer could it be rationally argued that disease had but one cause (a disorder of the humours with all its variations to suit the circumstances); it was now evident that many different morbid processes could incapacitate or destroy the body.

I felt a sense of great elation.

* * *

Telesphorus soon brought me down to earth.

"Master, you run too fast," was his response to my account of Morgagni's work. "Despite the title of his book, *De Sedibus et Causis Morborum per Anatomen Indagatis* [*The Seats and Causes of Diseases Investigated by Anatomy*], he has brought the physician no closer to understanding the causes of disease; the causes of the symptoms maybe, but not of disease. Has he brought you closer to your release or merely conceived another possible solution to the insoluble problems of disease and death?"

He saw the look of horror cross my face. "It may be, as I think you realize, that the problem is insoluble only to man, not to the gods."

What was I to make of this? As I understood him, Telesphorus was saying that as ideas about disease changed, man would believe himself closer to the truth. Yet the belief would be merely illusion. To paraphrase Morgagni: in the past man was in no doubt at all, but as his knowledge increased, so did his doubts.

I was relieved when Telesphorus let the subject drop. He knew he had given me much cause for thought.

After Morgagni's death, I returned to my Bologna home as the third generation of the Baldassare family to reside there. Once again, I found the place just as I had left it. But one morning, I forget how many years later, I awoke to a musty smell about the house; the curtains hung awry and would have fallen in shreds had they been drawn. My beautiful furniture looked to have lain for years in a leaking attic. The building itself had decayed and when I stepped into the garden I could not restrain my tears: the paths I had walked along were submerged in undergrowth and none of my chosen flowers would bloom again. The wall around my physic garden had crumbled. My home lay desolate. Telesphorus was nowhere to be seen.

I drew back indoors. The surface of the reception table in the hallway was surprisingly bright and shone in the sunlight; on it lay a brightly polished salver holding a note addressed to Doctor Paul Baldassare.

"It is time to move," the note read. "Nothing remains for you in Italy. Come to Paris."

How typical of Telesphorus! He first plays with time and then commands me without even troubling to sign the note. Nevertheless, I could imagine the twinkle in his eye as he planned a campaign that would both impress me with the passage of time and leave me no choice but to obey. Once this had sunk in, I even found it in my heart to forgive him the destruction of my home. He had, after all, been responsible for the halting of its natural decay and now had simply permitted time to catch up with itself.

* * *

When my coach slithered through the January mire into Paris, the Revolution that had torn France apart had long been over and the Republic was now ruled by an executive consisting of a three-man Consulate. The politics of the matter concerned neither Telesphorus nor myself.

"Paul," he said, before I had even had the opportunity to commend him on his choice of a fashionable house on the south bank of the river; from the upper rooms I had an excellent view over the city towards Montmartre in the distance. "I have arranged for you to meet Marie-François-Xavier Bichat [1771–1802] – though why the French indulge themselves in these strings of hyphenated names is beyond my comprehension – at the school of anatomy. He has progressed beyond Morgagni."

And so it was that I spent a pleasant morning in the company of Bichat. At once I realized he had an ungovernable urge to bring order to everything and in his latest outburst he had classified the tissues of the body into twenty-one groups. Quite how he managed this, still puzzles me as he disdained the use of a microscope, believing it to be responsible for distortion which could lead to false conclusions.

"If dissection does not give me satisfactory results, I resort to desiccation, maceration, putrefaction and the use of chemical agents."

Although I quickly grasped the reasoning behind these techniques, I could not stop my eyebrows rising in surprise, but he seemed not to notice.

"Medicine has been excluded from the exact sciences for a long time," he continued, "but it will have a right to be associated with them, at least as regards the diagnosis of disease, when we shall have combined clinical observation with the examination of the alterations suffered by the organs in every disease. Of what value is clinical observation if one is ignorant of the seat of the evil?"

I looked questioningly at Telesphorus. "But this is what Morgagni said," I muttered. His glance held the unmistakable message to be silent.

In the next moment my question was answered.

"You are aware, Dr Baldassare, are you not, that my anatomical studies have identified twenty-one different tissues in the body?"

I acknowledged that to be so.

"Morgagni related the clinical symptoms to the organs of the body. I have gone further and related them to the tissues. The more I observe diseases in the opened cadaver – and I have examined more than six hundred – the more am I convinced of the need to consider local disease, not from the point of view of complex organs but from that of the individual tissues.

"It is impossible ever to explore too deeply." His eyes held the look of a visionary. "Dissect in anatomy, experiment in physiology, follow the disease and perform the necropsy in medicine. This is the three-fold path without which there can be no anatomist, no physiologist, no physician."

Telesphorus had summoned me to Paris just in time. Two days after our meeting, Bichat cut himself with his scalpel while dissecting. At the age of thirty-one he became a casualty, in the words of Jean-Nicolas Corvisart [1755–1821], 'on the field of battle that numbers more than one victim'.

COMMENTARY

1) The Enlightenment (see Source 3, below) had a profound effect on many aspects of life. Not only did it lead to a change in social policy but also it created an environment which permitted a

freedom of intellectual thought that ultimately led to the world of today. Progress in all areas was enhanced, particularly in health-related issues where the over-riding belief was now that of health being the natural state of the body and it was the duty of patient and doctor alike to restore and maintain the rightful balance.

2) In *De Sedibus* Morgagni gave clear descriptions of numerous conditions including angina pectoris, mitral stenosis, aortic incompetence, aortic aneurysm, dissecting aortic aneurysm, endocarditis, the first clear description of heart-block (previously, Marcus Gerbezius, who died in 1718, had given a less convincing account), tuberculosis of the kidneys, acute yellow atrophy of the liver and gallstones. In summarizing Morgagni's achievements, it can be said that he did more than any of his contemporaries to demonstrate the union between anatomy, pathology and clinical medicine.

3) The excerpts from Morgagni's account of the epidemic in Padua leave no doubt that the disease was lobar pneumonia (the old man's friend, as it is sometimes called). They also identify the origin of the term hepatization (like liver) to describe the pathological state of the lungs in this disease. The full report would still bring considerable credit to today's physicians and morbid anatomists.

4) It might seem that by his refusal to use the microscope Bichat was being perverse or just plain bloody-minded. But he was a perfectionist and believed that the distortion introduced by the instruments of the time led to false judgments. What is amazing is that, without the help of a microscope, his work paved the way for the development of histology – defined as the study of the minute structure of tissues.

SOURCES

1) "He [the patient] was a man in his sixty-eighth year, of a habit moderately fat, and of a florid complexion, when he was first seiz'd with the epilepsy, which left behind it the greatest slowness of

pulse.... And, indeed, after he had pass'd a night of that kind [restlessness], which was far more troublesome than the rest, when to the greatest rarity of the pulse, which I mention'd in the beginning, an inequality had suddenly been added, so that very often they were perceiv'd to be much more rare, then not more so, than usual, and presently much much rarer again; which symptom made us the more uneasy, because the disease [the epilepsy], at that time, was wont, first of all, entirely to obscure the pulse, and then immediately to begin its attack."

Giovanni Battista Morgagni, *The Seats and Causes of Diseases*, 1769; original edition, 1761. Letter the ninth describing a patient who developed heart-block.

2) "Around 1800 clinical judgment was still drawing upon the threads and patches of humoralism. Disease theories remained multifactorial (later critics would say confused). Yet, thanks to developments in pathology, attention was newly being paid to normal and abnormal structures and functions, a trend that would come to fruition in the nineteenth century."

Roy Porter, The Eighteenth Century, *The Western Medical Tradition*, 1995

3) "The Enlightenment, according to Kant, was the period in the development of European civilization when 'Mankind grew out of its self-encumbered minority'. More simply, one might say that Europeans reached 'the age of discretion'. The metaphor is a powerful one, with medieval Christendom seen as the parent and Europe's secular culture as a growing child conceived in the Renaissance. Childhood had been encumbered by the baggage of parental and religious tradition and by family quarrels. The key attainment came with 'the autonomy of reason', the ability to think and act for oneself. But the child continued to possess a number of strong family traits."

Norman Davies, *Europe: A History*, 1996

Chapters 21 & 22

1800 ───

— Battle of Trafalgar 1805
— Corvisart's *Essai...* published 1806
— Auenbrugger's *Inventum* published in French 1808
— Death of Auenbrugger; birth of Jakob Henle 1809

1810 ─── Birth of Theodor Schwann
— Napoleon's retreat from Moscow 1812
— Battle of Waterloo 1815
  Restoration of French monarchy 1815
— Laennec's *De l'Auscultation* published 1819

1820 ───

— Birth of Louis Pasteur; death of Napoleon 1821
— Death of Laennec 1826
— Death of Beethoven 1827
— Birth of Julius Cohn 1828

1830 ───

— Deaths of Sir Walter Scott and Goethe 1832

— Queen Victoria succeeded to the throne 1837

1840 ─── Penny post (prepaid) introduced
— Birth of Robert Koch 1843
— Introduction of surgical anaesthesia 1846
— British Museum opened 1847

1850 ───

— Crimean War 1854–1855
— Indian Mutiny 1857
— Charles Darwin's *Origin of Species* published
  Battle of Solferino 1859

1860 ───

— Death of Sir John Forbes 1861
— American Civil War 1861– 1865
— Joseph Lister introduced antisepsis 1865

1870 ─── Franco–Prussian War 1870–1871

— Alexander Graham Bell invented telephone 1876

1880 ───

— Death of Theodor Schwann 1882
— Death of Jakob Henle 1885
— Asepsis introduced into surgery 1886

1890 ───

— ⎰ Death of Louis Pasteur 1895
  ⎱ Wilhelm Röntgen discovered X-rays 1895
— Marie and Pierre Curie discovered radium 1896
— Death of Julius Cohn 1898
— Boer War 1899–1902

Instruments are brought to the aid of diagnosis

(1815–1826)

The early years of the Second Restoration were hard for those who had sided with Napoleon – and lacked the influence or bare-faced effrontery to extricate themselves. Having been on the surgical staff of the Emperor's Imperial Guard and been made a Commander of the Legion of Honour, I was in distinct disfavour and contemplated leaving France.

When I mentioned this to Telesphorus, he donned his most enigmatic expression and simply said: "You should look to the physicians." And, since he refused to be any more forthcoming, I could only assume he was once again surreptitiously guiding my footsteps. But though I had kept my finger on the pulse of medical and scientific activities – and they were considerable, stimulated, as had been so much else, by the fervour of revolution – I had not the least idea of their destination.

There was one man, though, who might be able to help. I had known Jean-Nicolas Corvisart reasonably well during the years of the Consulate [1799–1804] and he had always been pleased to discuss medical concerns. In the intervening years he had published an important book on the heart [*Essai sur les Maladies et les Lesions Organique du Coeur et des Gross Vaisseaux – Essay on the Diseases and Organic Lesions of the Heart and Great Vessels*, 1806] which helped in differentiating between diseases of the heart and of the lungs. He had also translated from the Latin an obscure text on percussion by an Austrian physician, Leopold Auenbrugger [1722–1809]. Neither of these seemed to me at the time to be good enough reasons for Telesphorus's injunction. Nevertheless, I decided to seek him out as he was renowned for the excellence of his teaching and for the subsequent brilliance of his pupils. When I had last heard of him he had been Professor of Medicine at the Collège de France and my enquiries revealed that I would still find him there.

He welcomed me warmly. He had changed little; maybe his hair was whiter and the receding hairline was now closer to the back of his head, but his eyes had not lost their kindly quizzical look – a look I have often noticed in the eyes of born teachers. But to my consternation, he studied me more closely than I felt was strictly necessary.

"You have worn well," was all he remarked. "Presumably there is a reason you wish to see me again after all this time?" Did I detect a touch of humour in his voice?

"Yes," I answered. I saw no point in dissimulation even though I had concocted what I hoped would seem a compelling reason for my visit. "I have received a letter from a friend in America enquiring about the state of medicine in France now that we are no longer at war. I understand you have developed Morgagni's correlation between symptoms and post-mortem findings by eliciting signs of the disease during life and relating these to the findings after death?"

"I have, and that is why I regard my translation of Auenbrugger's treatise on percussion as of the first importance. His discovery – which was the application of the way he measured the level of wine in his father's casks to what he called hardening of the lungs – has enabled me to estimate during life not only the condition of the lungs, but also the size of the heart. And, what is more, I have confirmed the accuracy of these assessments at post-mortem. Although I am not the first to have translated his book, I am the first to appreciate its merit. In fact, I could have claimed credit for the discovery but, as I wrote in my Preface: 'By that I would sacrifice the name of Auenbrugger to my own vanity and that I do not wish to do: It belongs to him, it is his beautiful and rightful discovery (*Inventum Novum*, as he justly says) which I wish to bring to life.' [Auenbrugger's original Latin text was published in 1761; Corvisart's French translation in 1808.]

"Even so, there is a former student of mine who is pursuing the work of Morgagni, Auenbrugger and myself still further. The correlation of symptoms with post-mortem changes is only the first step in improving our method of diagnosis. It is essential to discover the signs of disease so that the picture may be completed. Auenbrugger realized that this was so, but his heart was not truly in his discovery and its disregard by his contemporaries was of small concern to him. Nevertheless, Doctor Baldassare, my translation has attracted attention and as time has moved on, I would recommend you to visit that ex-pupil of mine who is now a physician at the Hôpital Necker."

The next morning was herald to a glorious early autumn day so, looking upon it as a favourable omen, I took a leisurely stroll to the Hôpital. I should have known that René-Théophile-Hyacinth Laennec [1781–1826] always made an early start and consequently he was already well through his rounds. As I arrived he was deep in thought and I contrived to slip unnoticed among the students gathered around the bed. Apparently he was dissatisfied with his examination of a young lady. Percussion and palpation had revealed nothing on account of her fatness, and her age and sex ruled out the use of direct or immediate auscultation.

Slowly Laennec turned to face his students. I cannot say I was shocked by his appearance, but I could not prevent a silent gasp. He had the look of a man who knew his time was limited. Already the signs of the disease, pulmonary tuberculosis, the nature of which he himself was to elucidate, were apparent.

"Why," he said after a preliminary cough, "should we not make use of a well-known fact in acoustics? I refer, of course, to the speaking trumpet which enables the hard-of-hearing to be aware of the faintest whisper; to the ascending tube in the warehouse which conveys to the upper storeys the muttered directions of the master below; to the ticking of a watch placed at the end of a long beam or the scratching of a pin which is heard loudly by the ear applied to its other end. Therefore, if I place a tube on the chest over the lungs or the heart I ought to hear the sounds of the movements within more plainly."

And, without further ado, he snatched the notes from the hands of the nearest student and, rolling the papers lengthways, applied one end to his ear and the other, first to one side of the patient's chest, then to the other, and then to her back between and below the shoulder blades.

He raised his head and handed the still-rolled pages back to their owner. His elation was evident.

"I can hear the movements of respiration and the actions of the heart much more clearly and more distinctly than ever I could by the direct application of my ear to the chest." He paused for a moment, contemplating the significance of what he had heard. His drawn face lit up. "I believe we have here the means for enabling us to discover the character, not only of the heart's action, but also the manner of sound produced by every movement of the lungs: we can now explore the nature of respiration!"

As I left the ward, intending to return later in the day, I wondered whether Laennec was the physician Telesphorus had in mind. I decided to call on Corvisart on my way home to get his opinion of the importance of Laennec's discovery.

But before I could speak, Corvisart hurried me out through the door.

"Baldassare, your name is on the black list and it is only a matter of time before you will be arrested. I hear you insulted a returned royalist emigré. Is that true?"

"And with justification!" I replied with considerable vehemence. "M Carlin, a pompous idiot if ever I saw one, was holding forth on the military incompetence of the 'Corsican upstart'. I simply stared at him. 'The Emperor was worth a hundred of your Bourbon kings, as you would know if you had fought with him for the glory of France,' I said, and turned on my heel."

"Then you certainly must flee Paris, even France; stay away until I write that it is safe for you to return – passions may take a few years to cool. Even your services to France cannot save you from the consequences of a treasonable remark like that. Go to England while you are still at liberty."

With that advice ringing in my ears, I escaped to the country that had thwarted the Napoleonic ambition at every turn. In the same way that the English were making a rite of passage of the Grand Tour of Europe, so we made our own Grand Tour of the British Isles. In the course of this I learnt that Laennec had published his book on mediate auscultation [*De l'Auscultation Médiate*], as he called his new technique of examination. The stethoscope, the name he gave to his instrument, was at first simply a wooden version of the student's rolled-up notes.

Corvisart's letters eventually caught up with me and, to my dismay, he wrote that Laennec's treatise had failed to attract critical acclaim in France. Before long, however, copies of the book – and, just as important, of his stethoscope – began to reach England where their arrival was greeted with far greater enthusiasm. One review concluded: "To the enlightened author, of whom France may well be proud, the thanks of Europe are due."

To my regret, I was unable to obtain a copy of the book until, a few years later, I was pursuing an interest in cathedral architecture and found myself in Chichester in the County of Sussex. This city boasted a well-known practitioner by name, John Forbes [1787–1861], and, for what seemed no very good reason, I thought I would pay him a visit. My intuition was rewarded: Forbes had recently completed a translation of Laennec's book and was only too delighted to talk about his book to a fellow physician who had attended one of Laennec's rounds and whom he assumed to be French.

I cannot say that I warmed towards Dr Forbes; he was too sure of himself and regarded his 'translation' as an improvement on the original – as, indeed, did some English reviewers! For all his enthusiasm for the sounds – which he comprehensively revised for the benefit of the English reader – he had doubts whether the stethoscope would gain popular appeal.

"Notwithstanding the instrument's value, I confess that the sight of a grave physician solemnly listening through a long wooden tube to a patient's chest has about it an element of the ludicrous." The arrogance of the inhabitants of these Isles amazed me as he continued: "Besides, the method would seem to make a bold claim and to have a pretension to certainty and precision of diagnosis which cannot, at first sight, but be startling to a mind deeply versed in the knowledge and uncertainty of our art, and to the calm and cautious habits of philosophizing to which the English physician is accustomed." I held my tongue: I would have to wait until I could talk to Laennec himself before passing judgment on the matter of diagnostic certainty.

But Forbes continued talking; once launched on his own opinions there was no stopping him.

"Here," he said, his Scottish burr growing more and more irritating to my ears the longer he went on. He was rummaging about in his desk. "No, I cannot find it. I thought I had a copy of the letter I sent to Laennec. Still, no matter, I am reminded of its gist.

"I referred to my book as an abridgement, rather than a translation, of his immortal work. But it was, in fact, more than that. I took considerable liberties with the manner and matter of his treatise, for which the only substantial excuse I could offer was my conviction that a simple translation of so voluminous a work – I restrained myself from calling its style diffuse and verbose and by no means commendable in a scientific text. As I say, a simple translation would have met with little or no encouragement in this country and would therefore have frustrated the great and important object of making his immortal labours and discoveries known to a large number of British physicians."

I was glad to make my escape from Forbes's home. While he had been talking I had taken the opportunity to leaf through both books. He had, indeed, taken so many liberties that to refer to his 'abridgement' as a translation, as he did on his title page, was nothing short of sacrilege. I was now more impatient than ever for Corvisart to write assuring me of a safe return to France.

* * *

If I had been distressed before at Laennec's appearance, I was truly horrified now, eight years later. His face, never full, had fallen away until the skin was stretched tight over the bone. A hectic flush, combined with the determination in his bright blue eyes, gave him the look of a man not of this world. He had but a short time to live and he knew it – he had seen so many of his patients tread the same path before him. Yet he had so much to do, not the least of which was the completion of the second edition of his *De l'Auscultation Médiate*.

"The first edition appeared only three years after I had discovered the use of the baton," he was eager to talk about his work, not self-centredly as was Forbes, but informatively and constructively. "In that time, besides studying, describing and categorizing the sounds, I experimented with the instrument, using different materials and different lengths. I now use a wooden cylinder, an inch-and-a-half in diameter, and a foot long, perforated longitudinally and hollowed out to a funnel shape to a depth of one inch-and-a-half at one of its ends. It can be dismantled into two halves, partly for the convenience of carriage and partly to permit its being used at half its length.

"Although I usually speak of it as a baton or cylinder, I have named it the stethoscope – from the Greek. The precise dimensions are unimportant although I find the full length generally more convenient except when the patient is seated on a chair or in bed, when access is restricted." He was speaking rapidly and with that sense of urgency commonly encountered among those in the final grip of phthisis.

"But my life's work really began long before the arrival of my baton. I was a student of Corvisart at La Charité. He became more of a friend than a teacher and helped me greatly in my career. During the last few years of my formal medical training I prepared, under his supervision, more than four hundred case histories of patients from bedside to post-mortem. So, when I was appointed to the Necker, I had my students keep meticulous notes of the patients in their charge – notes which I supplemented with my own observations; these I dictated in Latin for reasons you will readily appreciate.

"My work at La Charité gave me an excellent grounding in the structural pathology of disease but, so far as the chest was concerned, it lacked the evidence provided during life by the baton...."

Without warning, he broke off in a fit of terrible coughing which nearly broke my heart to hear. When he had recovered, I offered to leave but he insisted on putting straight the matter of Forbes's translation – a copy of which lay open on the desk in front of him – and his charge about the claim made for auscultation.

"M Forbes would never have written those words in his Preface had he spent the three years between discovery and publication here with me at the Necker. Every day I worked to the point of exhaustion. My chief difficulty lay in describing and naming the different sounds I heard – never for one moment did I imagine a greater problem would arise over their translation. But gradually I was able to differentiate them and then to relate them to the pathology revealed at post-mortem. Should the post-mortem show any error in my interpretation, this was corrected immediately in the notes. At first, the sounds I heard merely indicated the nature of the underlying physical state – as you would expect. Then, as I gathered more and more evidence, I believed it safe to say that certain combinations of sounds and physical findings indicated the presence of certain diseases.

"Yes! In that sense, I am guilty of making the claims M Forbes suggests that I do, but they are based on sure evidence, as he would appreciate if he had taken the trouble to examine a sufficient number of patients rather than criticize the work of one who has!"

Laennec's calmness appeared in danger of evaporating. He remained silent for a minute or two and then indicated his readiness to continue.

"The matter of râles and rhonchi?" I queried.

"Ah!" he said, "now you come up against the obtuseness of the English." The ghost of a smile crossed his death-like features.

"In my book, I use the word râles," (when said by Laennec, the word had the hint of an onomatopoeic quality about it, which had been nowhere apparent in the sound produced by Forbes) "indeed, I only use the word in writing. I would never say it in front of a patient as he would associate it with râles de la mort – the death rattle. In England that is not a consideration. So, when speaking to students in front of a patient and dictating my notes in Latin, as I do, I speak of rhonchi, the Latin translation of rattle. M Forbes evidently is ignorant of this fact and believes râles and rhonchi to be two different sounds – no doubt influenced by the homophony of the words rhonchi and bronchi!

"Surely no one could have any problem with my description of the types of râles – or even wish to make a translation!" That ghostly smile appeared again. I liked Laennec.

"These various sounds occur when there are changes in the underlying lung. The râle sonore when there are changes in the shape or size of the medium or large bronchi – maybe compressed by tumorous growths, lymph nodes or inflammation. If the smallest bronchi are obstructed, the sound is different – more like a prolonged whistle – the râle sibilant.

"Or they may depend on what the air is passing through in the air passages; this may be mucus or tuberculous matter, for example – the râle muqueux; when I hear this in the trachea I imagine the sound is like the wheels of a carriage coming over the paved road to collect the dying patient. Often you can hear it quite plainly without a baton. The râle crépitant sec à grosse bulles is heard only during inspiration and is a crackling sound like the blowing up of a dried bladder; but, as I say, it is uncommon. The râle humide ou crépitation – and here I stand guilty of the charge laid by M Forbes – is the sound I find typical of pneumonia; I can reproduce it in the post-mortem room by gently squeezing the blood-and-air-filled lung.

"I also described most carefully changes in the sound of the voice in disease. The presence of a cavity is indicated by what I term pectoriloquy and I am quite confident that aegophony is heard in cases of pleurisy attended by a moderate effusion or in hydrothorax or other liquid effusion into that cavity.

"Now, M Baldassare, you shall come with me and listen for yourself to all these sounds and tell me whether an educated physician would require a translation."

I followed him into the ward where he led me from patient to patient, to listen while he told me what I should be hearing, often likening the sounds to the songs of the birds in his beloved Brittany. Since I am fortunate to have been blessed with a good ear I found it remarkably easy to picture in my mind the events within the lungs.

As I was about to leave, he detained me a moment longer.

"Some people think my *De l'Auscultation Médiate* deals only with my stethoscopic discoveries. This is far from being the case, though it might appear so to the casual reader of the first edition, since I adopted the analytical approach relating the signs in life to structural pathological changes at post-mortem. In my new edition, however, I have changed that to detailed descriptions of each disease, systematically working my way through diagnosis, pathology and treatment." [This edition has been described as the most important treatise on diseases of the thoracic organs ever written.]

* * *

I stood at Laennec's bedside. He was in the act of stepping into the ferryman's boat when he paused, removed the rings from his fingers and laid them gently on the table at his side.

"Because someone would have to render me this service, I wish to spare them the painful task."

I waited until he had arrived safely on the far bank.

COMMENTARY

1) The French Revolution (social upheaval) had done much to centralize hospitals and the opportunities this system introduced were seized by a group of outstanding French physicians, typified by Laennec.

2) The advances in France attracted medical students from other parts of Europe and from the USA. These men (there were no women) returned home competent not only in clinical medicine, but also in the new disciplines of microscopy, chemistry and pathology. Thus the ethos of scientific medicine was establishing itself in the curriculum.

3) The laboratory study of medical matters moved from being the domain of the 'gentleman scientist' (for example, Robert Boyle; see Chapter 18) to the proper place for the systematic study of disease, namely the hospital environment.

4) The modern hospital – a place where sickness can be identified, controlled and, hopefully, cured – can date its origins to this period. In such an institution the patient, it has been argued, often loses their autonomy and becomes of secondary importance to the problem they present to the medical profession. Recent debates have called into question the need to use hospitals in what is now

a traditional manner.

5) The ear has been applied directly to the chest wall on and off since Hippocrates described, mainly in culinary terms, some of the sounds he heard; but he did correctly identify the presence of dry pleurisy by likening the sound it produced to that of creaking leather. Difficult though it may be for the modern reader to appreciate, the concept of structural pathology scarcely existed before the18th–19th centuries and if any physician before then had even bothered to elicit evidence of structural changes within the body, it would have been a complete waste of time as he would have had no idea of its significance. Moreover, the niceties that had to be observed in the examination of the fair sex did little for the advancement of medicine or, indeed for discovering the best treatment that could be offered.

6) It may seem that Baldasarre was unduly harsh on Sir John Forbes considering that it was largely due to his 'translations' (which went through several revised editions – changing his choice of descriptive terms as the spirit moved him) that the English-speaking world came to know of Laennec's work on auscultation and his approach to diseases of the chest. But generations of long-suffering British medical students would have been better served and less confused had Laennec's own terminology for the breath sounds remained untranslated. After all, how many foreign terms are already part of the medical vocabulary? To quote from a popular student textbook of not so long ago: "Confusion has been caused by the different terminology employed in different schools." This confusion is far less significant than it used to be, now that the stethoscope is scarcely more than a screening instrument (except to the ears of the expert) before passing the patient on to the x-ray and other more exotic departments. To add insult to injury, all excerpts in English of Laennec's writings are in the Forbes 'translation'. A final comment on Forbes: he was also responsible for an English translation of Auenbrugger's treatise on percussion in which he paid scant regard to the subtleties of meanings of many of the terms.

7) The English poet and erstwhile surgeon, John Keats knew *The terror of death* from the self-same disease as Laennec. The opening lines of his poem of that name express the Frenchman's feelings all too well: "When I have fears that I may cease to be / Before my pen has glean'd my teeming brain, / Before high-piléd books, in charact'ry / Hold like rich garners the full-ripen'd grain;… "

8) Although Laennec discovered a cavity at post-mortem in all twenty patients in whom he had encountered pectoriloquy, time has shown that it can, in fact, be heard in other states in which there is no cavity. The choice of the word aegophony to describe a sound not unlike the bleating of a wild goat rather pleased Laennec.

9) Laennec himself did not use the dieresis (Laënnec) often found in the spelling of his name, though as he was a Breton it should be pronounced in three syllables.

SOURCES

1) "An important factor in the emergence of Paris as the leading clinical school was the French Revolution. As the old regime was swept away, so were ancient ideas and inhibitions, opening the way to new approaches by experiment, an emphasis on pragmatism rather than theory, and bedside observation instead of reasoning by concept. The hospital became more important as the focus of medical activity, public health measures were seen as a duty of government, and medical practice was open to all classes."
Albert S. Lyons and R. Joseph Petrucelli, *Medicine. An Illustrated History*, 1978

2) "Auenbrugger himself was too well poised and serene by nature to worry about his posthumous reputation. Grave, genial, inflexibly honest, unassuming and charitable, loving science for its own sake, writing the libretto of a little opera [*The Chimney Sweep* with music composed by Antonio Salieri (1750–1825)] for the delectation of Maria Theresa, and modestly waiving her request that he repeat the experiment on the ground that 'one was enough',

caring more for the society of his beautiful wife, good music, and *Gemüthlichkeit* generally than for any notoriety, he is, indeed, a noble example of the substantial worth and charm of old-fashioned German character at its very best."

Fielding H. Garrison, *An Introduction to the History of Medicine*, 1929 Auenbrugger was ennobled by the Austrian Emperor Joseph II with the title of Edler von Auenbrugg.

3) "The signs of hydrops of the chest [pleural effusion] on one side of the thorax – besides these general signs which I have just presented, the affected side (if it is entirely filled with fluid), is weakened, and is perceived to be less movable in inspiration. Moreover on percussion, there is no resonance in any part. But if it is half filled with fluid, a greater resonance is obtained in that part which is not filled with fluid."

Leopold Auenbrugger, *Inventum Novum*, 1761

Birth of bacteriology. The start of modern medicine

(Mid-19th century –1881)

The medical world – indeed, the world at large – was undergoing cataclysmic change – and I do not exaggerate. The years were gone when Telesphorus and I could wander leisurely from country to country, from town to town, enjoying the talk and experiences of men who were shaping the destiny of medicine. Now the tempo was fast increasing and the very devil of it was that I could not keep pace. But – and this I found infinitely more disturbing – I had an inexplicable sensation that as medicine became more complex, so the prospect of an understanding of disease was receding ever further. (Just like the expanding universe!) Had everything I had hoped for been damned from the start?

Or, I wondered in my more optimistic moods, could it be that light was there, awaiting its moment to illuminate this medical complexity, to guide mankind to a true understanding? Unfortunately, the one really unknown quantity in the equation was, inevitably, man himself. In consequence, I truly could not define the most important of the many directions medicine was pursuing. Telesphorus, as always, came to my rescue.

"Bal-sarra-uzur, I cannot, to my sorrow, disclose the future to you – my father would banish me from your mortal world for ever should I be so presumptuous and then how could I comfort and advise you? Besides it would remove much of the excitement from life, from both our lives!" It certainly would from his; I was not so sure about mine.

"Come back with me to our old friend Aristotle. You did not know, did you, that he and I spent many mutually enjoyable hours in his belvedere discussing highly abstruse aspects of science and philosophy – I didn't waste all my time in the gynaeceum as you probably believed!

Our conversation frequently came up against the nature of life and the topic on one occasion was, as I recall, the various methods of reproduction in the animal kingdom and he was quite adamant that spontaneous generation was a fact of life. This idea of his persisted and for centuries people believed that verminous creatures with no evident means of reproduction originated spontaneously from dung heaps, decaying flesh and vegetable matter and similar obnoxious masses."

"I know Aristotle's teachings have had a profound influence on scientific thinking," I interrupted, "but what in the name of your father has spontaneous generation to do with medicine today when diseases are being unravelled by men such as poor Laennec?"

"Patience, Master, patience. Allow me to pursue the story in my own way and you will see where it leads. But first, as you mentioned his name, what did Laennec believe to be the cause of tuberculosis?"

Telesphorus had caught me unawares.

"I cannot say. But I suppose he subscribed to the popular opinion that it was hereditary, since both his mother and his brother died from phthisis."

"Precisely!" He was triumphant.

I gave him a puzzled look and was about to open my mouth. He raised his hand to stop me.

"Please, Bal-sarra-uzur, I am trying to help you." There was actually a note of pleading in his voice. "For many centuries, spontaneous generation has been accepted as the cause of verminous infestation and decomposition. You have to admit it is a highly plausible explanation."

I refused to comment as I still failed to understand the relevance of his argument to my present predicament.

"An old friend of Malpighi's, Francesco Redi [1626–1697], opened the first crack in the belief." Telesphorus was not to be put off by my obtuse silence. Instead he adopted what I always regard as his professorial voice. "He showed that maggots would appear on meat in uncovered jars, whereas in other jars covered with wire gauze, they still appeared but on top of the gauze. This proved, for those prepared to listen, that it was not the rotting meat that spontaneously produced the larvae (or maggots) of flies; it was simply that the larvae were able to grow on the rotting meat.

"Then Leeuwenhoek put the fly in the ointment." Telesphorus could not contain his merriment and with tears streaming down his cherubic cheeks he nearly slid from his chair. So much for the professor!

When he had gathered himself, he continued: "You remember Malpighi telling you about the Dutchman's exquisite lenses? Yes? Good. Well, with these lenses Leeuwenhoek was able to describe, in detail, the yeast cell. He also reported his observations of minute structures, some of which were in formations like clumps or chains while others were motile. He believed that these 'animalcules', as he called them, came from the air, but his discovery did not, as you might have expected, help towards disproving spontaneous generation, it only made things worse. If, indeed, they did in fact exist outside Leeuwenhoek's imagination, how, people asked, could animalcules come into existence other than by spontaneous generation?

"Other experimenters – I won't bother with their names; you probably wouldn't remember those you had met, anyway – proved, mostly only to their own satisfaction, that spontaneous generation from dead organic matter did not occur. In their different experiments, air was excluded (with varying degrees of success): air was allowed free access. Experiments in which air was heated or passed through acid were condemned on the ground that the air had been deprived of its 'life force' and so animalcules could not be expected to develop.

"I'm sorry, Master, to regurgitate the past like this, but important discoveries rarely, if ever, come unheralded.

"Now, so far as you need be concerned, we are up to date, and what I cannot impress upon you too strongly is that the up-to-date science – and all the metaphors that go with it – is chemistry. Just as the metaphors of Descartes's day were mechanical." The professor was firmly in his chair again.

I thought, nevertheless, it was about time I made an intelligent, if only small, contribution.

"So, as I see it," I said, "there are two conflicting theories, with eminent chemists and scientists proposing convincing and sustainable arguments for both sides. In essence, disease may be caused by animalcules of one sort or another which, according to one theory, are generated spontaneously from organic matter and, according to the other are living organisms, or germs, from the start; they reproduce. Am I correct?"

To my relief and gratification, Telesphorus nodded. "I think you have grasped the essentials of the problem." He could be remarkably condescending when he set his mind to it! "At the present time, the climate of opinion favours the germ theory, though those who contest it have a powerful religious precedent on their side. Spontaneous generation is agreed by many to have occurred 'In the beginning'. So for true believers, it is inconceivable that the process cannot be repeated.

"The real problem confronting the upholders of the germ theory – and I risk incurring the wrath of my father in saying this – is that they have not the slightest idea of how they should study their germs. A theory remains a theory until it receives practical confirmation!"

"Obscurity flourishes in the realm of the invisible." After my intellectual battering by Telesphorus, I felt that was not a bad epigram.

"Quite correct," said the professor in a tone that only just avoided the patronizing. "The number of extremely peculiar ideas circulating among those who cannot accept that germs are able to reproduce themselves is beyond reasonable count. They say that the 'globules' Leeuwenhoek had seen were a form of chemical. They say that 'particles' of an unspecified nature catalyse the normal human chemistry to produce chemical poisons which then cause disease. Other 'particles' have actually been 'proved' experimentally to be the cause of infectious disease. They have been identified as 'spheroidal, transparent, of gelatinous consistence, of density nearly equal to that of the animal liquids in which they float, and that they are mainly, but perhaps not exclusively composed of albuminous matter.' Someone has even claimed he could isolate the poison of hospital fever in solid form! They argue that the growth of crystals in solutions is analogous to the origin of life! Oh, the infinite capacity of man for self-delusion!" Professor Telesphorus threw up his hands in despair.

Then a thought occurred to him. "Perhaps you are like all the others and are merely a child of the times – as, indeed, you would be if I didn't take you in hand once in a while – and agree with the chemists? The line between the living and the not-living is, in truth, finely drawn.

"Tell me this, Doctor, is yeast a living organism or not? After all, fermentation occupies an important place in our existence." And he took a long draught from the tankard of beer on the table in front of him. "Some chemists regard yeast as a decomposition product of malt and not the cause of fermentation. Have you an opinion on the matter, Dr Baldassare?"

I was silent for a while, thinking furiously. The chemists did seem to occupy the more favourable position. Then a thought occurred to me.

"Telesphorus, answer me this. We are now living in a time when scientific principles are paramount? You agree?" He did. "So theoretical considerations – which constitute most, if not all, the arguments on both sides – must be resolved by enquiries into the conditions under which these lowly organisms, if they exist, can develop and multiply."

"In that case we must visit the Professor of Geology and Chemistry at the Ecole des Beaux-Arts."

As we entered the laboratory, a fine-looking man in his mid-forties stood leaning against a work-bench gazing intently at a sealed flask in his right hand. He acknowledged our arrival with a nod before holding up the flask in our direction.

"I have kept this flask of boiled milk sealed for some time," Louis Pasteur [1822–1898] began, a look of controlled excitement taking over from the serious set of his features. "And I wait, I watch, I question it, begging it to recommence for me the beauteous spectacle of the first creation."

Oh, my gods! Telesphorus cannot have brought me to a latter-day alchemist's laboratory; to a reincarnation of Trithemius! Was this one of his little jokes? Was this otherwise intelligent-seeming chemist about to reveal yet another 'truth' of spontaneous generation? Yet you do not become a professor at a leading Paris institute without a certain degree of intellectual integrity.

"But," Pasteur proceeded, "it is dumb, dumb since these experiments were begun several years ago; it is dumb because I have kept from it the only thing Man cannot produce – I have kept from it the germs that float in the air; I have kept from it Life, for Life is a germ and a germ is Life!"

I sat down, uninvited, on a stool and stared at him.

"I have established," he was in earnest again. No matter how melodramatic his speech, there was nothing of the fanatic about him. "I have established," he said, "that yeast is a living organism and is responsible for fermentation. I have heated wine to fifty or sixty degrees centigrade – which affects neither bouquet nor taste – thus destroying the microscopic organisms that so nearly brought the industry to its knees through spoilage. Since I have proved the utter fallacy of spontaneous generation, I believe that not only have I discovered the causes of fermentation and spoilage, but I have also found the source of life itself!"

He put the flask down on the bench in the one available place between his books, his microscope and his equipment.

"You make no challenge?" He seemed surprised.

"No, since I have no reason," I responded with an encouraging smile.

"You are a strange man, Dr Baldassare." We had been announced by Pasteur's assistant. "Many so-called scientists would have raised trivial objections and continued with their argument that the microscopic organisms I found were produced by spoilage of the wine. Some years ago Thedor Schwann [1810–1882] showed yeast to be a living organism but he could not prove that it was responsible for fermentation. The technical difficulties were too many at the time, but time and techniques have moved on and I have been able to resolve the problems."

* * *

Pasteur had discovered bacteria and was putting the information he had gleaned to good practical use. Besides his work for the wine industry, he had been called upon to save the silkworm industry of France which was being crippled by disease. For five years he laboured and when eventually he discovered its cause and how to prevent the disease, his triumph was shattered: "Il y a deux maladies!" Pasteur's cry of despair was echoed by the industry. After more hard, infinitely painstaking work this second disease was also conquered.

Four years after our first meeting, Pasteur suffered a stroke brought on, his friends believed, by the harsh criticism he had had to endure on account of his 'failures'. I visited him frequently when I was in Paris, as we had developed a sympathetic rapport – he persisted in calling me 'you strange man', an indication, if such were needed, that his seriousness did not exclude, only hid, a genuinely warm character. Or did he, like so many intuitive men I had encountered, suspect that I was not what I seemed, yet could not say in what way or give a reason for their suspicions?

Meanwhile the controversy over spontaneous generation rumbled on. I asked Telesphorus why this had not been finally silenced by Pasteur's discoveries.

"It appears you listen neither to yourself nor to me." I feared I was about to be taken to task for a lapsus memoriae, though what particular snatch of conversation I had forgotten was a mystery, but one soon, no doubt, to be uncovered.

"When we were originally discussing the germ theory… "

"But that was twelve years ago." I was indignant. "I am only mortal with a mortal's memory."

"… you yourself said," he ignored my outburst, "that the theoretical arguments must be settled by enquiries into the conditions under which the micro-organisms develop and multiply. A remark obviously inspired by my having said previously that the supporters of the germ theory had not the slightest idea of how they should study their germs! Now argue your way out of that!"

And so I did, very rapidly indeed. "Ah, my dear Telesphorus, you were looking into your crystal ball so, to protect you from the wrath of your father, the words were erased from my memory as soon as they had served their purpose. Now, let us drink to each other and to Louis

Pasteur who has again saved from bacterial disaster yet another of mankind's solaces."

We touched beer mugs and muttering "Pasteur, Paul, Telesphorus" (except that Telesphorus spoke his name before mine – the gods do not surrender to mortals that easily), we drank to the last drop.

* * *

My fear that I might have so upset Telesphorus that it would be a long time before he would proffer even the most obscure of advice, proved quite unfounded – as I should have known it would. It was his suggestion that we should visit Prussia, specifically the region around Breslau [this is now in Poland and Breslau has been renamed Wroclaw]. He would say no more and would give me no reason.

As my clever curly-headed little professor had so amply demonstrated with his sermon on spontaneous generation, I could not keep up with all that was going on in medicine and, on our journey, he proved it once again.

"Dr Baldassare." I knew a lecture was about to be delivered. "Jakob Henle [1809–1885], now Professor of Anatomy at Göttingen, is an exceptionally talented and far-sighted man. His work on microscopic anatomy has carried Bichat's studies onward to include the developmental and functional aspects of the tissues, and his approach to gross anatomy has made it much simpler for students to understand. He is a charming man and possesses great artistic talent – it is a pity you never met him. His lectures are almost lessons in anatomical art; in consequence, his students leave his courses both knowledgeable and inspired.

"One of those students, however, was inspired by something quite other than Henle's anatomy classes. Early in his career, Henle had been fascinated by the problem of contagion and, having accepted that it was due to living micro-organisms, he drew up a set of conditions that had to be fulfilled before a causal association could be established between the suspect micro-organism and the disease in question: The organism had to be demonstrated in every case of the disease and in no other disease. The organism had to be isolated from all other micro-organisms and other extraneous matter. The isolated organism had to be shown to be capable of causing the original disease. Quite demanding criteria, don't you think? Is it any wonder that they were quietly left to simmer until someone found out how bacteria could be studied?

"It has taken a long while for Henle's inspiration to stir the student into action – and it has happened in the most unusual circumstances. Robert Koch [1843–1910], the ex-student, returned from service in the Franco-Prussian War [1870–1871] to become district physician at the small town of Wollstein [now also in Poland and renamed Wolsztyn]. He soon grew bored with the monotony of the job and began playing around with his microscope. Before long he realized where his interests and future lay.

"I may have misled you, Balthasar, in saying we were going to Breslau. That is so, but it is not our final destination as I would like you first to meet Julius Cohn [1828–1898]. As well as being the Professor of Botany, he is also an enthusiastic bacteriologist; he has already presented evidence that bacteria are constant in their form and has suggested that this could be used as a method of classifying them into genera and species."

But to Telesphorus's annoyance, Professor Cohn was away in Berlin – even the gods can sometimes nod! So on we went to Wollstein.

Koch received us in a fashion that made me feel he would rather be pursuing his studies than entertaining two apparently casual passers-by. Nevertheless, he made us welcome and once I had asked the right question, he agreed to give us a practical demonstration.

For the rest of the day we watched enthralled as he worked through his bacteriological techniques. After staining the fixed preparation with one of the aniline dyes – he used methyl violet, fuchsine or aniline brown, depending on the organism – he examined the slide under the microscope, moving from low power, to high power and then to the oil immersion lens which was quite a new-fangled idea and gave remarkable definition. Finally, he took photographs of the stained bacteria. (Staining the invisible to make it visible, you might say.)

"I owe so much to Julius Cohn who has become a good friend," he said. "When my first studies – they were on the life-cycle of the bacillus of anthrax – were complete, I wrote to him. He immediately invited me to demonstrate my methods of culture and staining at his Institute before some of his eminent colleagues. It was a great success. Soon afterwards, I proved conclusively that micro-organisms were the cause of wound infections. Although this gave the answer to a highly contentious issue, it also gave surgeons much to think about!"

The next time I met Koch – who, by then, was on the staff of the Imperial Health Department – was two or three years later at a medical congress in London where he demonstrated a novel method of obtaining pure cultures on a solid coagulum produced by spreading liquid gelatine and meat infusion on a glass dish.

I had, with difficulty, persuaded Pasteur who had an antipathy to all things Prussian – he had returned his Bonn MD at the outbreak of the Franco-Prussian War – to attend the demonstration. Patriot he may have been, but he was even more a great scientist: "C'est un grand progrès!" he exclaimed.

A great advance, it was, indeed. Mankind had at last begun to understand the cause of the array of diseases that had been his greatest affliction since he first appeared on earth. Could I, at last, truly see the beginning of the end of my existence on earth?

You may wonder why my story stops at this point well over a century ago. The reasons are simple. First, I cannot see any definite end-points in the era that began with the work of Pasteur – in the midst of events we lose perspective. And second, so much has happened in those years that I have been unable to determine which events have increased man's understanding of disease – as, after all, that is my only concern since it is his understanding that will influence my fate. Despite all that has been achieved, man is still groping in the dark in this regard – to which my continued presence here should testify. The achievements (observe that I do not refer to them as progress or advances), particularly in diagnosis and treatment, are a testament to man's ingenuity and industry and have done much to alleviate suffering. But I remain unconvinced that they have brought him any closer to an understanding of the nature of disease. And might what you think you understand perhaps be turned on its head by future generations – as has happened so often in the past?

Edward Gibbon [1737–1794] once wrote: "Insulted Nature sometimes vindicated her rights". This, I believe, is the crux of the matter: Nature will always remain a step or two ahead. You have only to look at the history of antibiotics; they have changed the pattern of infective disease and arguably not for the long-term better – the rise of virus diseases could be attributed to their use as more certainly could the development of pathogenicity among previously non-pathogenic organisms. Nature does not like to be disturbed!

If all my years on earth have taught me anything at all, it is that disease is an inescapable part of the human lot. And the past one hundred years, in particular, have persuaded me that Imhotep was wrong in his judgment. The true understanding of disease does rest with the gods and is beyond the comprehension of man.

COMMENTARY

1) Pasteur was a laboratory-based scientist who had been trained as a chemist (not as a medical doctor) and became an outstanding microscopist. His combination of skills enabled him to meet the demands of industry, in the course of which he discovered that air-borne organisms were responsible for spoilage in the case of wine and beer and for disease in that of silkworms. These discoveries contradicted the prevailing theory of spontaneous generation and culminated in his ground-breaking work to prove once and for all the validity of the germ theory.

2) Koch's meticulous studies enhanced Pasteur's microbial theory beyond measure. Furthermore, his standardization of procedure

(Koch's postulates) ensured that, following their identification, micro-organisms could be linked to specific conditions. The enemies had not simply been identified, the diseases they caused could now be fought rationally.

3) Apart from the overwhelming significance of the work of Pasteur and Koch in the fight against infectious diseases, it also revolutionized the practice of surgery – it was as if unseen chains holding it back had been severed. When Joseph Lister (1827–1912) studied Pasteur's writings he saw at once the analogy between putrefaction and hospital gangrene (wound infection): bacteria in the air were the cause of the infection; keep them away from the wound and the surgeon's troubles would be over. Reality was not quite as simple as this, but it did lead first to antiseptic surgery (which had its own problems) and then to aseptic surgery which underwent considerable development over the years.

4) In 1878 Koch published his important book on wound infections which detailed the pathological effects of the different varieties of bacteria. This was undoubtedly responsible for the rationalizing of asepsis which was beginning to take shape in the Berlin clinic of Ernst von Bergmann (1836–1907). Koch's work on the sterilizing actions of hot air and of steam was incorporated into the practice of asepsis.

5) Pasteur and Koch were the founding fathers of bacteriology, a science which in a very short space of time underwent an almost explosive expansion. Their work came at an opportune moment for rationalizing the public hygiene activities that had been in progress with increasing urgency since the 1830s. The ravages to the health of the labouring classes caused by cheap gin in the 18th century had given way to that due to the degrading urban squalor associated with the burgeoning growth of new towns and cities in the wake of the Industrial Revolution. Sir Edwin Chadwick (1800–1890) had produced reports on poor law reform, on the health of the labouring classes and on cemeteries which showed how censuses and mortality statistics could be used to diagnose public ailments. The combination of bacteriology and public

health measures eventually led to a greatly improved situation, although social classes IV and V are still at a considerable disadvantage as regards health.

SOURCES

1) "However, there is one limitation in this regard [that the student or physician should be well acquainted with the history of medicine]. It consists quite simply in the onrush of the development of new knowledge, the volume of which must tend to overpower the student and the practitioner alike. William Boyd in remarking on this, and noticing that medical literature seems to have reached the logarithmic phase of growth, aptly quotes *Alice Through the Looking Glass* 'it takes all the running you can do to keep in the same place. If you want to get somewhere else, you must run twice as fast as that.' The competition for the time of the student and practitioner by his studies on the one hand and by practice on the other, combined with the formidable continual increase in essential knowledge makes it unlikely that a large volume of medical history will be read at all thoroughly. Its very size and completeness may act as a deterrent to any such reading, no matter how much it is desired and how valuable it is realized to be in many respects. The solution may come in… the History of Ideas."
J.F.A. McManus, *The Fundamental Ideas of Medicine*, 1963

2) "The experiments of Pasteur again conclusively proved that the agents of putrefaction did not develop *de novo* in organic solutions but are either in these at the beginning of the experiment or reach them through the air. The controversy dragged on for many years being finally dissipated as attention was devoted to the more specialized phases of bacteriology. It is a good example of the principle that fewer questions in medicine are settled by conclusive proof than by loss of interest in one or another side of the problem."
Cecilia C. Mettler, *History of Medicine*, 1947

Characters and Chronology

[Some of the earlier dates in this listing are perforce approximations; of only two of the characters (Ebih-Il and Seneb) is there no historical record. Characters who are only mentioned en passant or only in the Commentaries are not included in this listing; their names will be found in the Index of Personal Names.]

CHAPTER 1 (*c*.2700BC)
Ebih-Il. Diviner – no historical record
Ishtar. Babylonian goddess – also identified with Astarte

CHAPTER 2 (*c*.2700–*c*.1500BC)
Imhotep. Physician, architect and grand vizier to King Zozer. c.2700BC Subsequently deified
Zoser. Pharoah. *c*.2700BC

CHAPTER 3 (*c*. 1500BC)
Amenophis I. Pharoah. *c*.1500BC
Seneb. Scribe – no historical record

CHAPTER 4 (*c*.1500BC)
Tammuz. Babylonian/Syrian god – also identified with Adonis
Astarte. Goddess of Eastern Mediterranean regions – also identified with Ishtar
Allatu. Goddess of the land of the dead in Eastern Mediterranean regions

CHAPTER 5 (*c*. 1500BC)
Hammurabi, King of Babylon. 1792–1750BC

CHAPTER 6 (*c*.1200–*c*.425BC)
Asklepios. Greek god of medicine
Telesphorus. Mythological son of Asklepios
Panacea and Hygeia. Goddess daughters of Asklepios
Pindar. Greek poet. *c*.552–*c*.442BC

CHAPTER 7 (430–*c*.425BC)
Thucydides. Historian. *c*.470–399BC
Hippocrates. Physician. 460–370BC
Isocrates. Orator and teacher of rhetoric. 436–338BC
Pythagoras. Scientist. *c*.582–*c*.507BC

CHAPTER 8 (370–321BC)
Aristotle. Philosopher scientist. 384–322BC
Alexander the Great, King of Macedonia. 356–323BC
Philip II, King of Macedonia. Father of Alexander. 382–336BC
Plato. Philosopher. 427–347BC
Hermeias, King of Mysia. *fl*.360BC
Ptolemy. Ruler and then king of Egypt. General under Alexander. *c*.367–283BC
Hephaestion. Friend of Alexander. *d*.324BC
Olympias. Mother of Alexander. *d.c*.321BC
Darius III, King of Persia. *d*.331BC
Oxyartes. Ruler of Bactria. *fl*.325BC
Roxana. Daughter of Oxyartes and wife of Alexander. *d.c*.321BC

CHAPTER 9 (321–30BC)
Herophilus. Anatomist. 335–280BC
Erasistratus. Physiologist. 310–250BC
Chrysippus of Cnidos. Greek physician. *fl*.340BC
Cicero. Roman writer and statesman. 106–43BC
Themison. Philosopher of the Methodist school. *fl*.50BC

Democritus. Philosopher. c.460–362BC

Anaxagoras. Philosopher. c.500–428 BC

CHAPTER 10 (166–169)

Gaius Julius Caesar. Sole ruler of Rome – marking the end of the Republic. c.101–44BC

Claudius Galen. Physician. 129–c.200/216

Aurelius Cornelius Celsus. Aristocratic lay compiler of, and commentator upon, available medical literature. AD25–50

Ovid. Poet. 43–17BC

Virgil. Epic poet. 70–19BC

Marcus Aurelius. Last of the Five Good Emperors of Rome. 121–180

Lucius Verus. Co-emperor with Marcus Aurelius. 130–175

Apollonius of Chalcedon. Stoic philosopher. fl.140

Aurelius Commodus. Son of Marcus Aurelius; co-emperor and successor. 161–192 (assassinated)

Annius Verus. Son of Marcus Aurelius. 162–169

CHAPTER 11 (169–177)

Epicurus. Greek philosopher. 341–270BC

Praxagoras of Cos. Philosopher scientist. fl.335BC

Pitholaus. Tutor to Commodus. fl.174

CHAPTER 12 (c.400–c.900)

Magnus of Emesa in Syria and/or Nisibis in Mesopotamia. Compiler of works of Galen. fl.370

CHAPTER 13 (c.900–1037)

Muhammed. The Prophet. c.570–632

al-Ma'mun. 7th Abbasid caliph. d.833

Qusta ibn Luqa. Christian polymath and translator. d.912

Hunayn ibn Ishaq. Nestorian priest and translator. 808–873

Rhazes (Abu Bakr Muhammed ibn Zakariyya al-Razi). Physician. c.865–925

Pedanius (Pedacius) Dioscorides. Turkish physician in the Roman army of Nero. Avid collector and recorder of medicines, mainly herbal. fl.60

Avicenna (Abu Ali al-Hasayn ibn-Sina). Physician. 980–1037

Albrecht von Haller. Swiss physiologist. 1708–1777

CHAPTER 14 (c.1037–c.1330)

Constantinus Africanus. Monk, scholar, translator. c.1020–1097

Mondino de Luzzi (Mundinus). Anatomist and surgeon at Bologna. 1270–1326

Alessandra Gilliani. Anatomical prosector and assistant to Mondino. fl.1300

Aretaeus of Cappadocia. Physician. fl.2nd–3rd century AD

CHAPTER 15 (c.1330–1348)

Fiammetta. Boccaccio's affectionate name for Maria d'Aquino, natural daughter of Robert the Wise, King of Naples. d.1348

Giovanni Boccaccio. Author of, inter alia, the *Decameron*. 1313–1375

St Francis of Assisi. Called Francis by his father, Pietro di Bernardone, but baptized John. Canonized two years after his death. 1182–1226

Giotto di Bendone. Artist. c.1267–1337

Cimabue, the nickname of Cenni di Pepo. Artist. c.1240–c.1302

Simone Martini. Siennese artist. c.1284–1344

Lorenzetti brothers. Siennese artists. Pietro, c.1280–c.1348. Ambrogio, fl.1320. It is possible that both died during the Black Death

Aesculapius. Roman god of medicine. Identified with the Greek Asklepios

CHAPTER 16 (1348–1516)

Hans Holbein the Younger. German-born painter and woodcut artist. 1497–1543

Geber (Jabir ibn-Hayyan). Arabian chemist and alchemist. *fl.*776

Juan Ponce de Léon. Spanish explorer and discoverer of Florida in 1513. *c.*1460–1521

Johannes Tritheim (Trithemius). Ecclesiastic and alchemist. 1462–1516

Moses Maimonides. Physician-philosopher of the Western Caliphate. 1135–1204

CHAPTER 17 (Second quarter 16th century)

Paracelsus (Theophrastus Philippus Aureolus Bombastus von Hohenheim). Swiss alchemist and physician (though whether qualified is uncertain). Bombastus was his father's family name, but he adopted the name of Paracelsus (superior to Celsus) in about 1529. 1493–1541

Joannes Oporinus. Swiss printer; Professor of Greek at Basle University; one-time amanuensis to Paracelsus. 1507–1568

Andreas Vesalius (André Wesel). Belgian anatomist; Professor of Anatomy at Padua 1514–1564

Jan Stephan van Calcar (Kalcar). Artist; student of Titian. 1499–1546

Leonardo da Vinci. One of the greatest figures of the Italian Renaissance. 1452–1519

Desiderius Erasmus. Dutch scholar and humanist. c.1466–1536

The identity of the Benedictine monk is obscure. He may have been Johann Estchenreuter who wrote under the pseudonym of Basil Valentine. *fl.*1500

Archbishop Ernst of Salzburg. *fl.*1540

Averroës (abu-al-Walid Muhammad ibn-Ahmad ibn-Rushd). Arabian philosopher and physician of the Western Caliphate. 1126-1198

Sylvius (Jacques Dubois). Parisian anatomist. 1478–1555

Masaccio (Tommaso di Giovanni di Simone Guidi). Florentine artist. 1401–1428

Filippo Brunelleschi. Italian architect. 1377–1446

Johann Gutenberg (Gensfleisch). German printer; inventor of moveable metal type. *c.*1400–1468

Charles V, Holy Roman Emperor. 1500–1558

Philip II, King of Spain. 1527–1598

Gabriele Fallopio. Anatomist. 1523–1562

CHAPTER 18 (Second half 16th century – first half 17th century)

William Harvey. English physician; discovered that the blood circulates. 1578–1657

Robert Boyle. Seventh son of the Earl of Cork. Chemist; intensely interested in medicine, especially experimental; obtained a medical degree in 1665. A founder of the Royal Society. 1627–1691

Giambattista Canano. Professor of Anatomy at Ferrara. 1515–1579

Amatus Lusitanus (Juan Rodriguez). Anatomist. 1511–1568

Heironymus Fabricius ab Aquapendente. Professor of Anatomy at Padua. 1533–1619

Andrea Cesalpino. Italian physician. 1519–1603

Pope Clement VIII. 1636–1605

Salomon Alberti. Professor of Medicine at Wittenberg. *fl.*1585

Matteo Realdo Colombo. Vesalius's prosector at Padua; later, Professor of Anatomy at Rome. 1516–1559

Jean Riolan the Younger. Professor of Anatomy at Paris. 1577–1657

René Descartes. French mathematician and philosopher. 1596–1650

Christina, Queen of Sweden from 1632 to 1654 when she abdicated. 1626–1689

CHAPTER 19 (Second half 17th century)

Marcello Malpighi. Italian physician and microscopist; Professor of Medicine at Bologna, Pisa and Messina. 1628–1694

Socrates. Athenian philosopher. c.469–399BC

Giovanni Alfonso Borelli. Italian mathematician. 1608–1679

Antonj van Leeuwenhoek. Dutch cloth merchant turned microscopist. 1632–1723

Thomas Sydenham. English physician (the 'English Hippocrates'). 1624–1689

CHAPTER 20 (18th century)

Théophile Bonet. Swiss physician. 1620–1689

Duc de Longueville. *fl.*1670

Giovanni Battista Morgagni. Professor of Anatomy at Padua. 1682–1771

Antonio Maria Valsalva. Professor of Anatomy at Padua. 1666–1723

Marie-François-Xavier Bichat. French anatomist. 1771–1802

Jean-Nicolas Corvisart des Marets. French physician. 1755–1821

CHAPTER 21 (1815–1826)

Leopold Auenbrugger. Austrian physician. 1722–1809

René-Théophile-Hyacinth Laennec. French physician. 1781–1826 (Laennec did not use the diaerisis (Laënnec) commonly found in the spelling of his name.)

Sir John Forbes. Scottish physician; practised in England; Physician to the Court of Queen Victoria. 1787–1861

John Keats. English poet. 1795–1821

CHAPTER 22 (Mid-19th century–1881)

Francesco Redi. Italian naturalist. 1626–1697

Louis Pasteur. French chemist; Director of the Institut Pasteur. 1822–1895

Theodor Schwann. Professor of Anatomy and Physiology at Liège. 1810–1882

Jakob Friedrich Gustav Henle. Professor of Anatomy at Zurich, Heidelberg and Göttingen. 1809–1885

Robert Koch. German physician. Professor of Hygeine and Bacteriology at the University of Berlin. 1843–1910

Ferdinand Julius Cohn. Professor of Botany at Breslau; bacteriologist.

Index of Personal Names

Subject Index

MESOPOTAMIA *C.* 2700BC

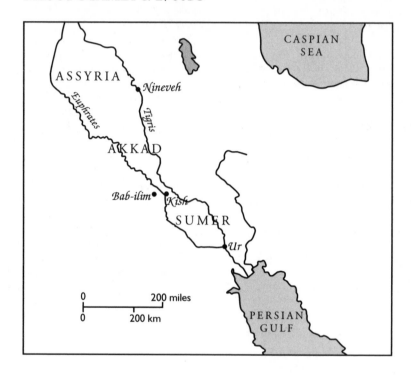

EGYPT *c.* 2700BC

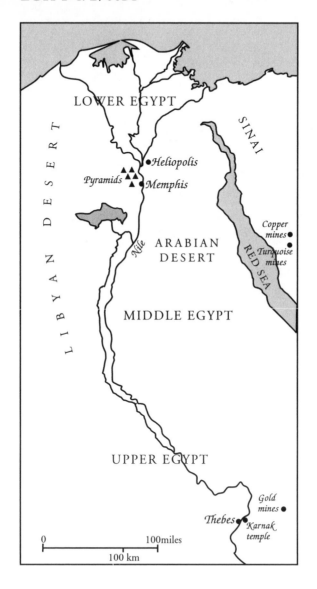

NILE AND EUPHRATES VALLEYS c. 1500BC

GREECE AND WESTERN ASIA MINOR 1120-400BC

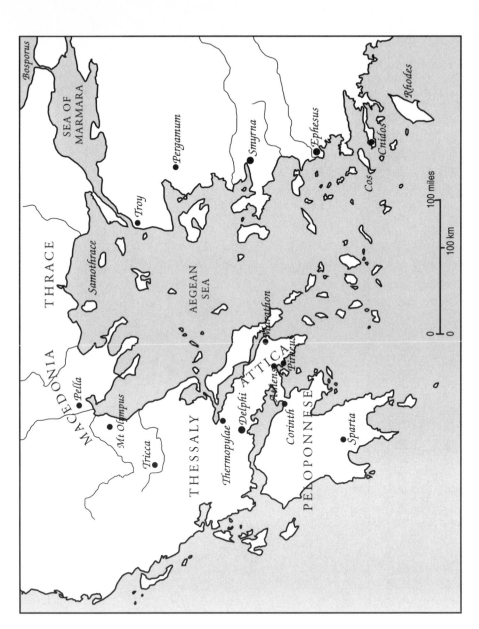

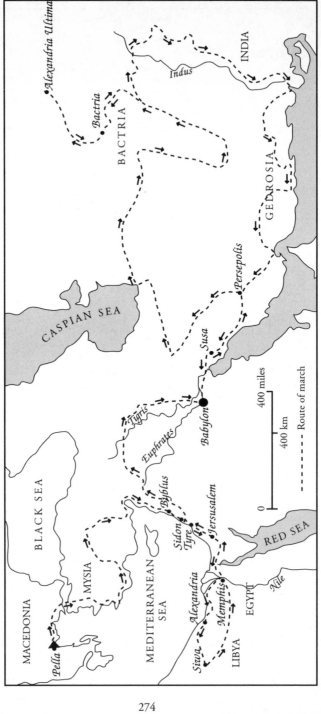

THE EMPIRE OF ALEXANDER THE GREAT
HIS MARCH OF LIBERATION AND CONQUEST

Alexandria Ultima

INDIA

Indus

Bactria

BACTRIA

GEDROSIA

Persepolis

CASPIAN SEA

Susa

Tigris

Euphrates

Babylon

400 miles

400 km

- - - - - Route of march

BLACK SEA

MYSIA

Byblus

Sidon
Tyre

Jerusalem

MEDITERRANEAN SEA

RED SEA

MACEDONIA

Pella

Alexandria

Siwa

Memphis

EGYPT

LIBYA

Nile

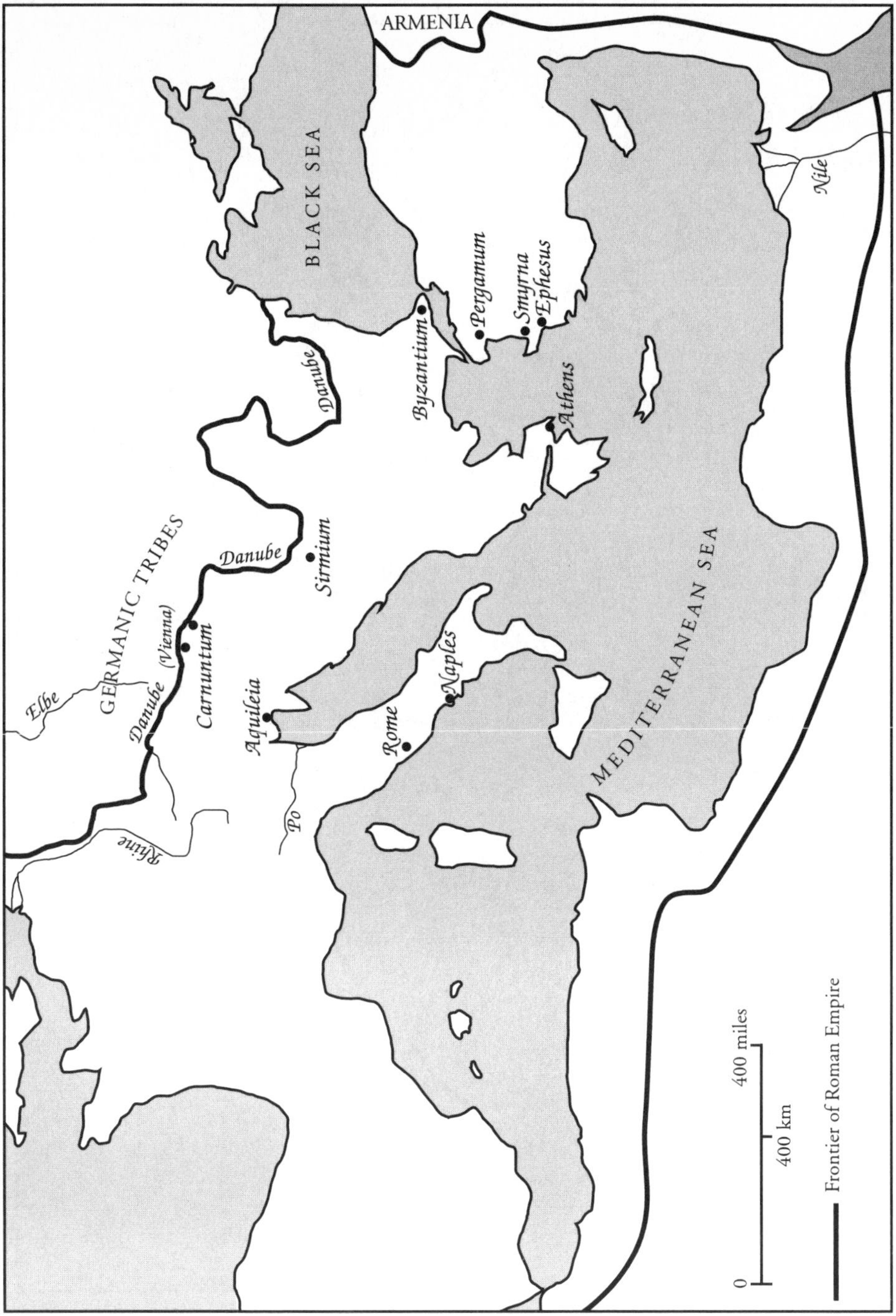
ARMENIA
BLACK SEA
Byzantium
Pergamum
Smyrna
Ephesus
Athens
Nile
Danube
Danube
Danube
GERMANIC TRIBES
Sirmium
(Vienna)
Carnuntum
Elbe
Aquileia
Po
Rhine
Rome
Naples
MEDITERRANEAN SEA
0
400 miles
400 km
Frontier of Roman Empire

THE CONQUESTS OF ISLAM

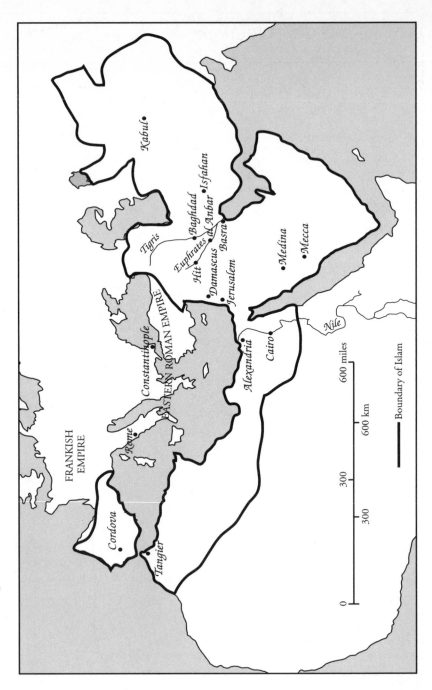